Object–Oriented Programming with Swift 2

Get to grips with object-oriented programming with Swift to efficiently build powerful real-world applications

Gastón C. Hillar

BIRMINGHAM - MUMBAI

Object-Oriented Programming with Swift 2

Copyright © 2016 Packt Publishing

All rights reserved. No part of this book may be reproduced, stored in a retrieval system, or transmitted in any form or by any means, without the prior written permission of the publisher, except in the case of brief quotations embedded in critical articles or reviews.

Every effort has been made in the preparation of this book to ensure the accuracy of the information presented. However, the information contained in this book is sold without warranty, either express or implied. Neither the author, nor Packt Publishing, and its dealers and distributors will be held liable for any damages caused or alleged to be caused directly or indirectly by this book.

Packt Publishing has endeavored to provide trademark information about all of the companies and products mentioned in this book by the appropriate use of capitals. However, Packt Publishing cannot guarantee the accuracy of this information.

First published: January 2016

Production reference: 1220116

Published by Packt Publishing Ltd.
Livery Place
35 Livery Street
Birmingham B3 2PB, UK.

ISBN 978-1-78588-569-3

www.packtpub.com

Credits

Author
Gastón C. Hillar

Reviewers
Vinod Madigeri
Hugo Solis

Commissioning Editor
Amarabha Banerjee

Acquisition Editors
Nadeem Bagban
Reshma Raman

Content Development Editor
Divij Kotian

Technical Editor
Parag Topre

Copy Editor
Shruti Iyer

Project Coordinator
Nikhil Nair

Proofreader
Safis Editing

Indexer
Monica Ajmera Mehta

Graphics
Disha Haria

Production Coordinator
Nilesh Mohite

Cover Work
Nilesh Mohite

About the Author

Gastón C. Hillar is an Italian and has been working with computers since he was 8 years old. In the early 80s, he began programming with the legendary Texas TI-99/4A and Commodore 64 home computers. Gaston has a bachelor's degree in computer science and graduated with honors. He also holds an MBA in which he graduated with an outstanding thesis. At present, Gaston is an independent IT consultant and a freelance author who is always looking for new adventures around the world.

He has been a senior contributing editor at Dr. Dobb's and has written more than a hundred articles on software development topics. Gatson was also a former Microsoft MVP in technical computing. He has received the prestigious Intel® Black Belt Software Developer award seven times.

He is a guest blogger at Intel® Software Network (http://software.intel.com). You can reach him at gastonhillar@hotmail.com and follow him on Twitter at http://twitter.com/gastonhillar. Gastón's blog is http://csharpmulticore.blogspot.com.

He lives with his wife, Vanesa, and his two sons, Kevin and Brandon.

About the Reviewers

Vinod Madigeri is a curious developer with a particular interest in object-oriented programming. He has worked in different industries (telecommunication, game technologies, and consumer electronics) writing software in C, C++, Objective-C, Swift, and C#.

Vinod is a passionate software engineer who writes code for fun. He has been doing this professionally for some 6 years and had been goofing with computers for 10 years before that.

Hugo Solis is an assistant professor in the physics department at University of Costa Rica. His current research interests are computational cosmology, complexity, and the influence of hydrogen on material properties. Hugo has wide experience with languages such as C/C++ and Python for scientific programming and visualization. He is a member of Free Software Foundation and has contributed code to a few free software projects. Hugo has also been a technical reviewer for *Mastering Object-Oriented Python, Learning Object-Oriented Programming* and *Kivy: Interactive Applications in Python* and the author of *Kivy Cookbook, Packt Publishing*. Currently, he is in charge of IFT, a Costa Rican scientific nonprofit organization for the multidisciplinary practice of physics (http://iftucr.org).

> I'd like to thank my beloved mother, Katty Sanchez, for her support and vanguard thoughts.

www.PacktPub.com

Support files, eBooks, discount offers, and more

For support files and downloads related to your book, please visit www.PacktPub.com.

Did you know that Packt offers eBook versions of every book published, with PDF and ePub files available? You can upgrade to the eBook version at www.PacktPub.com and as a print book customer, you are entitled to a discount on the eBook copy. Get in touch with us at service@packtpub.com for more details.

At www.PacktPub.com, you can also read a collection of free technical articles, sign up for a range of free newsletters and receive exclusive discounts and offers on Packt books and eBooks.

https://www2.packtpub.com/books/subscription/packtlib

Do you need instant solutions to your IT questions? PacktLib is Packt's online digital book library. Here, you can search, access, and read Packt's entire library of books.

Why subscribe?

- Fully searchable across every book published by Packt
- Copy and paste, print, and bookmark content
- On demand and accessible via a web browser

Free access for Packt account holders

If you have an account with Packt at www.PacktPub.com, you can use this to access PacktLib today and view 9 entirely free books. Simply use your login credentials for immediate access.

To my sons, Kevin and Brandon, and my wife, Vanesa

Table of Contents

Preface	**v**
Chapter 1: Objects from the Real World to Playground	**1**
Installing the required software	1
Capturing objects from the real world	4
Generating classes to create objects	11
Recognizing variables and constants to create properties	14
Recognizing actions to create methods	17
Organizing classes with UML diagrams	20
Working with API objects in the Xcode Playground	26
Exercises	31
Test your knowledge	31
Summary	32
Chapter 2: Structures, Classes, and Instances	**33**
Understanding structures, classes, and instances	33
Understanding initialization and its customization	34
Understanding deinitialization and its customization	36
Understanding automatic reference counting	36
Declaring classes	37
Customizing initialization	38
Customizing deinitialization	41
Creating the instances of classes	45
Exercises	46
Test your knowledge	46
Summary	47
Chapter 3: Encapsulation of Data with Properties	**49**
Understanding the elements that compose a class	49
Declaring stored properties	51
Generating computed properties with setters and getters	54

[i]

Combining setters, getters, and a related property	**62**
Understanding property observers	**65**
Transforming values with setters and getters	**69**
Using type properties to create values shared by all the instances of a class	**70**
Creating mutable classes	**74**
Building immutable classes	**78**
Exercises	**81**
Test your knowledge	**81**
Summary	**82**

Chapter 4: Inheritance, Abstraction, and Specialization — 83

Creating class hierarchies to abstract and specialize behavior	**83**
Understanding inheritance	**88**
Declaring classes that inherit from another class	**90**
Overriding and overloading methods	**96**
Overriding properties	**101**
Controlling whether subclasses can or cannot override members	**103**
Working with typecasting and polymorphism	**108**
Taking advantage of operator overloading	**121**
Declaring operator functions for specific subclasses	**126**
Exercises	**128**
Test your knowledge	**128**
Summary	**129**

Chapter 5: Contract Programming with Protocols — 131

Understanding how protocols work in combination with classes	**131**
Declaring protocols	**133**
Declaring classes that adopt protocols	**137**
Taking advantage of the multiple inheritance of protocols	**142**
Combining inheritance and protocols	**144**
Working with methods that receive protocols as arguments	**152**
Downcasting with protocols and classes	**155**
Treating instances of a protocol type as a different subclass	**159**
Specifying requirements for properties	**162**
Specifying requirements for methods	**164**
Combining class inheritance with protocol inheritance	**166**
Exercises	**178**
Test your knowledge	**179**
Summary	**180**

Table of Contents

Chapter 6: Maximization of Code Reuse with Generic Code — 181
- Understanding parametric polymorphism and generic code — 181
- Declaring a protocol to be used as a constraint — 183
- Declaring a class that conforms to multiple protocols — 184
- Declaring subclasses that inherit the conformance to protocols — 188
- Declaring a class that works with a constrained generic type — 190
- Using a generic class for multiple types — 195
- Combining initializer requirements in protocols with generic types — 201
- Declaring associated types in protocols — 202
- Creating shortcuts with subscripts — 204
- Declaring a class that works with two constrained generic types — 206
- Using a generic class with two generic type parameters — 209
- Inheriting and adding associated types in protocols — 213
- Generalizing existing classes with generics — 214
- Extending base types to conform to custom protocols — 223
- Test your knowledge — 225
- Exercises — 226
- Summary — 227

Chapter 7: Object-Oriented Programming and Functional Programming — 229
- Refactoring code to take advantage of object-oriented programming — 229
- Understanding functions as first-class citizens — 241
- Working with function types within classes — 243
- Creating a functional version of array filtering — 245
- Writing equivalent closures with simplified code — 247
- Creating a data repository with generics and protocols — 248
- Filtering arrays with complex conditions — 253
- Using map to transform values — 256
- Combining map with reduce — 259
- Chaining filter, map, and reduce — 262
- Solving algorithms with reduce — 262
- Exercises — 264
- Test your knowledge — 265
- Summary — 266

Chapter 8: Extending and Building Object-Oriented Code — 267
- Putting together all the pieces of the object-oriented puzzle — 267
- Adding methods with extensions — 269
- Adding computed properties to a base type with extensions — 273
- Declaring new convenience initializers with extensions — 278
- Defining subscripts with extensions — 280

Working with object-oriented code in apps	**281**
Adding an object-oriented data repository to a project	**290**
Interacting with an object-oriented data repository through Picker View	**294**
Exercises	**299**
Test your knowledge	**299**
Summary	**300**
Appendix: Exercise Answers	**301**
Chapter 1, Objects from the Real World to Playground	301
Chapter 2, Structures, Classes, and Instances	301
Chapter 3, Encapsulation of Data with Properties	302
Chapter 4, Inheritance, Abstraction, and Specialization	302
Chapter 5, Contract Programming with Protocols	302
Chapter 6, Maximization of Code Reuse with Generic Code	302
Chapter 7, Object-Oriented Programming and Functional Programming	303
Chapter 8, Extending and Building Object-Oriented Code	303
Index	**305**

Preface

Object-oriented programming, also known as OOP, is a required skill in any modern software developer job. It makes a lot of sense because object-oriented programming allows you to maximize code reuse and minimize maintenance costs. However, learning object-oriented programming is challenging because it includes too many abstract concepts that require real-life examples to be easy to understand. In addition, object-oriented code that doesn't follow best practices can easily become a maintenance nightmare.

Swift is a multi-paradigm programming language, and one of its most important paradigms is OOP. If you want to create great applications and apps for Mac, iPhone, iPad, Apple TV, and Apple Watch, you need to master OOP in Swift. In addition, as Swift also grabs the nice features found in functional programming languages, it is convenient to know how to mix OOP code with functional programming code.

This book will allow you to develop high-quality reusable object-oriented code in Swift 2.2. You will learn the object-oriented programming principles and how Swift implements them. You will learn how to capture objects from real-world elements and create object-oriented code that represents them. You will understand Swift's approach towards object-oriented code. You will maximize code reuse and reduce maintenance costs. Your code will be easy to understand, and it will work with representations of real-life elements.

What this book covers

Chapter 1, *Objects from the Real World to Playground*, teaches you the principles of object-oriented paradigms. We will discuss how real-world objects can become part of the fundamental elements of code. We will translate elements into the different components of the object-oriented paradigm supported in Swift: classes, protocols, properties, methods, and instances.

Preface

Chapter 2, *Structures, Classes, and Instances*, starts generating blueprints to create objects. You will learn about an object's life cycle, and we will work with many examples to understand how object initializers and deinitializers work.

Chapter 3, *Encapsulation of Data with Properties*, introduces you to organizing data in the blueprints that generate objects. We will understand the different members of a class and how they are reflected by members of the instances generated from a class. You will learn the difference between mutable and immutable classes.

Chapter 4, *Inheritance, Abstraction, and Specialization*, introduces you to creating a hierarchy of blueprints that generate objects. We will take advantage of inheritance and many related features to specialize behavior.

Chapter 5, *Contract Programming with Protocols*, discusses how Swift works with protocols in combination with classes. We will declare and combine multiple blueprints to generate a single instance. We will declare protocols with different types of requirements, and then we will create classes that conform to these protocols.

Chapter 6, *Maximization of Code Reuse with Generic Code*, teaches you how to maximize code reuse by writing code capable of working with objects of different types—that is, instances of classes that conform to specific protocols or whose class hierarchy includes specific superclasses. We will work with protocols and generics.

Chapter 7, *Object-Oriented Programming and Functional Programming*, teaches you how to refactor existing code to take full advantage of object-oriented code. We will prepare the code for future requirements, reduce maintenance costs, and maximize code reuse. We will also work with many functional programming features included in Swift combined with object-oriented programming.

Chapter 8, *Extending and Building Object-Oriented Code*, puts together all the pieces of the object-oriented puzzle. We will take advantage of extensions to add features to types, classes, and protocols in which we don't have access to the source code. We will make sure that the code exposes only the things that it has to expose, and you will learn how everything you learned about object-oriented programming is useful in any kind of app we might create.

What you need for this book

In order to work with Xcode and the Swift Playground, you will need a Mac OS computer capable of running OS X 10.10.5 or later with 8 GB of RAM.

In order to work with the Swift open source version on the Linux platform, you will need any computer capable of running Ubuntu 14.04 or later or Ubuntu 15.10 or later. These are the Linux distributions where the Swift open source binaries are built and tested. It is also possible to run the Swift compiler and utilities on other Linux distributions. You must take a look at the latest available documentation at the Swift open source website, `https://swift.org`.

Who this book is for

If you are an IOS developer who has a basic idea of OOP and want to incorporate OOP concepts with Swift to optimize your application's performance, then this book is for you. This is a very useful resource for developers who want to shift from Objective C, C#, Java, Python, JavaScript, or other object-oriented languages to Swift.

Conventions

In this book, you will find a number of text styles that distinguish between different kinds of information. Here are some examples of these styles and an explanation of their meaning.

Code words in text, database table names, folder names, filenames, file extensions, pathnames, dummy URLs, user input, and Twitter handles are shown as follows: "We can assign `20` to `regularHexagon1.lengthOfSide` and `50` to `regularHexagon2.lengthOfSide`."

A block of code is set as follows:

```
let degCUnitFromStr = HKUnit(fromString: "degC")
let degFUnitFromStr = HKUnit(fromString: "degF")
```

When we wish to draw your attention to a particular part of a code block, the relevant lines or items are set in bold:

```
Animal created
Mammal created
DomesticMammal created
Dog created
TerrierDog created
SmoothFoxTerrier created
I am 7 years old.
I am 14 years old.
I am 21 years old.
I am 4 years old.
I am 5 years old.
```

Preface

New terms and **important words** are shown in bold. Words that you see on the screen, for example, in menus or dialog boxes, appear in the text like this: "Start Xcode, navigate to **File** | **New** | **Playground....**"

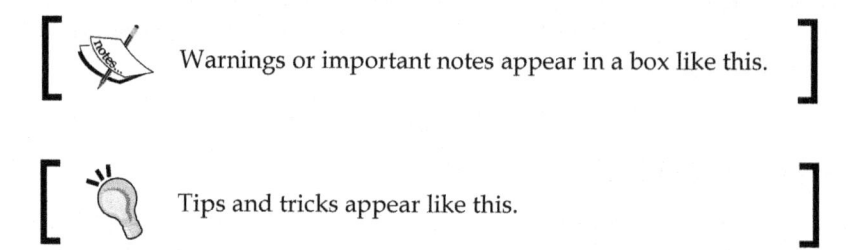

> Warnings or important notes appear in a box like this.

> Tips and tricks appear like this.

Reader feedback

Feedback from our readers is always welcome. Let us know what you think about this book—what you liked or disliked. Reader feedback is important for us as it helps us develop titles that you will really get the most out of.

To send us general feedback, simply e-mail `feedback@packtpub.com`, and mention the book's title in the subject of your message.

If there is a topic that you have expertise in and you are interested in either writing or contributing to a book, see our author guide at `www.packtpub.com/authors`.

Customer support

Now that you are the proud owner of a Packt book, we have a number of things to help you to get the most from your purchase.

Downloading the example code

You can download the example code files from your account at `http://www.packtpub.com` for all the Packt Publishing books you have purchased. If you purchased this book elsewhere, you can visit `http://www.packtpub.com/support` and register to have the files e-mailed directly to you.

Errata

Although we have taken every care to ensure the accuracy of our content, mistakes do happen. If you find a mistake in one of our books—maybe a mistake in the text or the code—we would be grateful if you could report this to us. By doing so, you can save other readers from frustration and help us improve subsequent versions of this book. If you find any errata, please report them by visiting http://www.packtpub.com/submit-errata, selecting your book, clicking on the **Errata Submission Form** link, and entering the details of your errata. Once your errata are verified, your submission will be accepted and the errata will be uploaded to our website or added to any list of existing errata under the Errata section of that title.

To view the previously submitted errata, go to https://www.packtpub.com/books/content/support and enter the name of the book in the search field. The required information will appear under the **Errata** section.

Piracy

Piracy of copyrighted material on the Internet is an ongoing problem across all media. At Packt, we take the protection of our copyright and licenses very seriously. If you come across any illegal copies of our works in any form on the Internet, please provide us with the location address or website name immediately so that we can pursue a remedy.

Please contact us at copyright@packtpub.com with a link to the suspected pirated material.

We appreciate your help in protecting our authors and our ability to bring you valuable content.

eBooks, discount offers, and more

Did you know that Packt offers eBook versions of every book published, with PDF and ePub files available? You can upgrade to the eBook version at www.PacktPub.com and as a print book customer, you are entitled to a discount on the eBook copy. Get in touch with us at customercare@packtpub.com for more details.

At www.PacktPub.com, you can also read a collection of free technical articles, sign up for a range of free newsletters, and receive exclusive discounts and offers on Packt books and eBooks.

Questions

If you have a problem with any aspect of this book, you can contact us at questions@packtpub.com, and we will do our best to address the problem.

Objects from the Real World to Playground

Whenever you have to solve a problem in the real world, you use elements and interact with them. For example, when you are thirsty, you take a glass, you fill it up with water, soda, or your favorite juice, and then you drink. Similarly, you can easily recognize elements, known as objects, from real-world actions and then translate them into object-oriented code. In this chapter, we will start learning the principles of object-oriented programming to use them in the Swift programming language to develop apps and applications.

Installing the required software

In this book, you will learn to take advantage of all the object-oriented features included in the Swift programming language version 2.2. Most of the examples are compatible with previous Swift versions, such as 1.0, 1.1, 1.2, 2.0, and 2.1, but it is convenient to use **Swift 2.0** or later because it has added error-handling features and many performance and stability improvements as compared to its predecessors.

We will use **Xcode** as our **IDE (Integrated Development Environment)**. All the examples work with Xcode version 7 or higher. The latest versions of the IDE include Swift 2.2 as one of the supported programming languages to build iOS apps, watchOS apps, and Mac OS X applications. It is important to note that Xcode only runs on Mac OS X, and all the instructions provided in this chapter consider that we are running this operating system on a Mac computer. However, after Apple launched Swift 2.2, it made the language open source and added a port to Linux. Thus, we can apply everything we learn about object-oriented programming with Swift when targeting other platforms to which the language is ported.

Objects from the Real World to Playground

>  In case you want to work with the Swift open source release, you can download the latest development snapshot in the **Downloads** section at http://swift.org. You can run all the code examples included in the book in the **Swift Read Evaluate Print Loop** command-line environment instead of working with **Xcode Playground**. The Swift Read Evaluate Print Loop command-line environment is also known as Swift REPL.

In order to install Xcode, you just need to launch Mac App Store, enter **Xcode** in the search box, click on the Xcode application icon shown in the results, and make sure that it is the application developed by Apple and not an Xcode helper application. The following screenshot shows the details of the Xcode application in Mac App Store:

Then, click on **GET** and wait until Mac App Store downloads Xcode. Note that it is necessary to download a few GBs, and therefore, it may take some time to finish the download process. Once the download is finished, click on **INSTALL APP** and follow the necessary steps to complete the application's installation process. Finally, you will be able to launch the Xcode application as you would execute any other application in your Mac OS X operating system.

Apple usually launches Xcode beta versions before releasing the final stable versions. It is highly recommended to avoid working with beta versions to test the examples included in the book because beta versions are unstable, and some examples might crash or generate unexpected outputs. Mac App Store only offers the latest stable version of Xcode, and therefore, there is no risk of installing a beta version by mistake when following the previously explained steps.

Chapter 1

In case we have any Xcode beta version installed on the same computer in which we will run the book samples, we have to make sure that the configuration for the stable Xcode version uses the appropriate command-line tools. We won't work with the command-line tools, but we will take advantage of Playground, and this feature uses the command-line tools under the hood.

Launch Xcode and navigate to **Xcode | Preferences…** and click on **Locations**. Make sure that the **Command Line Tools** drop-down menu displays the stable Xcode version that you installed as the selected option. The following screenshot shows **Xcode 7.2 (7C68)** as the selected version for **Command Line Tools**:

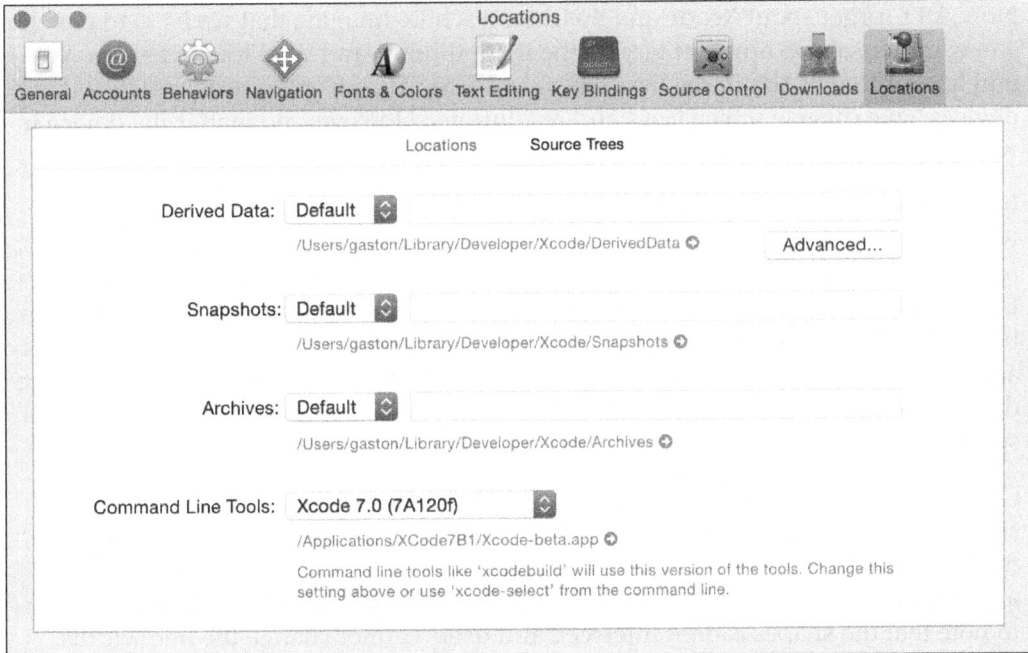

 We don't need an iOS Developer Program membership to run the examples included in this book. However, in case we want to distribute the apps or applications coded in Swift to any App Store or activate certain capabilities in Xcode, we will require an active membership.

[3]

We don't need any previous experience with the Swift programming language to work with the examples in the book and learn how to model and create object-oriented code with Swift. If we have some experience with Objective-C, Java, C#, Python, Ruby, or JavaScript, we will be able to easily learn Swift's syntax and understand the examples. Swift borrows many features from these and other modern programming languages, and therefore, any knowledge of these languages will be extremely useful.

Capturing objects from the real world

Now, let's forget about Xcode and Swift for a while. Imagine that we have to develop a new universal iOS app that targets the iPad, iPhone, and iPod touch devices. We will have different **UIs** (**User Interfaces**) and **UXs** (**User eXperiences**) because these devices have diverse screen sizes and resolutions. However, no matter the device in which the app runs, it will have the same goal.

Imagine that Vanessa is a very popular YouTuber, painter, and craftswoman who usually uploads videos on a YouTube channel. She has more than a million followers, and one of her latest videos had a huge impact on social networking sites. In this video, she sketched basic shapes and then painted them with acrylic paint to build patterns. She worked with very attractive colors, and many famous Hollywood actresses uploaded pictures on Instagram sharing their creations with the technique demonstrated by Vanessa and with the revolutionary special colors developed by a specific acrylic paint manufacturer.

Obviously, the acrylic paint manufacturer wants to take full advantage of this situation, so he specifies the requirements for an app. The app must provide a set of predefined 2D shapes that the user can drag and drop in a document to build a pattern so that he/she can change both the 2D position and size. It is important to note that the shapes cannot intersect, and users cannot change the line widths because they are the basic requirements of the technique introduced by Vanessa. A user can select the desired line and fill colors for each shape. At any time, the user can tap a button, and the app must display a list of the acrylic paint tubes, bottles, or jars that the user must buy to paint the drawn pattern. Finally, the user can easily place an online order to request the suggested acrylic paint tubes, bottles, or jars. The app also generates a tutorial to explain to the user how to generate each of the final colors for the lines and fills by thinning the appropriate amount of acrylic paint with water, based on the colors that the user has specified.

The following image shows an example of a pattern. Note that it is extremely simple to describe the objects that compose the pattern: four 2D shapes—specifically, two rectangles and two circles. If we measure the shapes, we would easily realize that they aren't two squares and two ellipses; they are two rectangles and two circles.

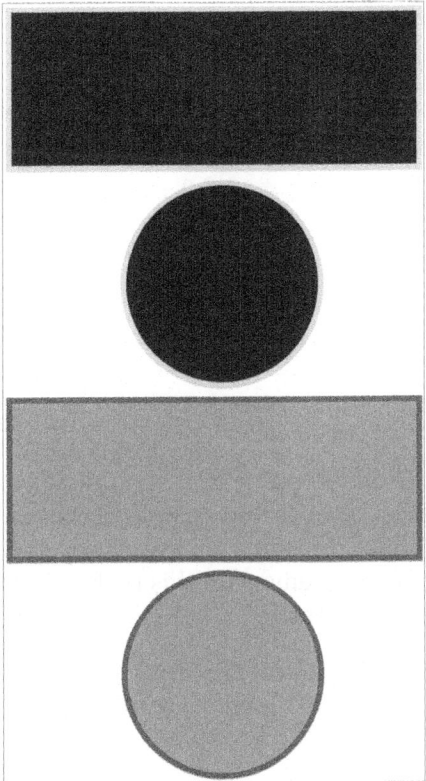

We can easily recognize objects; we understand that the pattern is composed of many 2D geometric shapes. Now, let's focus on the core requirement for the app, which is calculating the required amounts of acrylic paint. We have to take into account the following data for each shape included in the pattern in order to calculate the amount of acrylic paint:

- The perimeter
- The area
- The line color
- The fill color

Objects from the Real World to Playground

The app allows users to use a specific color for the line that draws the borders of each shape. Thus, we have to calculate the perimeter in order to use it as one of the values that will allow us to estimate the amount of acrylic paint that the user must buy to paint each shape's border. Then, we have to calculate the area to use it as one of the values that will allow us to estimate the amount of acrylic paint that the user must buy to fill each shape's area.

We have to start working on the backend code that calculates areas and perimeters. The app will follow Vanessa's guidelines to create the patterns, and it will only support the following six shapes:

- Squares
- Equilateral triangles
- Rectangles
- Circles
- Ellipses
- Regular hexagons

We can start writing Swift code—specifically, six functions that calculate the areas of the previously enumerated shapes and another six to calculate their perimeters. Note that we are talking about functions, and we stopped thinking about objects; therefore, we will face some problems with this path, which we will solve with an object-oriented approach from scratch.

For example, if we start thinking about functions to solve the problem, one possible solution is to code the following 12 functions to do the job:

- `calculateSquareArea`
- `calculateEquilateralTriangleArea`
- `calculateRectangleArea`
- `calculateCircleArea`
- `calculateEllipseArea`
- `calculateRegularHexagonArea`
- `calculateSquarePerimeter`
- `calculateEquilateralTrianglePerimeter`
- `calculateRectanglePerimeter`
- `calculateCirclePerimeter`
- `calculateEllipsePerimeter`
- `calculateRegularHexagonPerimeter`

Each of the previously enumerated functions has to receive the necessary parameters of each shape and return either its calculated area or perimeter.

Now, let's forget about functions for a bit. Let's recognize the real-world objects from the application's requirements that we were assigned. We have to calculate the areas and perimeters of six elements, which are six nouns in the requirements that represent real-life objects—specifically 2D shapes. Our list of real-world objects is exactly the same that Vanessa's specification uses to determine the shapes allowed to be used to create patterns. Take a look at the list:

- Squares
- Equilateral triangles
- Rectangles
- Circles
- Ellipses
- Regular hexagons

After recognizing the real-life objects, we can start designing our application by following an object-oriented paradigm. Instead of creating a set of functions that perform the required tasks, we can create software objects that represent the state and behavior of a square, equilateral triangle, rectangle, circle, ellipse, and regular hexagon. This way, the different objects mimic the real-world 2D shapes. We can work with the objects to specify the different attributes required to calculate the area and perimeter. Then, we can extend these objects to include the additional data required to calculate other required values, such as the quantity of acrylic paint required to paint the borders.

Now, let's move to the real world and think about each of the previously enumerated six shapes. Imagine that we have to draw each of the shapes on paper and calculate their areas and perimeters. After we draw each shape, which values will we use to calculate their areas and perimeters? Which formulas will we use?

We started working on an object-oriented design before we started coding, and therefore, we will work as if we didn't know many concepts of geometry. For example, we can easily generalize the formulas that we use to calculate the perimeters and areas of regular polygons. However, we will analyze the requirements in most cases; we still aren't experts on the subject, and we need to dive deeper into the subject before we can group classes and generalize their behavior.

The following figure shows a drawn square and the formulas that we will use to calculate the perimeter and area. We just need the length of side value, usually identified as **a**.

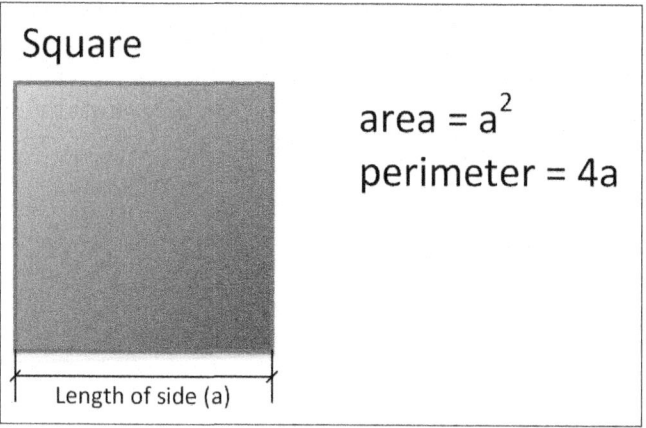

The following figure shows a drawn equilateral triangle and the formulas that we will use to calculate the perimeter and area. This type of triangle has equal sides, and the three internal angles are equal to 60 degrees. We just need the length of side value, usually identified as **a**.

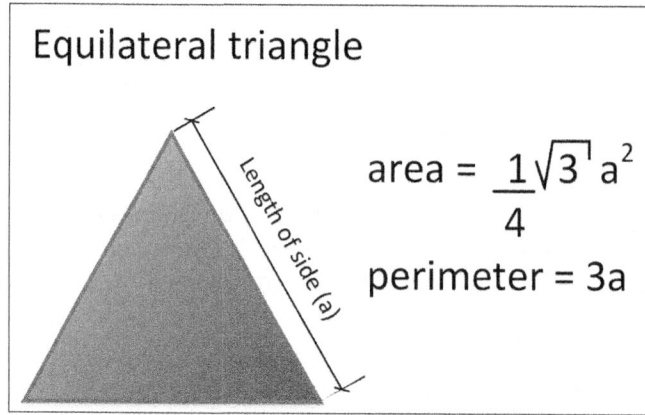

The following figure shows a drawn rectangle and the formulas that we will use to calculate the perimeter and area. We need the width and height values.

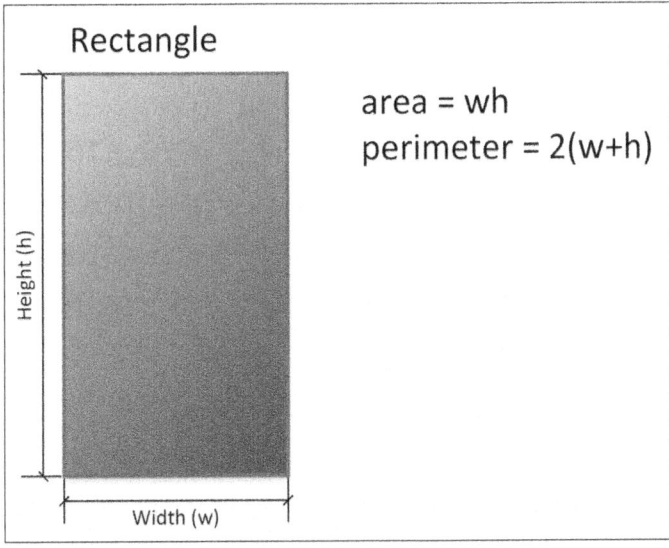

The following figure shows a drawn circle and the formulas that we will use to calculate the perimeter and area. We just need the radius value, usually identified as **r**.

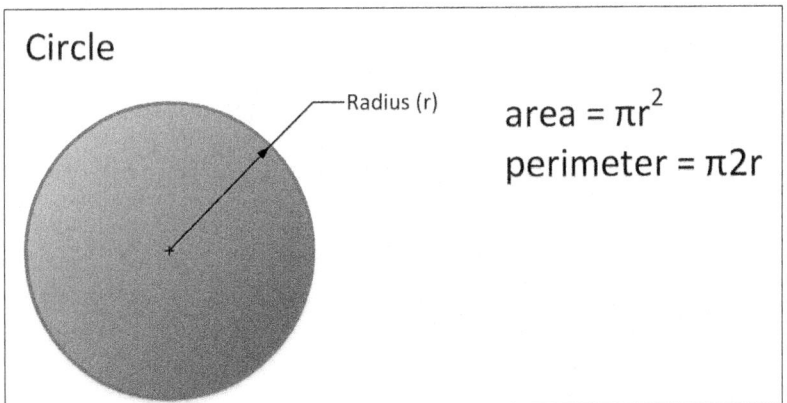

Objects from the Real World to Playground

The following figure shows a drawn ellipse and the formulas that we will use to calculate the perimeter and area. We need the semimajor axis (usually labelled as **a**) and semiminor axis (usually labelled as **b**) values.

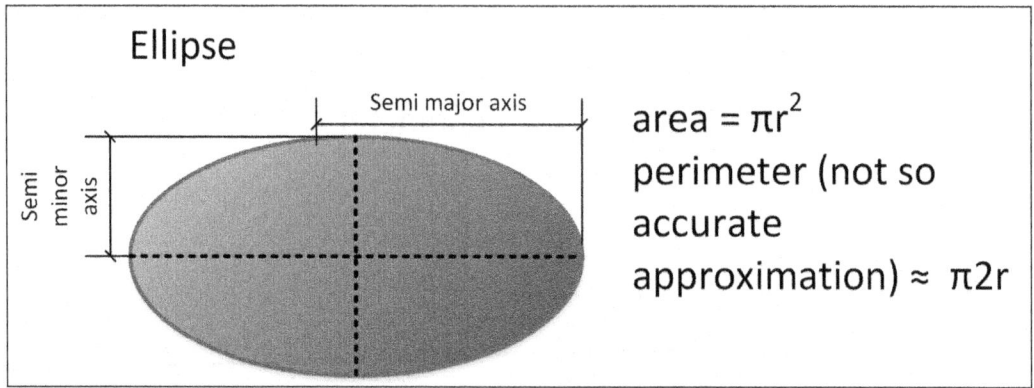

The following figure shows a drawn regular hexagon and the formulas that we will use to calculate the perimeter and area. We just need the length of the side value, usually labelled as **a**.

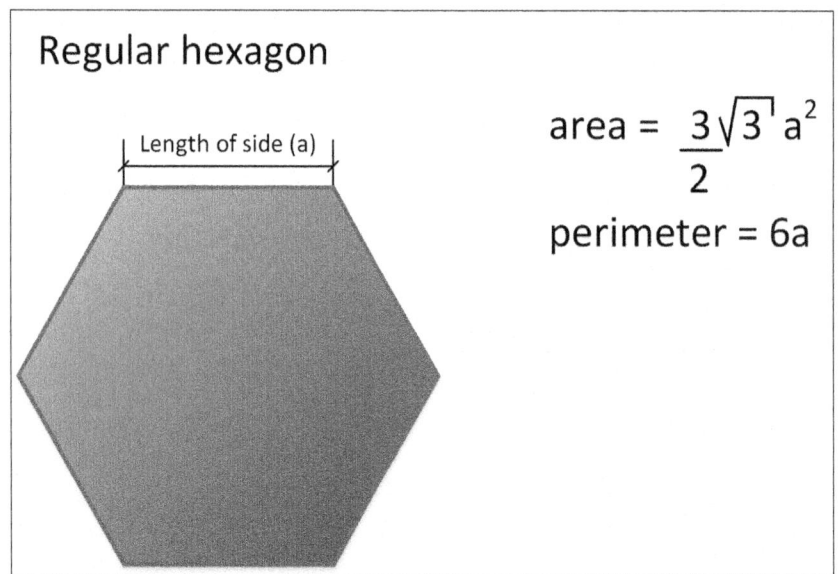

The following table summarizes the data required for each shape:

Shape	Required data
Square	The length of a side
Equilateral triangle	The length of a side
Rectangle	The width and height
Circle	The radius
Ellipse	The semimajor and semiminor axes
Regular hexagon	The length of a side

Each object that represents a specific shape encapsulates the required data that we identified. For example, an object that represents an ellipse will encapsulate the ellipse's semimajor and semiminor axes.

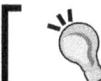

> *Data encapsulation* is one of the major pillars of object-oriented programming.

Generating classes to create objects

Imagine that you want to draw and calculate the areas of six different ellipses. You will end up with six ellipses drawn, their different semimajor axis and semiminor axis values, and their calculated areas. It would be great to have a blueprint to simplify the process of drawing each ellipse with their different semimajor axis and semiminor axis values.

In object-oriented programming, a class is a template definition or blueprint from which objects are created. Classes are models that define the state and behavior of an object. After declaring a class that defines the state and behavior of an ellipse, we can use it to generate objects that represent the state and behavior of each real-world ellipse.

> Objects are also known as instances. For example, we can say each *circle* object is an instance of the *Circle* class.

The following picture shows two circle instances drawn with their radius values specified: **Circle #1** and **Circle #2**. We can use a Circle class as a blueprint to generate the two different Circle instances. Note that **Circle #1** has a radius value of **175**, and **Circle #2** has a radius value of **350**. Each instance has a different radius value.

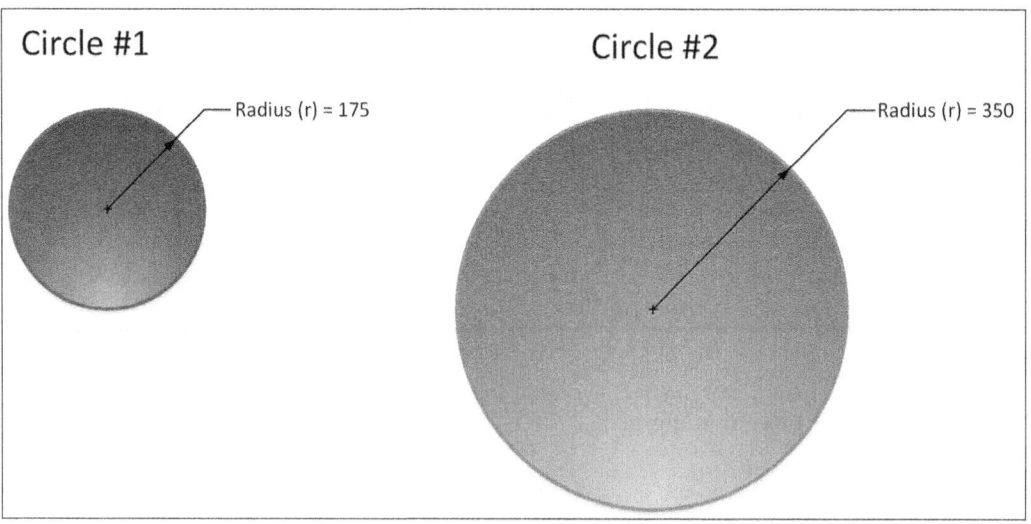

The following image shows three ellipse instances drawn with their semimajor axis and semiminor axis values specified: **Ellipse #1**, **Ellipse #2**, and **Ellipse #3**. In this case, we can use an *Ellipse* class as a blueprint to generate the three different ellipse instances. It is very important to understand the difference between a class and the objects or instances generated through its usage. The object-oriented programming features supported in Swift allow us to discover which blueprint we used to generate a specific object. We will use these features in many examples in the upcoming chapters. Thus, we can know that each object is an instance of the *Ellipse* class. Each ellipse has its own specific values for the semimajor and semiminor axes.

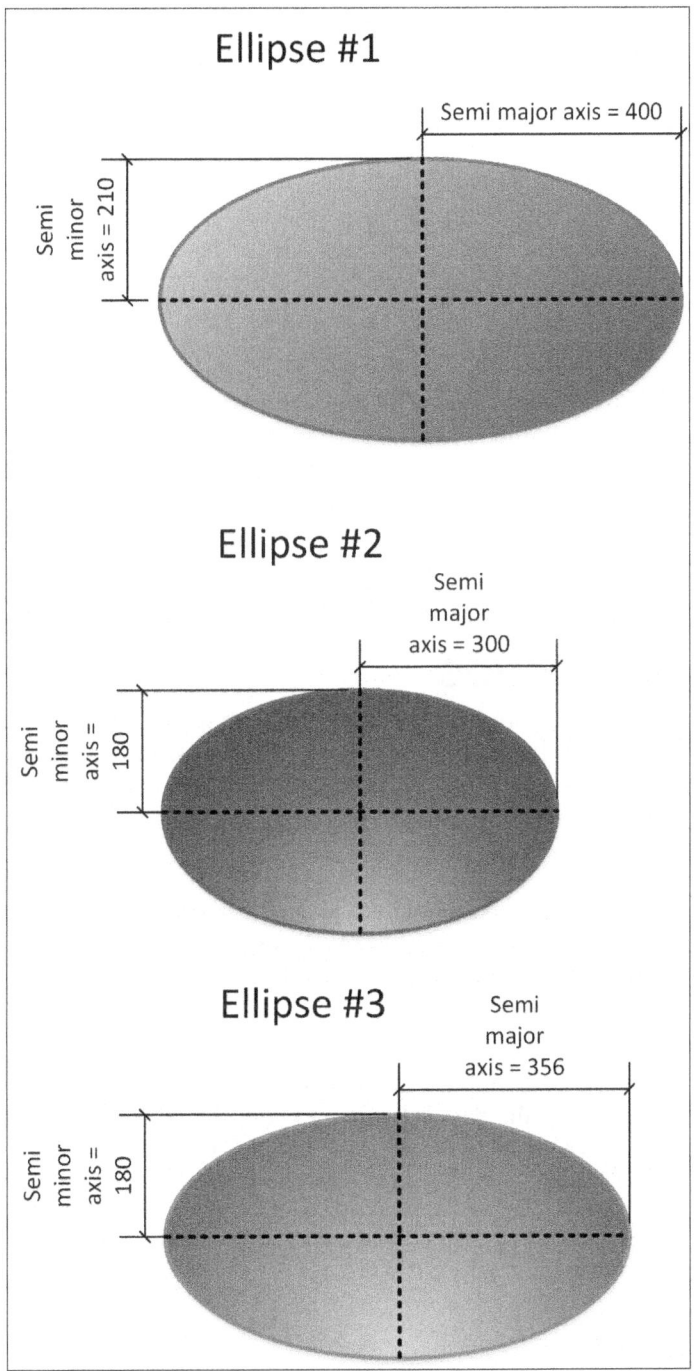

Objects from the Real World to Playground

We recognized six completely different real-world objects from the application's requirements, and therefore, we can generate the following six classes to create the necessary objects:

- `Square`
- `EquilateralTriangle`
- `Rectangle`
- `Circle`
- `Ellipse`
- `RegularHexagon`

Note the usage of Pascal case for class names; this means that the first letter of each word that composes the name is capitalized, while the other letters are in lowercase. This is a coding convention in Swift. For example, we use the `RegularHexagon` name for the class that will generate regular hexagons.

Recognizing variables and constants to create properties

We know the information required for each of the shapes to achieve our goals. Now, we have to design the classes to include the necessary properties that provide the required data to each instance. We have to make sure that each class has the necessary variables that encapsulate all the data required by the objects to perform all the tasks based on our application domain.

Let's start with the `RegularHexagon` class. It is necessary to know the length of a side for each instance of this class—that is, for each regular hexagon object. Thus, we need an encapsulated variable that allows each instance of the `RegularHexagon` class to specify the value for the length of a side.

> The variables defined in a class to encapsulate the data for each instance of the class in Swift are known as **properties**. Each instance has its own independent value for the properties defined in the class. The properties allow us to define the characteristics for an instance of the class. In other programming languages, these variables defined in a class are known as either **attributes** or **fields**.

Chapter 1

The `RegularHexagon` class defines a floating point property named `lengthOfSide`, whose initial value is equal to 0 for any new instance of the class. After we create an instance of the `RegularHexagon` class, it is possible to change the value of the `lengthOfSide` attribute.

Note the usage of Camel case, which is using a lowercase first letter, for class property names. The first letter is lowercase, and then, the first letter for each word that composes the name is capitalized, while the other letters are in lowercase. It is a coding convention in Swift for both variables and properties. For example, we use the name `lengthOfSide` for the property that stores the value of the length of side.

Imagine that we create two instances of the `RegularHexagon` class. One of the instances is named `regularHexagon1` and the other `regularHexagon2`. The instance names allow us to access the encapsulated data for each object, and therefore, we can use them to change the values of the exposed properties.

Swift uses a dot (`.`) to allow us to access the properties of instances. So, `regularHexagon1.lengthOfSide` provides access to the length of side for the `RegularHexagon` instance named `regularHexagon1`, and `regularHexagon2.lengthOfSide` does the same for the `RegularHexagon` instance named `regularHexagon2`.

Note that the naming convention makes it easy for us to differentiate an instance name—that is, a variable from a class name. Whenever we see the first letter in uppercase or capitalized, it means that we are talking about a class.

We can assign `20` to `regularHexagon1.lengthOfSide` and `50` to `regularHexagon2.lengthOfSide`. This way, each `RegularHexagon` instance will have a different value for the `lengthOfSide` attribute.

Now, let's move to the `Ellipse` class. We can define two floating point attributes for this class: `semiMajorAxis` and `semiMinorAxis`. Their initial values will also be 0. Then, we can create three instances of the `Ellipse` class named `ellipse1`, `ellipse2`, and `ellipse3`.

We can assign the values summarized in the following table to the three instances of the `Ellipse` class:

Instance name	semiMinorAxis **value**	semiMajorAxis **value**
ellipse1	210	400
ellipse2	180	300
ellipse3	180	356

Objects from the Real World to Playground

This way, `ellipse1.semiMinorAxis` will be equal to `210`, while `ellipse3.semiMinorAxis` will be equal to `180`. The `ellipse1` instance represents an ellipse with `semiMinorAxis` of `210` and `semiMajorAxis` of `400`.

The following table summarizes the floating point properties defined for each of the six classes that we need for our application:

Class name	Properties list
`Square`	`lengthOfSide`
`EquilateralTriangle`	`lengthOfSide`
`Rectangle`	`width` and `height`
`Circle`	`radius`
`Ellipse`	`semiMinorAxis` and `semiMajorAxis`
`RegularHexagon`	`lengthOfSide`

> The properties are members of their respective classes. However, properties aren't the only members that classes can have.

Note that three of these classes have the same property: `lengthOfSide` — specifically, the following three classes: `Square`, `EquilateralTriangle`, and `RegularHexagon`. We will dive deep into what these three classes have in common later and take advantage of object-oriented features to reuse code and simplify our application's maintenance. However, we are just starting our journey, and we will make improvements as we learn additional object-oriented features included in Swift.

The following image shows a **UML (Unified Modeling Language)** class diagram with the six classes and their properties. This diagram is very easy to understand. The class name appears on the top of the rectangle that identifies each class. A rectangle below the same shape that holds the class name displays all the property names exposed by the class with a plus sign (+) as a prefix. This prefix indicates that what follows it is an attribute name in UML and a property name in Swift.

Square		EquilateralTriangle
+lengthOfSide		+lengthOfSide

Rectangle		Circle
+width +height		+radius

Ellipse		RegularHexagon
+semiMinorAxis +semiMajorAxis		+lengthOfSide

Recognizing actions to create methods

So far, we designed six classes and identified the necessary properties for each of them. Now, it is time to add the necessary pieces of code that work with the previously defined properties to perform all the tasks. We have to make sure that each class has the necessary encapsulated functions that process the property values specified in the objects to perform all the tasks.

Let's forget a bit about similarities between the different classes. We will work with them individually as if we didn't have the necessary knowledge of geometric formulas. We will start with the Square class. We need pieces of code that allow each instance of this class to use the value of the lengthOfSide property to calculate the area and perimeter.

> The functions defined in a class to encapsulate the behavior of each instance of the class are known as **methods**. Each instance can access the set of methods exposed by the class. The code specified in a method can work with the properties specified in the class. When we execute a method, it will use the properties of the specific instance. Whenever we define methods, we must make sure that we define them in a logical place—that is, in the place where the required data is kept.

[17]

Objects from the Real World to Playground

When a method doesn't require parameters, we can say that it is a parameterless method. In this case, all the methods we will initially define for the classes will be parameterless methods that just work with the values of the previously defined properties and use the formulas shown in the figures. Thus, we will be able to call them without arguments. We will start creating methods, but we will be able to explore additional options based on specific Swift features later.

The `Square` class defines the following two parameterless methods. We will declare the code for both methods within the definition of the `Square` class so that they can access the `lengthOfSide` property value, as follows:

- `calculateArea`: This method returns a floating point value with the calculated area for the square. It returns the square of the `lengthOfSide` attribute value (*lengthOfSide^2* or *lengthOfSide ^ 2*).
- `calculatePerimeter`: This method returns a floating point value with the calculated perimeter for the square. It returns the `lengthOfSide` attribute value multiplied by 4 (*4 * lengthOfSide*).

Note the usage of Camel case — that is, using a lowercase first letter — for method names. The first letter is in lowercase, and then, the first letter for each word that composes the name is capitalized, while the other letters are in lowercase. As it happened with property names, it is a coding convention in Swift for methods.

Swift uses a dot (.) to allow us to execute the methods of the instances. Imagine that we have two instances of the `Square` class: `square1` with the `lengthOfSide` property equal to 20 and `square2` with the `lengthOfSide` property equal to 40. If we call `square1.calculateArea`, it will return the result *20^2*, which is 400. If we call `square2.calculateArea`, it will return the result *40^2*, which is 1600. Each instance has a diverse value for the `lengthOfSide` attribute, and therefore, the results of executing the `calcualteArea` method are different.

If we call `square1.calculatePerimeter`, it will return the result of *4 * 20*, which is 80. On the other hand, if we call `square2.calculatePerimeter`, it will return the result of *4 * 40*, which is 160.

Now, let's move to the `EquilateralTriangle` class. We need exactly two methods with the same names specified for the `Square` class: `calculateArea` and `calculatePerimeter`. In addition, the methods return the same type and don't need parameters, so we can declare both of them as parameterless methods, as we did in the `Square` class. However, these methods have to calculate the results in a different way; that is, they have to use the appropriate formulas for an equilateral triangle. The other classes also need the same two methods. However, each of them will use the appropriate formulas for the related shape.

We have a specific problem with the `calculatePerimeter` method that the `Ellipse` class generates. Perimeters are complex to calculate for ellipses, so there are many formulas that provide approximations. An exact formula requires an infinite series of calculations. We can use an initial formula that isn't very accurate, which we will have to improve later. The initial formula will allow us to return a floating point value with the calculated approximation of the perimeter for the ellipse.

The following figure shows an updated version of the UML diagram with the six classes, their attributes, and their methods:

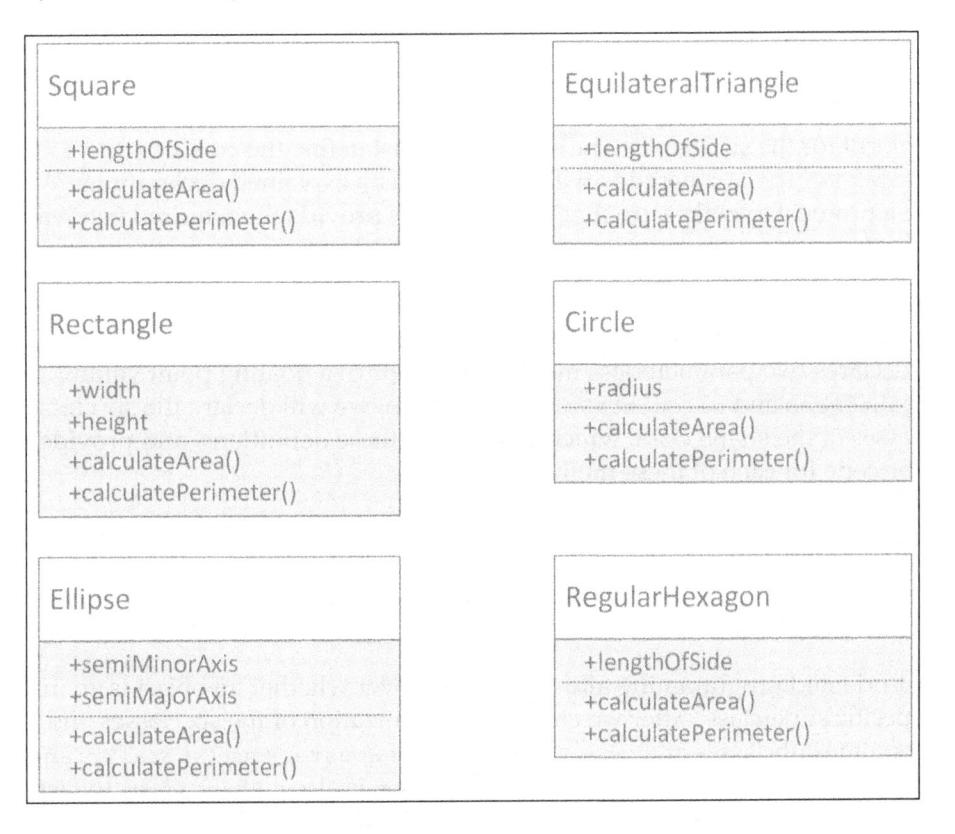

Square	EquilateralTriangle
+lengthOfSide	+lengthOfSide
+calculateArea() +calculatePerimeter()	+calculateArea() +calculatePerimeter()

Rectangle	Circle
+width +height	+radius
+calculateArea() +calculatePerimeter()	+calculateArea() +calculatePerimeter()

Ellipse	RegularHexagon
+semiMinorAxis +semiMajorAxis	+lengthOfSide
+calculateArea() +calculatePerimeter()	+calculateArea() +calculatePerimeter()

Organizing classes with UML diagrams

So far, our object-oriented solution includes six classes with their properties and methods. However, if we take another look at these six classes, we will notice that all of them have the same two methods: `calculateArea` and `calculatePerimeter`. The code for the methods in each class is different because each shape uses a special formula to calculate either the area or perimeter. However, the declarations, contracts, or protocols for the methods are the same. Both methods have the same name, are always parameterless, and return a floating point value. Thus, all of them return the same type.

When we talked about the six classes, we said we were talking about six different geometrical shapes or simply shapes. Thus, we can generalize the required behavior or protocol for the six shapes. The six shapes must define the `calculateArea` and `calculatePerimeter` methods with the previously explained declarations. We can create a protocol to make sure that the six classes provide the required behavior.

The protocol is a special class named `Shape`, and it generalizes the requirements for the geometrical shapes in our application. In this case, we will work with a special class, but in the future, we will use protocols for the same goal. The `Shape` class declares two parameterless methods that return a floating point value: `calculateArea` and `calculatePerimeter`. Then, we will declare the six classes as subclasses of the `Shape` class, which will inherit these definitions, and provide the specific code for each of these methods.

The subclasses of `Shape` (`Square`, `EquilateralTriangle`, `Rectangle`, `Circle`, `Ellipse`, and `RegularHexagon`) implement the methods because they provide code while maintaining the same method declarations specified in the `Shape` superclass. *Abstraction* and *hierarchy* are two major pillars of object-oriented programming.

Object-oriented programming allows us to discover whether an object is an instance of a specific superclass. After we chang the organization of the six classes and they become subclasses of `Shape`, any instance of `Square`, `EquilateralTriangle`, `Rectangle`, `Circle`, `Ellipse`, or `RegularHexagon` is also a `Shape` class. In fact, it isn't difficult to explain the abstraction because we speak the truth about the object-oriented model when we say that it represents the real world. It makes sense to say that a regular hexagon is indeed a shape, and therefore, an instance of `RegularHexagon` is a `Shape` class. An instance of `RegularHexagon` is both a `Shape` (the superclass of `RegularHexagon`) and a `RegularHexagon` (the class that we used to create the object) class.

The following figure shows an updated version of the UML diagram with the superclass or base class (`Shape`), its six subclasses, and their attributes and methods. Note that the diagram uses a line that ends in an arrow that connects each subclass to its superclass. You can read the line that ends in an arrow as the following: the class where the line begins "*is a subclass of*" the class that has the line ending with an arrow. For example, `Square` is a subclass of `Shape`, and `EquilateralTriangle` is a subclass of `Shape`.

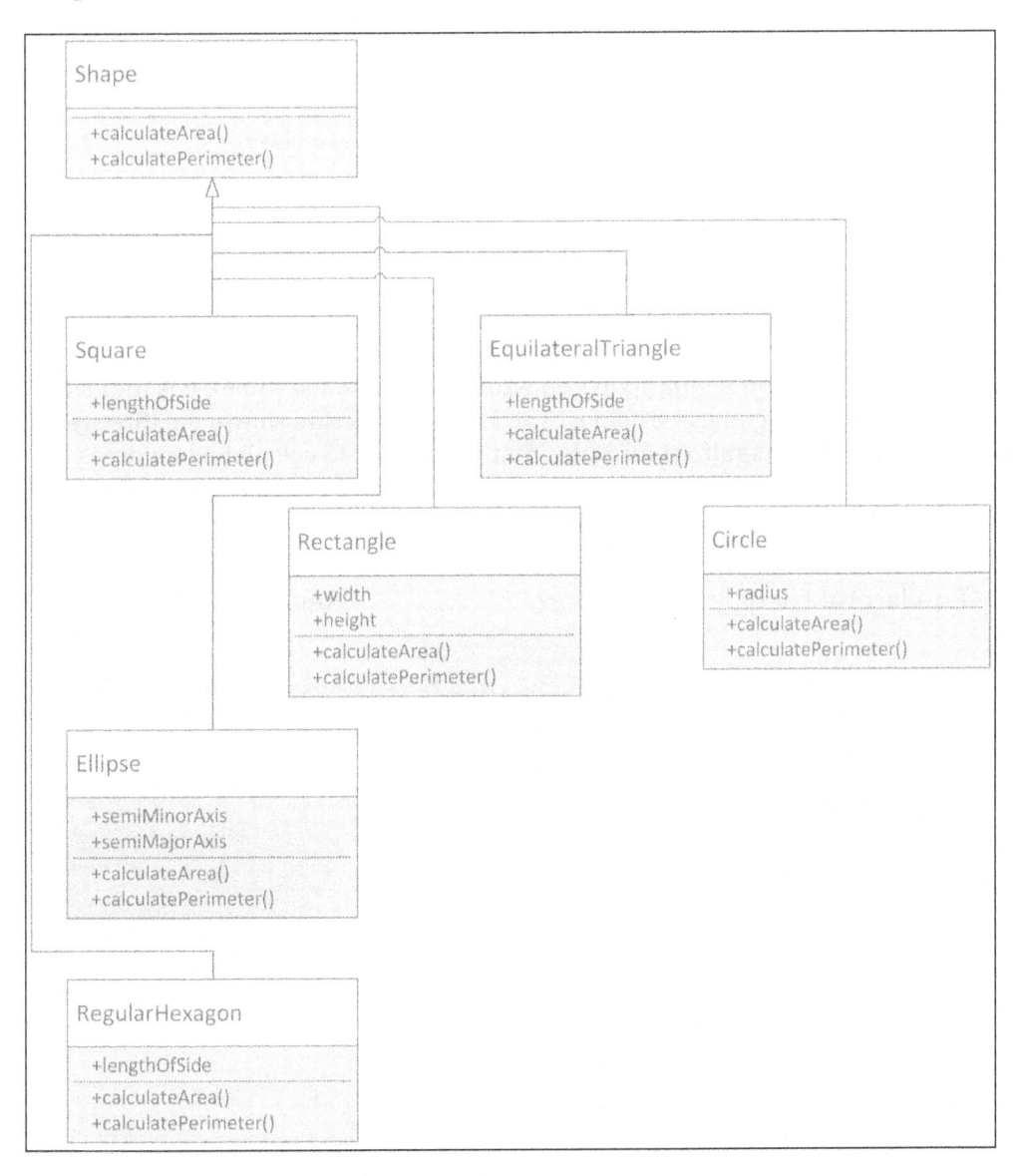

Shape
- +calculateArea()
- +calculatePerimeter()

Square
- +lengthOfSide
- +calculateArea()
- +calculatePerimeter()

EquilateralTriangle
- +lengthOfSide
- +calculateArea()
- +calculatePerimeter()

Rectangle
- +width
- +height
- +calculateArea()
- +calculatePerimeter()

Circle
- +radius
- +calculateArea()
- +calculatePerimeter()

Ellipse
- +semiMinorAxis
- +semiMajorAxis
- +calculateArea()
- +calculatePerimeter()

RegularHexagon
- +lengthOfSide
- +calculateArea()
- +calculatePerimeter()

Objects from the Real World to Playground

> [💡 A single class can be the superclass of many subclasses.]

Now, it is time to have a meeting with a domain expert—that is, someone that has an excellent knowledge of geometry. We can use the UML diagram to explain the object-oriented design for the solution. After we explain the different classes that we will use to abstract behavior, the domain expert explains to us that many of the shapes have something in common and that we can generalize behavior even further. The following three shapes are regular polygons:

- An equilateral triangle (the `EquilateralTriangle` class)
- A square (the `Square` class)
- A regular hexagon (the `RegularHexagon` class)

Regular polygons are polygons that are both equiangular and equilateral. All the sides that compose a regular polygon have the same length and are placed around a common center. This way, all the angles between any two sides are equal. An equilateral triangle is a regular polygon with three sides, the square has four sides, and the regular hexagon has six sides. The following picture shows the three regular polygons and the generalized formulas that we can use to calculate their areas and perimeters. The generalized formula to calculate the area requires us to calculate a cotangent, which is abbreviated as **cot**:

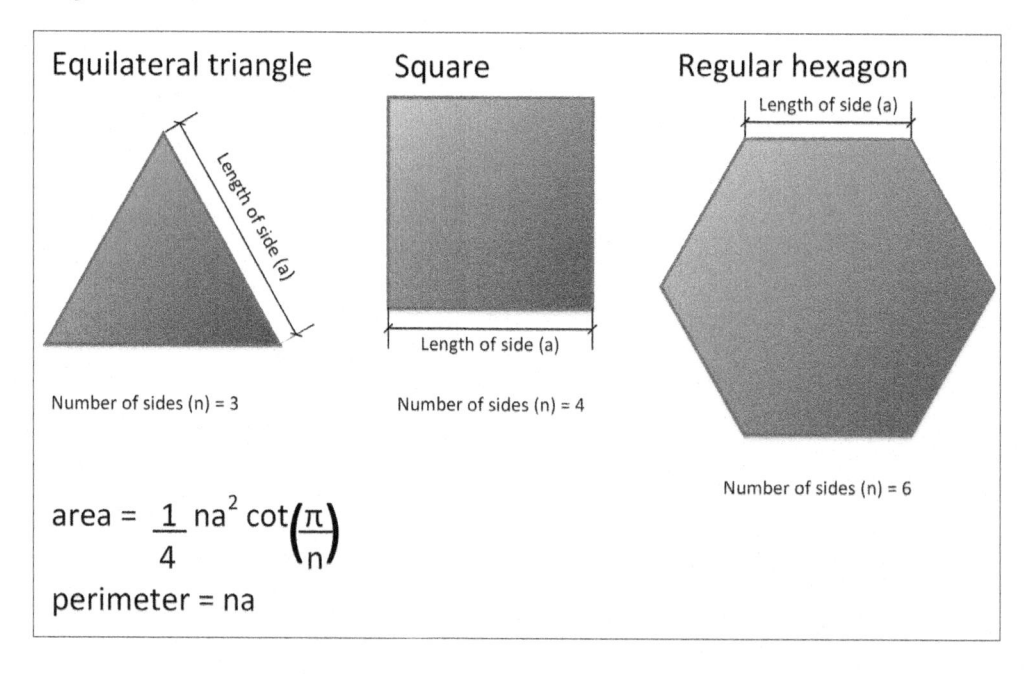

Equilateral triangle
Length of side (a)
Number of sides (n) = 3

Square
Length of side (a)
Number of sides (n) = 4

Regular hexagon
Length of side (a)
Number of sides (n) = 6

$$\text{area} = \frac{1}{4} na^2 \cot\left(\frac{\pi}{n}\right)$$

$$\text{perimeter} = na$$

As the three shapes use the same formula with just a different value for the number of sides (**n**) parameter, we can generalize the required protocol for the three regular polygons. The protocol is a special class named `RegularPolygon` that defines a new `numberOfSides` property that specifies the number of sides with an integer value. The `RegularPolygon` class is a subclass of the previously defined `Shape` class. It makes sense because a regular polygon is indeed a shape. The three classes that represent regular polygons become subclasses of `RegularPolygon`. However, both the `calculateArea` and `calculatePerimeter` methods are coded in the `RegularPolygon` class using the generalized formulas. The subclasses just specify the right value for the inherited `numberOfSides` property, as follows:

- `EquilateralTriangle`: 3
- `Square`: 4
- `RegularHexagon`: 6

The `RegularPolygon` class also defines the `lengthOfSide` property that was previously defined in the three classes that represent regular polygons. Now, the three classes become subclasses or `RegularPolygon` and inherit the `lengthOfSide` property. The following figure shows an updated version of the UML diagram with the new `RegularPolygon` class and the changes in the three classes that represent regular polygons. The three classes that represent regular polygons do not declare either the `calculateArea` or `calculatePerimeter` methods because these classes inherit them from the `RegularPolygon` superclass and don't need to make changes to these methods that apply a general formula.

```
Shape
---
+calculateArea()
+calculatePerimeter()
```

```
Rectangle
---
+width
+height
---
+calculateArea()
+calculatePerimeter()
```

```
Ellipse
---
+semiMinorAxis
+semiMajorAxis
---
+calculateArea()
+calculatePerimeter()
```

```
Circle
---
+radius
---
+calculateArea()
+calculatePerimeter()
```

```
RegularPolygon
---
+numberOfSides
+lengthOfSide
---
+calculateArea()
+calculatePerimeter()
```

```
EquilateralTriangle
---
+numberOfSides
```

```
Square
---
+numberOfSides
```

```
RegularHexagon
---
+numberOfSides
```

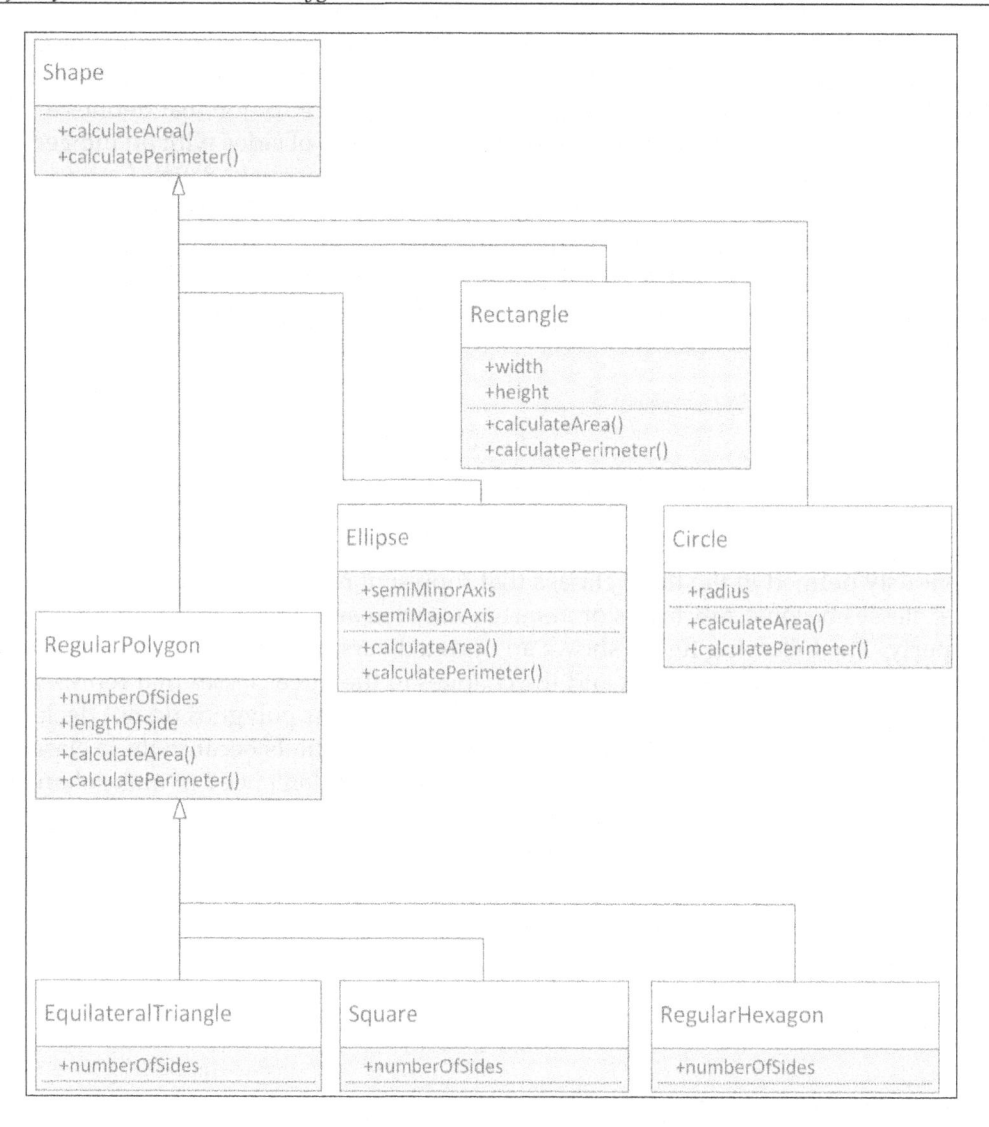

Our domain expert also explains to us a specific issue with ellipses. There are many formulas that provide approximations of the perimeter value for this shape. Thus, it makes sense to add additional methods that calculate the perimeter using other formulas. He suggests us to make it possible to calculate the perimeters with the following formulas:

- The second version of the formula developed by Srinivasa Aiyangar Ramanujan
- The formula proposed by David W. Cantrell

We will define the following two additional parameterless methods to the `Ellipse` class. The new methods will return a floating point value and solve the specific problem of the ellipse shape:

- `CalculatePerimeterWithRamanujanII`
- `CalculatePerimeterWithCantrell`

This way, the `Ellipse` class will implement the methods specified in the `Shape` superclass and also add two specific methods that aren't included in any of the other subclasses of `Shape`. The following figure shows an updated version of the UML diagram with the new methods for the `Ellipse` class:

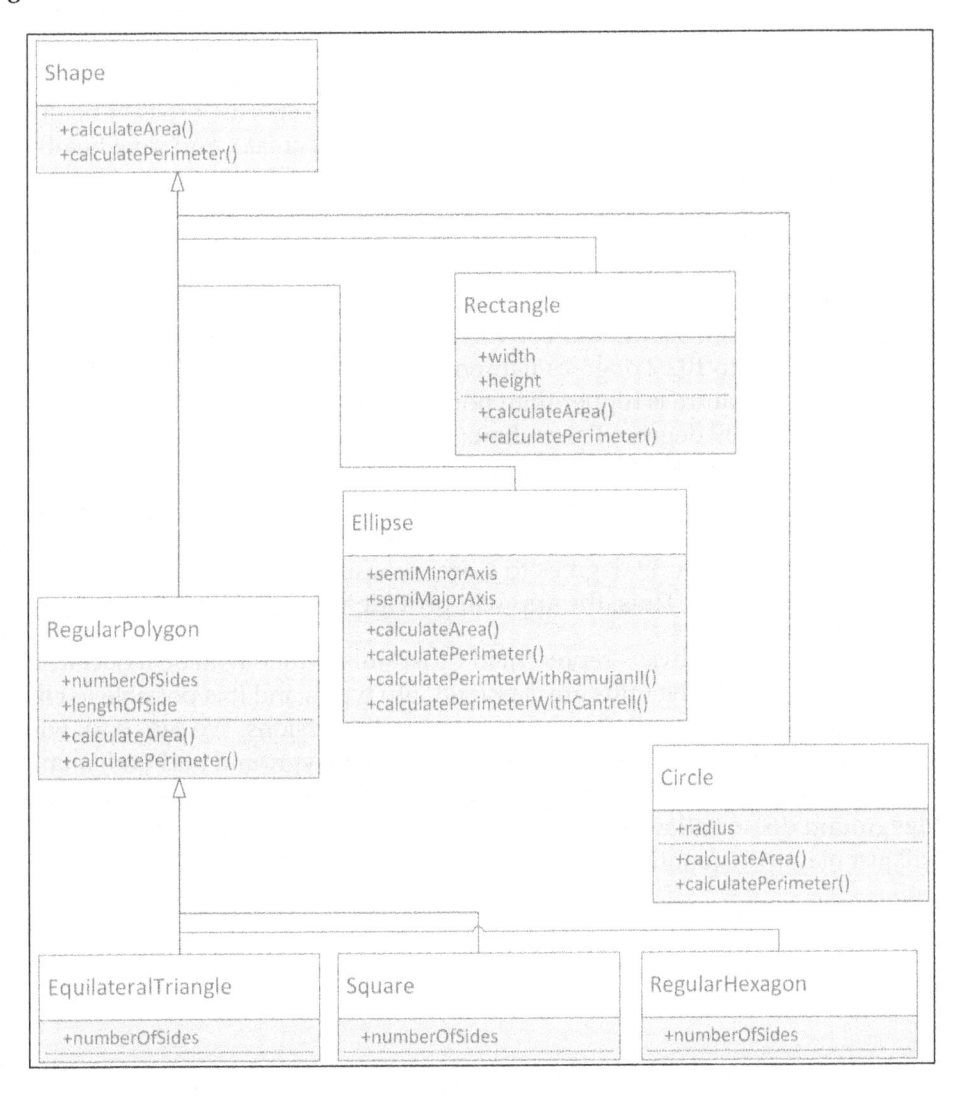

```
┌─────────────────────────────┐
│ Shape                       │
├─────────────────────────────┤
│ +calculateArea()            │
│ +calculatePerimeter()       │
└─────────────────────────────┘

┌─────────────────────────────┐
│ Rectangle                   │
├─────────────────────────────┤
│ +width                      │
│ +height                     │
├─────────────────────────────┤
│ +calculateArea()            │
│ +calculatePerimeter()       │
└─────────────────────────────┘

┌─────────────────────────────────────┐
│ Ellipse                             │
├─────────────────────────────────────┤
│ +semiMinorAxis                      │
│ +semiMajorAxis                      │
├─────────────────────────────────────┤
│ +calculateArea()                    │
│ +calculatePerimeter()               │
│ +calculatePerimterWithRamujanII()   │
│ +calculatePerimeterWithCantrell()   │
└─────────────────────────────────────┘

┌─────────────────────────────┐
│ RegularPolygon              │
├─────────────────────────────┤
│ +numberOfSides              │
│ +lengthOfSide               │
├─────────────────────────────┤
│ +calculateArea()            │
│ +calculatePerimeter()       │
└─────────────────────────────┘

┌─────────────────────────────┐
│ Circle                      │
├─────────────────────────────┤
│ +radius                     │
├─────────────────────────────┤
│ +calculateArea()            │
│ +calculatePerimeter()       │
└─────────────────────────────┘

┌──────────────────┐  ┌──────────────────┐  ┌──────────────────┐
│ EquilateralTriangle │ Square           │  │ RegularHexagon   │
├──────────────────┤  ├──────────────────┤  ├──────────────────┤
│ +numberOfSides   │  │ +numberOfSides   │  │ +numberOfSides   │
└──────────────────┘  └──────────────────┘  └──────────────────┘
```

Working with API objects in the Xcode Playground

Now, let's forget a bit about geometry, shapes, polygons, perimeters, and areas. We will interact with API objects in the Xcode Playground. You still need to learn many things before we can start creating object-oriented code. However, we will write some code in the Playground to interact with an existing API before we move forward with our journey into the object-oriented programming world.

Object-oriented programming is extremely useful when you have to interact with API objects. When Apple launched iOS 8, it introduced a Health app that provided iPhone users access to a dashboard of health and fitness data. The **HealthKit** framework introduced in the iOS SDK 8 allows app developers to request permissions from the users themselves to read and write specific types of health and fitness data. The framework makes it possible to ask for, create, and save health and fitness data that the users will see summarized in the Health app.

When we store and query health and fitness data, we have to use the framework to work with the units in which the values are expressed, their conversions, and localizations. For example, let's imagine an app that stores body temperature data without considering units and their conversions. A value of 39 degrees Celsius (which is equivalent to 102.2 degrees Fahrenheit) in an adult would mean that his/her body temperature is higher than normal (that is, he/she may have a fever). However, a value of 39 degrees Fahrenheit (equivalent to 3.88 degrees Celsius) would mean that his/her body is close to its freezing point. If our app just stores values without considering the related units and user preferences, we can have huge mistakes. If the app just saves 39 degrees and thinks that the user will always display Celsius, it will still display 39 degrees to a user whose settings use Fahrenheit as the default temperature unit. Thus, the app will provide wrong information to the user.

The data in HealthKit is always represented by a double value with an associated simple or complex unit. The units are classified into types, and it is possible to check the compatibility between units before performing conversions. We can work with HealthKit quantities and units in the Swift interactive Playground and understand how simple it is to work with an object-oriented framework. It is important to note that the Playground doesn't allow us to interact with the HealthKit data store. However, we will just play with quantities and units with a few object-oriented snippets.

Start Xcode, navigate to **File** | **New** | **Playground...**, enter a name for the **Playground**, select **iOS** as the desired platform, click on **Next**, select the desired location for the Playground file, and click on **Create**. Xcode will display a Playground window with a line that imports `UIKit` and creates a `string` variable. You just need to add the following line to be able to work with quantities and units from the `HealthKit` framework, as shown in the subsequent screenshot:

```
import HealthKit
```

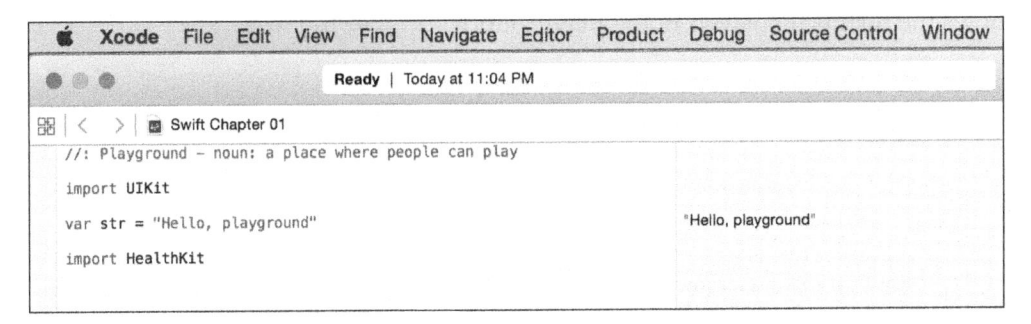

All `HealthKit` types start with the `HK` prefix. `HKUnit` represents a particular unit that can be either simple or complex. Simple units for Temperature are degrees Celsius and degrees Fahrenheit. A complex unit for Mass/Volume is ounces per liter (oz/L). `HKUnit` supports many standard **SI units** (**Système Internationale d'Unités** in French, **International System of Units** in English) and nonSI units.

Add the following two lines to the Swift Playground and check the results on the right-hand side of the window; you will notice that they generate instances of `HKTemperatureUnit`. Thus, you created two objects that represent temperature units, as follows:

```
let degCUnit = HKUnit.degreeCelsiusUnit()
let degFUnit = HKUnit.degreeFahrenheitUnit()
```

However, there are other ways to create objects that represent temperature units. It is also possible to use the `HKUnit` initializer, which returns the appropriate unit instance from its string representation. For example, the following lines also generate instances of `HKTemperatureUnit` for degrees in Celsius and Fahrenheit:

```
let degCUnitFromStr = HKUnit(fromString: "degC")
let degFUnitFromStr = HKUnit(fromString: "degF")
```

The following lines generate two instances of `HKEnergyUnit` — one for kilocalories and the other for kilojoules:

```
let kiloCaloriesUnit = HKUnit(fromString: "kcal")
let joulesUnit = HKUnit(fromString: "kJ")
```

Objects from the Real World to Playground

The next two lines generate two instances of `HKMassUnit` — one for kilograms and the other for pounds:

```
let kiloGramsUnit = HKUnit.gramUnitWithMetricPrefix(HKMetricPrefix.Kilo)
let poundsUnit = HKUnit.poundUnit()
```

The next line generates an instance of `_HKCompoundUnit` because the string specifies a complex unit for Mass/Volume: ounces per liter (oz/L). The subsequent screenshot shows the results displayed in the Playground:

```
let ouncesPerLiter = HKUnit(fromString: "oz/L")
```

```
import UIKit
var str = "Hello, playground"                                              "Hello, playground"
import HealthKit
let degCUnit = HKUnit.degreeCelsiusUnit()                                  degC
let degFUnit = HKUnit.degreeFahrenheitUnit()                               degF

let degCUnitFromStr = HKUnit(fromString: "degC")                           degC

let degFUnitFromStr = HKUnit(fromString: "degF")                           degF

let kiloCaloriesUnit = HKUnit(fromString: "kcal")                          kcal

let joulesUnit = HKUnit(fromString: "kJ")                                  kJ

let kiloGramsUnit = HKUnit.gramUnitWithMetricPrefix(HKMetricPrefix.        kg
    Kilo)

let poundsUnit = HKUnit.poundUnit()                                        lb

let ouncesPerLiter = HKUnit(fromString: "oz/L")                            oz/L
```

`HKQuantity` encapsulates a quantity value (`Double`) and the unit of measurement (`HKUnit`). This class doesn't provide all the operations you might expect to work with quantities and their units of measure, but it allows you to perform some useful compatibility checks and conversions.

The following lines create two `HKQuantity` instances with temperature units named `bodyTemperature1` and `bodyTemperature2`. The former uses degrees Celsius (`degCUnit`) and the latter degrees Fahrenheit (`degFUnit`). Then, the code calls the `isCompatibleWithUnit` method to make sure that each `HKQuantity` instance can be converted to degrees Fahrenheit (`degFUnit`). If `isCompatibleWithUnit` returns `true`, it means that you can convert to `HKUnit`, which is specified as an argument. We always have to call this method before calling the `doubleValueForUnit` method. This way, we will avoid errors when the units aren't compatible.

The `doubleValueForUnit` method returns the quantity value converted to the unit specified as an argument. In this case, the two calls make sure that the value is expressed in degrees Fahrenheit no matter the temperature unit specified in each `HKQuantity` instance. The screenshot that follows the given code shows the results displayed in the Playground:

```
let bodyTemperature1 = HKQuantity(unit: degCUnit, doubleValue: 35.2)
let bodyTemperature2 = HKQuantity(unit: degFUnit, doubleValue: 95)
print(bodyTemperature1.description)
print(bodyTemperature2.description)

if bodyTemperature1.isCompatibleWithUnit(degFUnit) {
    print("Temperature #1 in Fahrenheit degrees:
\(bodyTemperature1.doubleValueForUnit(degFUnit))")
}

if bodyTemperature2.isCompatibleWithUnit(degFUnit) {
    print("Temperature #2 in Fahrenheit degrees: \(bodyTemperature2.doubleValueForUnit(degFUnit))")
}
```

Code	Output
`import HealthKit`	
`let degCUnit = HKUnit.degreeCelsiusUnit()`	degC
`let degFUnit = HKUnit.degreeFahrenheitUnit()`	degF
`let degCUnitFromStr = HKUnit(fromString: "degC")`	degC
`let degFUnitFromStr = HKUnit(fromString: "degF")`	degF
`let kiloCaloriesUnit = HKUnit(fromString: "kcal")`	kcal
`let joulesUnit = HKUnit(fromString: "kJ")`	kJ
`let kiloGramsUnit = HKUnit.gramUnitWithMetricPrefix(HKMetricPrefix.Kilo)`	kg
`let poundsUnit = HKUnit.poundUnit()`	lb
`let ouncesPerLiter = HKUnit(fromString: "oz/L")`	oz/L
`let bodyTemperature1 = HKQuantity(unit: degCUnit, doubleValue: 35.2)`	35.2 degC
`let bodyTemperature2 = HKQuantity(unit: degFUnit, doubleValue: 95)`	95 degF
`print(bodyTemperature1.description)`	"35.2 degC\n"
`print(bodyTemperature2.description)`	"95 degF\n"
`if bodyTemperature1.isCompatibleWithUnit(degFUnit) { print("Temperature #1 in Fehrenheit degrees: \(bodyTemperature1.doubleValueForUnit(degFUnit))") }`	"Temperature #1 in Fehrenheit degrees: 95.3599999999999\n"
`if bodyTemperature2.isCompatibleWithUnit(degFUnit) { print("Temperature #2 in Fahrenheit degrees: \(bodyTemperature2.doubleValueForUnit(degFUnit))") }`	"Temperature #2 in Fahrenheit degrees: 95.0\n"

Objects from the Real World to Playground

The following line shows an example of the code that creates a new `HKQuantity` instance with a quantity and temperature unit converted from degrees Fahrenheit to degrees Celsius. There is no convert method that acts as a shortcut, so we have to call `doubleValueForUnit` and use it in the `HKQuantity` initializer, as follows:

```
let bodyTemperature2InDegC = HKQuantity(unit: degCUnit, doubleValue:
bodyTemperature2.doubleValueForUnit(degCUnit))
```

The compare method returns an `NSComparisonResult` value that indicates whether the receiver is greater than, equal to, or less than the compatible `HKQuantity` value specified as an argument. For example, the following lines compare `bodyTemperature1` with `bodyTemperature2` and print the results of the comparison. Note that it isn't necessary to convert both the `HKQuantity` instances to the same unit; they just need to be compatible, and the compare method will be able to perform the comparison by making the necessary conversions under the hood. In this case, one of the temperatures is in degrees Celsius, and the other is in degrees Fahrenheit. The screenshot that follows the given code shows the results displayed in the Playground:

```
let comparisonResult = bodyTemperature1.compare(bodyTemperature2)
switch comparisonResult {
    case NSComparisonResult.OrderedDescending:
        print("Temperature #1 is greater than #2")
    case NSComparisonResult.OrderedAscending:
        print("Temperature #2 is greater than #1")
    case NSComparisonResult.OrderedSame:
        print("Temperature #1 is equal to Temperature #2")
}
```

Code	Output
`let bodyTemperature2InDegC = HKQuantity(unit: degCUnit, doubleValue: bodyTemperature2.doubleValueForUnit(degCUnit))`	35 degC

`let comparisonResult = bodyTemperature1.compare(bodyTemperature2)`
`switch comparisonResult {`
`    case NSComparisonResult.OrderedDescending:`
`        print("Temperature #1 is greater than #2")`
`    case NSComparisonResult.OrderedAscending:`
`        print("Temperature #2 is greater than #1")`
`    case NSComparisonResult.OrderedSame:`
`        print("Temperature #1 is equal to Temperature #2")`
`}`
	C.NSComparisonResult
	"Temperature #1 is greater than #2\n"

Exercises

Now that you understand what an object is, it is time to recognize objects in different applications.

- **Exercise 1**: Work with an iOS app and recognize its objects. Work with an app that has both an iPhone and iPad version. Execute the app in both versions and recognize the different objects that the developers might have used to code the app. Create an UML diagram with the classes that you would use to create the app. Think about the methods and properties that you would require for each class. If the app is extremely complex, just focus on a specific feature.
- **Exercise 2**: Work with a Mac OS X application and recognize its objects. Execute the app and work with a specific feature. Recognize the objects that interact to enable you to work with the feature. Write down the objects you recognized and their required behaviors.

Test your knowledge

1. Objects are also known as:
    1. Classes.
    2. Subclasses.
    3. Instances.
2. The code specified in a method within a class:
    1. Cannot access the properties specified in the class.
    2. Can access the properties specified in the class.
    3. Cannot interact with other members of the class.
3. A subclass:
    1. Inherits all members from its superclass.
    2. Inherits only methods from its superclass.
    3. Inherits only properties from its superclass.
4. The variables defined in a class to encapsulate data for each instance of the class in Swift are known as:
    1. Subclasses.
    2. Properties.
    3. Methods.

5. The functions defined in a class to encapsulate behavior for each instance of the class are known as:
    1. Subclasses.
    2. Properties.
    3. Methods.

Summary

In this chapter, you learned how to recognize real-world elements and translate them into the different components of the object-oriented paradigm supported in Swift: classes, protocols, properties, methods, and instances. You understood that the classes represent blueprints or templates to generate the objects, also known as instances.

We designed a few classes with properties and methods that represent blueprints for real-life objects. Then, we improved the initial design by taking advantage of the power of abstraction and specialized different classes. We generated many versions of the initial UML diagram as we added superclasses and subclasses. Finally, we wrote some code in the Swift Playground to understand how we can interact with API objects.

Now that you have learned some of the basics of the object-oriented paradigm, we are ready to start creating classes and instances in Swift, which is the topic of the next chapter.

2
Structures, Classes, and Instances

In this chapter, you will learn the differences between structures and classes. We will start working with examples on how to code classes and customize the initialization and deinitialization of instances. We will understand how classes work as blueprints to generate instances and dive deep on all the details of automatic reference counting, also known as ARC.

Understanding structures, classes, and instances

In the previous chapter, you learned some of the basics of the object-oriented paradigm, including classes and objects, which are also known as instances. We started working on an app required by an acrylic paint manufacturer that wanted to take full advantage of the popularity of a popular YouTuber, painter, and craftswoman. We ended up creating a UML diagram with the structure of many classes, including their hierarchy, properties, and methods. It is time to take advantage of the Playground to start coding the classes and work with them.

In Swift, a class is always the type and blueprint. The object is the working instance of the class, and one or more variables can hold a reference to an instance. An object is an instance of the class, and the variables can be of a specific type (that is, a class) and hold objects of the specific blueprint that we generated when declaring the class.

It is very important to mention some of the differences between a class and structure in Swift. A structure is also a type and blueprint. In fact, structures in Swift are very similar to classes. You can add methods and properties to structures as you do with classes with the same syntax.

> However, there is a very important difference between structures and classes: Swift always copies structures when you pass them around the code because structures are value types. For example, whenever you pass a structure as an argument to a method or function, Swift copies the structure. When you work with classes, Swift passes them by reference because classes are reference types. In addition, classes support inheritance, while structures don't.

There are other differences between classes and structures. However, we will focus on the capabilities of classes because they will be the main building blocks of our object-oriented solutions.

Now, let's move to the world of superheroes. If we want to model an object-oriented app to work with superheroes, we will definitely have a `SuperHero` base class. Each superhero available in our app will be a subclass of the `SuperHero` superclass. For example, let's consider that we have the following subclasses of `SuperHero`:

- `SpiderMan`: This is a blueprint for Spider-Man
- `AntMan`: A blueprint for Ant-Man

So, each superhero becomes a subclass of `SuperHero` and a type in Swift. Each superhero is a blueprint that we will use to create instances. Suppose Kevin, Brandon, and Nicholas are three players that select a superhero as their preferred character to play a game in our app. Kevin and Brandon choose Spider-Man, and Nicholas selects Ant-Man. In our application, Kevin will be an instance of the `SpiderMan` subclass, Brandon will be an instance of the `SpiderMan` subclass, and Nicholas will be an instance of the `AntMan` subclass.

As Kevin, Brandon, and Nicholas are superheroes, they share many properties. Some of these properties will be initialized by the class, because the superhero they belong to determines some features—for example, the super powers, strength, running speed, flying speed (in case the superhero has flight abilities), attack power, and defense power. However, other properties will be specific to the instance, such as the name, weight, age, costume, and hair colors.

Understanding initialization and its customization

When you ask Swift to create an instance of a specific class, something happens under the hood. Swift creates a new instance of the specified type, allocates the necessary memory, and then executes the code specified in the initializer.

> You can think of initializers as equivalents of constructors in other programming languages such as C# and Java.

When Swift executes the code within an initializer, there is already a live instance of the class. Thus, we have access to the properties and methods defined in the class. However, we must be careful in the code we put in the initializer because we might end up generating huge delays when we create instances of the class.

> Initializers are extremely useful to execute setup code and properly initialize a new instance.

So, for example, before you can call either the `CalculateArea` or `CalculatePerimeter` method, you want both the `semiMajorAxis` and `semiMinorAxis` fields for each new `Ellipse` instance to have a value initialized to the appropriate values that represent the shape. Initializers are extremely useful when we want to define the values for the properties of the instances of a class right after their creation and before we can access the variables that reference the created instances.

Sometimes, we need specific arguments to be available at the time we create an instance. We can design different initializers with the necessary arguments and use them to create instances of a class. This way, we can make sure that there is no way of creating specific classes without using the provided initializers that make the necessary arguments required.

Swift uses a two-phase initialization process for classes. The first phase makes each class in the hierarchy that defines a property assign the initial value for each of them. Once all the properties are assigned their initial value, the second phase allows each class in the hierarchy to customize each of its defined properties. After the second phase finishes, the new instance is ready to be used, and Swift allows us to access the variable that references this instance to access its properties and/or call its methods.

> In case you have experience with Objective-C, the two-phase initialization process in Swift is very similar to the procedure in Objective-C. However, Swift allows us to set customized initial values.

Understanding deinitialization and its customization

At some specific times, our app won't require to work with an instance anymore. For example, once you calculate the perimeter of a regular hexagon and display the results to the user, you don't need the specific `RegularHexagon` instance anymore. Some programming languages require you to be careful about leaving live instances alive, and you have to explicitly destroy them and deallocate the memory that it consumed.

Swift uses an automatic reference counting, also known as ARC, to automatically deallocate the memory used by instances that aren't referenced anymore. When Swift detects that you aren't referencing an instance anymore, Swift executes the code specified within the instance's deinitializer before the instance is deallocated from memory. Thus, the deinitializer can still access all of the instance's resources.

> You can think of deinitializers as equivalents of destructors in other programming languages such as C# and Java. You can use deinitializers to perform any necessary cleanup before the objects are deallocated and removed from memory.

For example, think about the following situation: you need to count the number of instances of a specific class that are being kept alive. You can have a variable shared by all the classes. Then, customize the class initializer to atomically increase the value for the counter—that is, increase the value of the variable shared by all the classes. Finally, customize the class deinitializer to atomically decrease the value for the counter. This way, you can check the value of this variable to know the objects that are being referenced in your application.

Understanding automatic reference counting

Automatic reference counting is very easy to understand. Imagine that we have to distribute the items that we store in a box. After we distribute all the items, we must throw the box in a recycle bin. We cannot throw the box to the recycle bin when we still have one or more items in it. Seriously, we don't want to lose the items we have to distribute because they are very expensive.

The problem has a very easy solution; we just need to count the number of items that remain in the box. When the number of items in the box reaches zero, we can get rid of the box.

> One or more variables can hold a reference to a single instance of a class. Thus, it is necessary to count the number of references to an instance before Swift can get rid of an instance. When the number of references to a specific instance reaches zero, Swift can automatically and safely remove the instance from memory because nobody needs this specific instance anymore.

For example, you can create an instance of a class and assign it to a variable. The automatic reference counting mechanism registers the reference and knows that there is one reference to this instance. Then, you can assign the same instance to another variable, and therefore, the automatic reference counting mechanism will increase the reference count for the single instance to two.

After the first variable runs out of scope, the second variable that holds a reference to the instance will still be accessible. The automatic reference counting mechanism will decrease the reference count for the single instance to one as a result of the first variable running out of scope. At this point, the reference count for the single instance is equal to one, and therefore, the instance must still be available—that is, we need it alive.

After the second variable runs out of scope, there are no more variables that hold a reference to the instance; therefore, the automatic reference counting mechanism will decrease the reference count for the single instance to zero and mark it as disposable. At this point, the instance can be safely removed from memory.

> The automatic reference counting mechanism can remove the instance from memory at any time after the reference count for the instance reaches zero.

Declaring classes

The following lines declare a new minimal Circle class in Swift:

```
class Circle {
}
```

The class keyword, followed by the class name (Circle), composes the header of the class definition. In this case, the class doesn't have a parent class or superclass; therefore, there are neither superclasses listed after the class name, nor a colon (:). A pair of curly braces ({}) encloses the class body after the class header. In the forthcoming chapters, we will declare classes that inherit from another class, and therefore, they will have a superclass. In this case, the class body is empty. The Circle class is the simplest possible class we can declare in Swift.

Structures, Classes, and Instances

> Any new class you create that doesn't specify a superclass is considered a base class. Whenever you declare a class without a subclass, the class doesn't inherit from a universal base class, as it happens in other programming languages such as C#. Thus, the `Circle` class is known as a base class in Swift.

Customizing initialization

We want to initialize instances of the `Circle` class with the radius value. In order to do so, we can take advantage of customized initializers. Initializers aren't methods, but we will write them with syntax that is very similar to the instance methods. They will use the `init` keyword to differentiate from instance methods, and Swift will execute them automatically when we create an instance of a given type. Swift runs the code within the initializer before any other code within a class.

We can define an initializer that receives the radius value as an argument and use it to initialize a property with the same name. We can define as many initializers as we want to, and therefore, we can provide many different ways of initializing a class. In this case, we just need one initializer.

The following lines create a `Circle` class and define an initializer within the class body:

```
class Circle {
    var radius: Double
    init(radius: Double)
    {
        print("I'm initializing a new Circle instance with a radius value of \(radius).")
        self.radius = radius
    }
}
```

The initializer is declared with the `init` keyword. The initializer receives a single argument: `radius`. The code within the initializer prints a message on the console indicating that the code is initializing a new `Circle` instance with a specific radius value. This way, we will understand when the code within the initializer is executed. As the initializer has an argument, we can call it a parameterized initializer.

Then, the following line assigns the radius the `Double` value received as an argument to the `radius` classes' `Double` property. We will use `self.radius` to access the `radius` property for the instance and `radius` to reference the argument. In Swift, the `self` keyword provides access to the instance that is created and we want to initialize. The line before the initializer declares the `radius` double property. We will dive deep into the proper usage of properties in *Chapter 3, Encapsulation of Data with Properties*.

The following lines create two instances of the `Circle` class named `circle1` and `circle2`. Note that it is necessary to use the `radius` argument label each time we create an instance because we use the previously declared initializer. The initializer specifies `radius` as the name of the argument of the `Double` type that it requires. When we create an instance, we have to use the same argument name indicated in the initializer declaration, `radius`, followed by a colon (`:`) and the value we want to pass for the parameter. The first line specifies `radius: 25`; therefore, we will pass 25 to the radius parameter. The second line specifies `radius: 50`; and therefore, we will pass 50 to the `radius` parameter:

```
var circle1 = Circle(radius: 25)
var circle2 = Circle(radius: 50)
```

When we enter all the lines that declare the class and create the two instances in the Playground, we will see two messages that say "`I'm initializing a new Circle instance with a radius value of`" followed by the radius value specified in the call to the initializer of each instance, as shown in the following screenshot:

```
class Circle {
    var radius: Double
    init(radius: Double)
    {
        print("I'm initializing a new Circle instance with a radius value of \(radius).")     (2 times)
I'm initializing a new Circle instance with a radius value of
                          25.0.

I'm initializing a new Circle instance with a radius value of
                          50.0.


        self.radius = radius
    }
}
var circle1 = Circle(radius: 25)                                                              Circle

    radius 25





var circle2 = Circle(radius: 50)                                                              Circle

    radius 50


```

Structures, Classes, and Instances

Each line that creates an instance uses the class name followed by the argument label and the desired value for the `radius` class as an argument enclosed in parentheses. Swift automatically assigns the `Circle` type for each of the variables (`circle1` and `circle2`). After we execute the two lines that create the instances of `Circle`, we can take a look at the values for `circle1.radius` and `circle2.radius` in the Playground. We can click on the **Quick Look** icon and a popup will display the property and its value for the instance. The following screenshot shows the results of inspecting `circle1`:

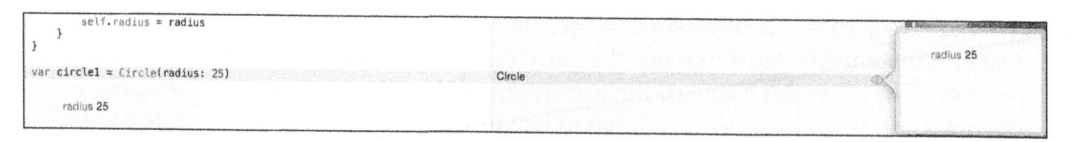

```
        self.radius = radius
    }
}
var circle1 = Circle(radius: 25)                    Circle                                                      radius 25

    radius 25
```

The following line won't allow the Playground to compile the code and will display a build error because the compiler cannot find a parameterless initializer declared in the `Circle` class. The specific error message is the following: "`Missing argument for parameter 'radius' in call.`" The subsequent screenshot shows the error icon on the left-hand side of the line that tries to create a `Circle` instance and the detailed Playground execution error displayed within the **Debug** area at the bottom of the window:

    var circleError = Circle()

```
 ⓘ  var circleError = Circle()          ⓘ Missing argument for parameter 'radius' in call

                                                                                            - 30 sec +
Playground execution failed: /var/folders/kv/5mbg_v3x6_l7ysvkvtvq5yxm0000gn/T/./lldb/5013/playground11.swift:19:25: error: missing argument
for parameter 'radius' in call
var circleError = Circle()
                         ^
```

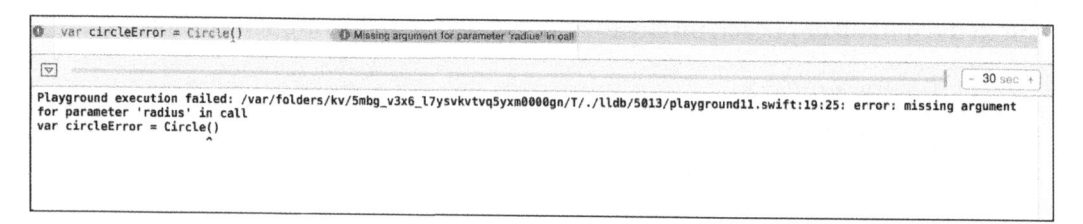

Remove the previous line that generated an error and enter the following two lines:

    print(circle1.dynamicType)
    print(circle2.dynamicType)

The Playground will display "**Circle\n**" as a result for both the lines because both the variables hold instances of the `Circle` class, as shown in the following screenshot. The `dynamicType` expression allows us to retrieve the runtime type as a value.

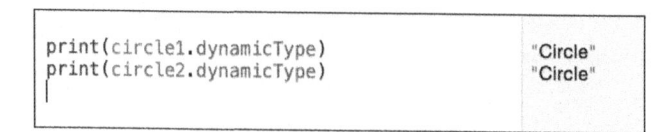

```
print(circle1.dynamicType)                    "Circle"
print(circle2.dynamicType)                    "Circle"
```

Customizing deinitialization

We want to know when the instances of the `Circle` class will be removed from memory—that is, when the objects aren't referenced by any variable and the automatic reference count mechanism decides that they have to be removed from memory. Deinitializers are special parameterless class methods that are automatically executed just before the runtime destroys an instance of a given type. Thus, we can use them to add any code we want to run before the instance is destroyed. We cannot call a deinitializer; they are only available for the runtime.

The deinitializer is a special class method that uses the `deinit` keyword in its declaration. The declaration must be parameterless, and it cannot return a value.

The following lines declare a deinitializer within the body of the `Circle` class:

```
deinit {
    print("I'm destroying the Circle instance with a radius value of \(radius).")
}
```

The following lines show the new complete code for the `Circle` class:

```
class Circle {
    var radius: Double
    init(radius: Double)
    {
        print("I'm initializing a new Circle instance with a radius value of \(radius).")
        self.radius = radius
    }

    deinit {
        print("I'm destroying the Circle instance with a radius value of \(radius).")
    }

}
```

Structures, Classes, and Instances

The code within the deinitilizer prints a message on the console indicating that the runtime will destroy a `Circle` instance with a specific radius value. This way, we will understand when the code within the deinitializer is executed.

The following lines create two instances of the `Circle` class named `circleToDelete1` and `circleToDelete2`. Then, the next lines assign new instances to both variables; therefore, the reference count for both objects reaches 0, and the automatic reference counting mechanism destroys them. Before the destruction takes place, Swift executes the deinitialization code. Enter the following lines in the Playground after adding the code for the destructor to the `Circle` class:

```
var circleToDelete1 = Circle(radius: 25)
var circleToDelete2 = Circle(radius: 50)
circleToDelete1 = Circle(radius: 32)
circleToDelete2 = Circle(radius: 47)
```

We will see the following messages in the Playground, as shown in the screenshot that follows them:

```
I'm initializing a new Circle instance with a radius value of 25.0.
I'm initializing a new Circle instance with a radius value of 50.0.
I'm initializing a new Circle instance with a radius value of 32.0.
I'm destroying the Circle instance with a radius value of 25.0.
I'm initializing a new Circle instance with a radius value of 47.0.
I'm destroying the Circle instance with a radius value of 50.0.
```

```
import UIKit

class Circle {
    var radius: Double
    init(radius: Double)
    {
        print("I'm initializing a new Circle instance with a radius
            value of \(radius).")

        self.radius = radius
    }
    deinit {
        print("I'm destroying the Circle instance with a radius value of
            \(radius).")
    }
}

var circleToDelete1 = Circle(radius: 25)

var circleToDelete2 = Circle(radius: 50)

circleToDelete1 = Circle(radius: 32)

circleToDelete2 = Circle(radius: 47)
```

```
I'm initializing a new Circle instance with a radius value of 25.0.
I'm initializing a new Circle instance with a radius value of 50.0.
I'm initializing a new Circle instance with a radius value of 32.0.
I'm destroying the Circle instance with a radius value of 25.0.
I'm initializing a new Circle instance with a radius value of 47.0.
I'm destroying the Circle instance with a radius value of 50.0.
```

The first two lines appear because we created instances of Circle, and Swift executed the initialization code. Then, we assigned the result of creating a new instance of the Circle class to the circleToDelete1 variable, and therefore, we removed the only existing reference to the instance with a radius value of 25.0. Swift printed a line that indicates that it initialized a new instance with a radius value of 32.0. After this line, Swift printed the line generated by the execution of the deinitializer of the Circle instance that had a radius value of 25.0.

Structures, Classes, and Instances

Then, we assigned the result of creating a new instance of the `Circle` class to the `circleToDelete2` variable, and therefore, we removed the only existing reference to the instance with a radius value of `50.0`. Swift printed a line that indicates that it initialized a new instance with a radius value of `47.0`. After this line, Swift printed the line generated by the execution of the deinitializer of the `Circle` instance that had a radius value of `50.0`.

The following lines create an instance of the `Circle` class named `circle3` and then assign a reference of this object to `referenceToCircle3`. Thus, the reference count to the object increases to 2. The next line assigns a new instance of the `Circle` class to `circle3`; therefore, the reference count for the object goes down from 2 to 1. As the `referenceToCircle3` variable stills holds a reference to the `Circle` instance, Swift doesn't destroy the instance, and we don't see the results of the execution of the deinitializer. Note that the screenshot only displays the results of the execution of the initializer, and there is no execution for the deinitializer:

```
var circle3 = Circle(radius: 42)
var referenceToCircle3 = circle3
circle3 = Circle(radius: 84)
```

```
import UIKit

class Circle {
    var radius: Double
    init(radius: Double)
    {
        print("I'm initializing a new Circle instance with a radius
            value of \(radius).")
        self.radius = radius
    }
    deinit {
        print("I'm destroying the Circle instance with a radius value of
            \(radius).")
    }
}

var circle3 = Circle(radius: 42)
var referenceToCircle3 = circle3
circle3 = Circle(radius: 84)
```

```
I'm initializing a new Circle instance with a radius value of 42.0.
I'm initializing a new Circle instance with a radius value of 84.0.
```

Creating the instances of classes

The following lines create an instance of the `Circle` class named `circle` within the scope of a `getGeneratedCircleRadius` function. The code within the function uses the created instance to access and return the value of its radius property. In this case, the code uses the `let` keyword to declare an immutable reference to the `Circle` instance named `circle`. An immutable reference is also known as a constant reference because we cannot replace the reference hold by the `circle` constant to another instance of `Circle`. When we use the `var` keyword, we declare a reference that we can change later.

After we define the new function, we will call it. Note that the screenshot displays the results of the execution of the initializer and then the deinitializer. Swift destroys the instance after the `circle` constant becomes out of scope because its reference count goes down from 1 to 0; therefore, there is no reason to keep the instance alive:

```
func getGeneratedCircleRadius() -> Double {
    let circle = Circle(radius: 20)
    return circle.radius
}

print(getGeneratedCircleRadius())
```

The following lines show the results displayed in the Playground's debug area after we executed the previously shown code. The following screenshot shows the results displayed at the right-hand side of the lines of code in the Playground:

```
I'm initializing a new Circle instance with a radius value of 20.0.
I'm destroying the Circle instance with a radius value of 20.0.
20.0
```

`func getGeneratedCircleRadius() -> Double {`
`    let circle = Circle(radius: 20)`
`    return circle.radius`
`}`
 	
`print(getGeneratedCircleRadius())`
	Circle
	20
	
	"20.0\n"

Note that it is extremely easy to code a function that creates an instance and uses it to call a method because we don't have to worry about removing the instance from memory. The automatic reference counting mechanism does the necessary cleanup work for us.

Exercises

Now that you understand an instance's life cycle, it is time to spend some time in the Playground creating new classes and instances:

- **Exercise 1**: Create a new `Employee` class with a custom initializer that requires two string arguments: `firstName` and `lastName`. Use the arguments to initialize properties with the same names as the arguments. Display a message with the values for `firstName` and `lastName` when an instance of the class is created. Display a message with the values for `firstName` and `lastName` when an instance of the class is destroyed.

  Create an instance of the `Employee` class and assign it to a variable. Check the messages printed in the Playground's Debug area. Assign a new instance of the `Employee` class to the previously defined variable. Check the messages printed in the Playground's Debug area.

- **Exercise 2**: Create a function that receives two `string` arguments: `firstName` and `lastName`. Create an instance of the previously defined `Employee` class with the received arguments as parameters for the creation of the instance. Use the instance properties to print a message with the first name followed by a space and the last name. You will be able to create a method and add it to the `Employee` class later to perform the same task. However, first, you must understand how you can work with the properties defined in a class.

Test your knowledge

1. Swift uses one of the following mechanisms to automatically deallocate the memory used by instances that aren't referenced anymore:
    1. Automatic Random Garbage Collector.
    2. Automatic Reference Counting.
    3. Automatic Instance Map Reduce.

2. Swift executes an instance's deinitializer:
    1. Before the instance is deallocated from memory.
    2. After the instance is deallocated from memory.
    3. After the instance memory is allocated.

3. A deinitializer:
    1. Can still access all of the instance's resources.
    2. Can only access the instance's methods but no properties.
    3. Cannot access any of the instance's resources.
4. Swift allows us to define:
    1. Only one initializer per class.
    2. A main initializer and two optional secondary initializers.
    3. Many initializers with different arguments.
5. Each time we create an instance:
    1. We must use argument labels.
    2. We can optionally use argument labels.
    3. We don't need to use argument labels.

Summary

In this chapter, you learned about an object's life cycle. You also learned how object initializers and deinitializers work. We declared our first class to generate a blueprint for objects. We customized object initializers and deinitializers and tested their personalized behavior in action with live examples in Swift's Playground. We understood how they work in combination with automatic reference counting.

Now that you have learned to start creating classes and instances, we are ready to share, protect, use and hide data with the data encapsulation features included in Swift, which is the topic of the next chapter.

3
Encapsulation of Data with Properties

In this chapter, you will learn about all the elements that might compose a class. We will start organizing data in blueprints that generate instances. We will work with examples to understand how to encapsulate and hide data by working with properties combined with access control. In addition, you will learn about properties, methods, and mutable versus immutable classes.

Understanding the elements that compose a class

So far, we worked with a very simple class and many instances of this class in the Playground. Now, it is time to dive deep into the different members of a class.

The following list enumerates the most common element types that you can include in a class definition in Swift and their equivalents in other programming languages. We already worked with a few of these elements:

- **Initializers**: These are equivalent to constructors in other programming languages
- **Deinitializer**: This is equivalent to destructors in other programming languages
- **Type properties**: These are equivalent to class fields or class attributes in other programming languages
- **Type methods**: These are equivalent to class methods in other programming languages
- **Subscripts**: These are also known as shortcuts

- **Instance properties**: This is equivalent to instance fields or instance attributes in other programming languages
- **Instance methods**: This is equivalent to instance functions in other programming languages
- **Nested types**: These are types that only exist within the class in which we define them

We already learned how basic initializers and deinitializers work in the previous chapter. So far, we used an instance-stored property to encapsulate data in our instances. We could access the instance property without any kind of restrictions as a variable within an instance.

However, as it happens sometimes in real-world situations, restrictions are necessary to avoid serious problems. Sometimes, we want to restrict access or transform specific instance properties into read-only attributes. We can combine the restrictions with computed properties that can define getters and/or setters.

> Computed properties can define get and/or set methods, also known as **getters** and **setters**. **Setters** allow us to control how values are set; that is, these methods are used to change the values of related properties. **Getters** allow us to control the values that we return when computed properties are accessed. Getters don't change the values of related properties.

Sometimes, all the members of a class share the same attribute, and we don't need to have a specific value for each instance. For example, the superhero types have some profile values, such as the average strength, average running speed, attack power, and defense power. We can define the following type properties to store the values that are shared by all the instances: `averageStrength`, `averageRunningSpeed`, `attackPower`, and `defensePower`. All the instances have access to the same type properties and their values. However, it is also possible to apply restrictions to their access.

It is also possible to define methods that don't require an instance of a specific class to be called; therefore, you can invoke them by specifying both the class and method names. These methods are known as **type** methods, operate on a class as a whole, and have access to type properties, but they don't have access to any instance members, such as instance properties or methods, because there is no instance at all. Type methods are useful when you want to include methods related to a class and don't want to generate an instance to call them. Type methods are also known as static or class methods. However, we have to pay attention to the keyword we use to declare type methods in Swift, because a type method declared with the `static` keyword has a different behavior than a type method declared with the `class` keyword. We will understand their difference as we move forward with the examples in this and the forthcoming chapters.

Declaring stored properties

When we design classes, we want to make sure that all the necessary data is available to the methods that will operate on this data; therefore, we encapsulate data. However, we just want relevant information to be visible to the users of our classes that will create instances, change values of accessible properties, and call the available methods. Thus, we want to hide or protect some data that is just needed for internal use. We don't want to make accidental changes to sensitive data.

For example, when we create a new instance of any superhero, we can use both its name and birth year as two parameters for the constructor. The constructor initializes the values of two properties: name and birthYear. The following lines show a sample code that declares the SuperHero class:

```
class SuperHero {
    var name: String
    var birthYear: Int
    
    init(name: String, birthYear: Int) {
        self.name = name
        self.birthYear = birthYear
    }
}
```

The next lines create two instances that initialize the values of the two properties and then use the print function to display their values in the Playground:

```
var antMan = SuperHero(name: "Ant-Man", birthYear: 1975)
print(antMan.name)
print(antMan.birthYear)
var ironMan = SuperHero(name: "Iron-Man", birthYear: 1982)
print(ironMan.name)
print(ironMan.birthYear)
```

Encapsulation of Data with Properties

The following screenshot shows the results of the declaration of the class and the execution of the lines in the Playground:

```
import UIKit

class SuperHero {
    var name: String
    var birthYear: Int
    
    init(name: String, birthYear: Int) {
        self.name = name
        self.birthYear = birthYear
    }
}

var antMan = SuperHero(name: "Ant-Man", birthYear: 1975)     SuperHero
print(antMan.name)                                           "Ant-Man\n"
print(antMan.birthYear)                                      "1975\n"
var ironMan = SuperHero(name: "Iron-Man", birthYear: 1982)   SuperHero
print(ironMan.name)                                          "Iron-Man\n"
print(ironMan.birthYear)                                     "1982\n"
```

We don't want a user of our `SuperHero` class to be able to change a superhero's name after an instance is initialized because the name is not supposed to change. There is a simple way to achieve this goal in our previously declared class. We can use the `let` keyword to define an immutable `name` stored property of type string instead of using the `var` keyword. We can also replace the `var` keyword with `let` when we define the `birthYear` stored property because the birth year will never change after we initialize a superhero instance.

The following lines show the new code that declares the `SuperHero` class with two stored immutable properties: `name` and `birthYear`. Note that the initializer code hasn't changed, and it is possible to initialize both the immutable stored properties with the same code:

```
class SuperHero {
    let name: String
    let birthYear: Int
    
    init(name: String, birthYear: Int) {
        self.name = name
        self.birthYear = birthYear
    }
}
```

The next lines create an instance that initializes the values of the two immutable stored properties and then use the print function to display their values in the Playground. Then, two lines of code try to assign a new value to both properties and fail to do so because they are immutable properties:

```
var antMan = SuperHero(name: "Ant-Man", birthYear: 1975)
print(antMan.name)
print(antMan.birthYear)

antMan.name = "Batman"
antMan.birthYear = 1976
```

The Playground displays the following two error messages for the last two lines, as shown in the next screenshot:

- **Cannot assign to property: 'name' is a 'let' constant**
- **Cannot assign to property: 'birthYear' is a 'let' constant**

> When we use the `let` keyword to declare a stored property, we can initialize the property, but it becomes immutable — that is, a constant — after its initialization.

Generating computed properties with setters and getters

As previously explained, we don't want a user of our superhero class to be able to change a superhero's birth year after an instance is initialized because the superhero won't be born again at a different date. In fact, we want to calculate and make the superhero's age available to users. We use an approximated age in order to keep the focus on the properties and don't complicate our lives with the manipulation of complete dates and the NSDate class.

We can define a property called age with a getter method but without a setter method; that is, we will create a read-only computed property. This way, it is possible to retrieve the superhero's age, but we cannot change it because there isn't a setter defined for the property. The getter method returns the result of calculating the superhero's age based on the current year and the value of the birthYear stored property.

The following lines show the new version of the SuperHero class with the new age calculated read-only property. Note that the code for the getter method appears after the property declaration with its type and the get keyword. All the lines enclosed in curly brackets after the get keyword define the code that will be executed when we request the value for the age property. The method creates a new instance of the NSDate class, date, and retrieves the current calendar, calendar. Then, the method retrieves the year, month and date components for date and returns the difference between the current year and the value of the birthYear property:

```swift
class SuperHero {
    let name: String
    let birthYear: Int

    var age: Int {
        get {
            let date = NSDate()
            let calendar = NSCalendar.currentCalendar()
            let components = calendar.components([.Year, .Month, .Day]
, fromDate: date)

            return components.year - birthYear
        }
    }

    init(name: String, birthYear: Int) {
        self.name = name
        self.birthYear = birthYear
    }
}
```

> We must use the `var` keyword to declare computed properties, such as the previously defined `age` computed property.

The next lines create an instance that initializes the values of the two immutable stored properties and then use the `print` function to display the value of the `age` calculated property in the Playground. Then, a line of code tries to assign a new value to the `age` property and fails to do so because the property doesn't declare a setter method:

```
var antMan = SuperHero(name: "Ant-Man", birthYear: 1975)
print(antMan.age)
var ironMan = SuperHero(name: "Iron-Man", birthYear: 1982)
print(ironMan.age)

antMan.age = 32
```

The Playground displays the following error message for the last line, as shown in the next screenshot:

Cannot assign to property: 'age' is a get-only property

```
import UIKit

class SuperHero {
    let name: String
    let birthYear: Int

    var age: Int {
        get {
            let date = NSDate()                                                 (2 times)
            let calendar = NSCalendar.currentCalendar()                         (2 times)
            let components = calendar.components([.Year, .Month, .Day], fromDate:  (2 times)
                date)

            return components.year - birthYear                                  (2 times)
        }
    }

    init(name: String, birthYear: Int) {
        self.name = name
        self.birthYear = birthYear
    }
}
var antMan = SuperHero(name: "Ant-Man", birthYear: 1975)            SuperHero
print(antMan.age)                                                   "40\n"
var ironMan = SuperHero(name: "Iron-Man", birthYear: 1982)          SuperHero
print(ironMan.age)                                                  "33\n"
antMan.age = 32                          Cannot assign to property: 'age' is a get-only property
```

[55]

Encapsulation of Data with Properties

> A computed property with a getter method and without a setter method is known as a get-only property.

Later, we will decide that it would be nice to allow the user to customize a superhero and allow it to change either its age or birth year. We can add a setter method to the `age` property with code that calculates the birth year based on the specified age and assigns this value to the `birthYear` property. Of course, the first thing we need to do is replace the `let` keyword with `var` when we define the `birthYear` stored property as we want it to become a mutable property.

The following lines show the new version of the `SuperHero` class with the new `age` calculated property. Note that the code for the setter method appears after the code for the getter method within the curly brackets that enclose the getter and setter declarations. We can place the setter method before the getter method. All the lines enclosed in curly brackets after the `set` keyword define the code that will be executed when we assign a new value to the `age` property, and the implicit name for the new value is `newValue`. So, the code enclosed in curly brackets after the `set` keyword receives the value that will be assigned to the property in the `newValue` argument. As we didn't specify a different name for the implicit argument, we can access the value using the `newValue` argument. Note that we don't see the argument name in the code; it is a default convention in Swift:

```
class SuperHero {
    let name: String
    var birthYear: Int

    var age: Int {
        get {
            let date = NSDate()
            let calendar = NSCalendar.currentCalendar()
            let components = calendar.components([.Year] , fromDate: date)

            return components.year - birthYear
        }
        set {
            let date = NSDate()
            let calendar = NSCalendar.currentCalendar()
```

[56]

```
            let components = calendar.components([.Year] , fromDate:
    date)
            self.birthYear = components.year - newValue
        }
    }
    init(name: String, birthYear: Int) {
        self.name = name
        self.birthYear = birthYear
    }
}
```

The setter method creates a new instance of the `NSDate` class, `date`, and retrieves the current calendar, `calendar`. Then, the method retrieves the year component for `date` and returns the difference between the current year, `components.year`, and the new age value that is specified: `newValue`.

The next lines create two instances of the `SuperHero` class, assign a value to the age computed property, and then use the print function to display the value of both the `age` calculated property and the `birthYear` stored property in the Playground:

```
var antMan = SuperHero(name: "Ant-Man", birthYear: 1975)
print(antMan.age)
var ironMan = SuperHero(name: "Iron-Man", birthYear: 1982)
print(ironMan.age)

antMan.age = 32
print(antMan.age)
print(antMan.birthYear)

ironMan.age = 45
print(ironMan.age)
print(ironMan.birthYear)
```

Encapsulation of Data with Properties

As a result of assigning a new value to the `age` computed property, its setter method changes the value of the `birthYear` stored property, as shown in the following screenshot:

```swift
import UIKit

class SuperHero {
    let name: String
    var birthYear: Int

    var age: Int {
        get {
            let date = NSDate()                                         (4 times)
            let calendar = NSCalendar.currentCalendar()                 (4 times)
            let components = calendar.components([.Year] , fromDate: date)  (4 times)

            return components.year - birthYear                          (4 times)
        }
        set {
            let date = NSDate()                                         (2 times)
            let calendar = NSCalendar.currentCalendar()                 (2 times)
            let components = calendar.components([.Year] , fromDate: date)  (2 times)

            self.birthYear = components.year - newValue                 (2 times)
        }
    }

    init(name: String, birthYear: Int) {
        self.name = name
        self.birthYear = birthYear
    }
}

var antMan = SuperHero(name: "Ant-Man", birthYear: 1975)        SuperHero
print(antMan.age)                                               "40\n"
var ironMan = SuperHero(name: "Iron-Man", birthYear: 1982)      SuperHero
print(ironMan.age)                                              "33\n"

antMan.age = 32                                                 SuperHero
print(antMan.age)                                               "32\n"
print(antMan.birthYear)                                         "1983\n"

ironMan.age = 45                                                SuperHero
print(ironMan.age)                                              "45\n"
print(ironMan.birthYear)                                        "1970\n"
```

Both the getter and setter methods use the same code to retrieve the current year. We can add a get-only property that retrieves the current year and call it from both the getter and setter methods for the `age` computed property. We will declare the function as a get-only property for the `SuperHero` class. We know that this class isn't the best place for this get-only property as it would be better to have it added to a date-related class, such as the `NSDate` class. We will be able to do so later after we learn additional things.

The following lines show the new version of the `SuperHero` class with the new `currentYear` calculated property. Note that the code for both the setter and getter methods for the age property are simpler because they use the new `currentYear` calculated property instead of repeating code:

```
class SuperHero {
    let name: String
    var birthYear: Int

    var age: Int {
        get {
            return currentYear - birthYear
        }
        set {
            birthYear = currentYear - newValue
        }
    }

    var currentYear: Int {
        get {
            let date = NSDate()
            let calendar = NSCalendar.currentCalendar()
            let components = calendar.components([.Year] , fromDate: date)

            return components.year
        }
    }

    init(name: String, birthYear: Int) {
        self.name = name
        self.birthYear = birthYear
    }
}
```

Encapsulation of Data with Properties

> Declarations that use the `let` keyword cannot be computed properties; therefore, we must always use the `var` keyword when we declare computed properties, even when they are get-only properties.

The next lines create two instances of the `SuperHero` class, assign a value to the age computed property, and then use the print function to display the value of both the `age` calculated property and the `birthYear` stored property in the Playground:

```
var superBoy = SuperHero(name: "Super-Boy", birthYear: 2008)
print(superBoy.age)
var superGirl = SuperHero(name: "Super-Girl", birthYear: 2009)
print(superGirl.age)

superBoy.age = 9
print(superBoy.age)
print(superBoy.birthYear)

superGirl.age = 8
print(superGirl.age)
print(superGirl.birthYear)

print(superBoy.currentYear)
print(superGirl.currentYear)
```

Note the number of times that each property's getter and setter methods are executed in the Playground. In this case, the `currentYear` getter method is executed eight times, as shown in the following screenshot:

```swift
import UIKit

class SuperHero {
    let name: String
    var birthYear: Int

    var age: Int {
        get {
            return currentYear - birthYear                              (4 times)
        }
        set {
            birthYear = currentYear - newValue                          (2 times)
        }
    }

    var currentYear: Int {
        get {
            let date = NSDate()                                         (8 times)
            let calendar = NSCalendar.currentCalendar()                 (8 times)
            let components = calendar.components([.Year] , fromDate: date)  (8 times)

            return components.year                                      (8 times)
        }
    }

    init(name: String, birthYear: Int) {
        self.name = name
        self.birthYear = birthYear
    }
}

var superBoy = SuperHero(name: "Super-Boy", birthYear: 2008)            SuperHero
print(superBoy.age)                                                     "7\n"
var superGirl = SuperHero(name: "Super-Girl", birthYear: 2009)          SuperHero
print(superGirl.age)                                                    "6\n"

superBoy.age = 9                                                        SuperHero
print(superBoy.age)                                                     "9\n"
print(superBoy.birthYear)                                               "2006\n"

superGirl.age = 8                                                       SuperHero
print(superGirl.age)                                                    "8\n"
print(superGirl.birthYear)                                              "2007\n"

print(superBoy.currentYear)                                             "2015\n"
print(superGirl.currentYear)                                            "2015\n"
```

Encapsulation of Data with Properties

The recently added `currentYear` computed property is get-only; therefore, we won't add a set clause to it. We can simplify the code that declares this property by omitting the `get` clause, as shown in the following lines:

```
var currentYear: Int {
    let date = NSDate()
    let calendar = NSCalendar.currentCalendar()
    let components = calendar.components([.Year] , fromDate: date)

    return components.year
}
```

> We only have to specify the `get` clause when we provide a `set` clause for the property.

Combining setters, getters, and a related property

Sometimes, we want to have more control over the values that are set to properties and retrieved from them, and we can take advantage of getters and setters to do so. In fact, we can combine a getter and setter, which generate a computed property and a related property that stores the computed value, and access protection mechanisms to prevent the user from making changes to the related property and force him to always use the computed property.

The superhero's sneakers might change over time. However, we always have to make sure that the sneakers' name is an uppercase string. We can define a `sneakers` property with a getter method that always converts the string value to an uppercase string and stores it in a private `sneakersField` property.

Whenever we assign a value to the `sneakers` property, the setter method is called under the hood with the value to be assigned as an argument. Whenever we specify the `sneakers` property in any expression, the getter method is called under the hood to retrieve the actual value. The following lines show a new version of the `SuperHero` class that adds a `sneakers` calculated property. Note that the code doesn't include the `age` and `currentYear` properties to avoid repeating the code that we analyzed before:

```
public class SuperHero {
    public let name: String
```

```
    public var birthYear: Int

    private var sneakersField = "NOT SPECIFIED"

    public var sneakers: String {
        get {
            return sneakersField
        }
        set {
            sneakersField = newValue.uppercaseString
        }
    }

    init(name: String, birthYear: Int, sneakers: String) {
        self.name = name
        self.birthYear = birthYear
        self.sneakers = sneakers
    }
}
```

The new version of the class is declared as `public class`; therefore, we declared `name`, `birthYear`, and `sneakers` as public properties. We should also declare both the `age` and `currentYear` properties that don't appear in the previous code as public. This way, when someone creates instances of the `SuperHero` class outside the source file that declares it, he will be able to access the public members—that is, the public properties have declared. However, the code declares the `sneakersField` property as a private property; therefore, only the code included in the same source file that declared the `SuperHero` class will be able to access this property. This way, the `sneakersField` property will be hidden for those who create instances of the `SuperHero` class outside of the source file that declares it.

When we declare the `sneakersField` private property, we will specify its initial value as `"NOT SPECIFIED"` and not declare its type because the type-inference mechanism determines that it is of type `String` based on the initial value. The following line of code is equivalent to the second line of code. We used the first line for the declaration to simplify our code and avoid redundancy whenever possible:

```
private var sneakersField = "NOT SPECIFIED"
private var sneakersField: String = "NOT SPECIFIED"
```

> We should take advantage of the type inference mechanism included in Swift as much as possible to reduce unnecessary boilerplate code.

Encapsulation of Data with Properties

The initializer for the class added a new argument that provides an initial value for the new `sneakers` property. The next lines create two instances of the `SuperHero` class, assign a value to the `sneakers` computed property, and then use the print function to display the value of the property in the Playground. In both cases, we will initialize sneakers with a string that the setter method converts to an uppercase string. Thus, when we print the values returned by the getter method, the Playground will print the uppercase string that is stored in the `sneakerField` private property:

```
var superBoy = SuperHero(name: "Super-Boy", birthYear: 2008, sneakers: "Running 2016")
print(superBoy.sneakers)
var superGirl = SuperHero(name: "Super-Girl", birthYear: 2009, sneakers: "Jumping Super Girl")
print(superGirl.sneakers)
```

Note the number of times that each property's getter and setter methods are executed in the Playground. In this case, the `sneakers` getter method is executed two times, as shown in the following screenshot:

```
public class SuperHero {
    public let name: String
    public var birthYear: Int
    
    private var sneakersField = "NOT SPECIFIED"
    
    public var sneakers: String {
        get {
            return sneakersField                                    (2 times)
        }
        set {
            sneakersField = newValue.uppercaseString                (2 times)
        }
    }
    
    public var age: Int {
        get {
            return currentYear - birthYear
        }
        set {
            birthYear = currentYear - newValue
        }
    }
    
    public var currentYear: Int {
        let date = NSDate()
        let calendar = NSCalendar.currentCalendar()
        let components = calendar.components([.Year] , fromDate: date)
        
        return components.year
    }
    
    init(name: String, birthYear: Int, sneakers: String) {
        self.name = name
        self.birthYear = birthYear
        self.sneakers = sneakers
    }
}

var superBoy = SuperHero(name: "Super-Boy", birthYear: 2008, sneakers:       SuperHero
    "Running 2016")
print(superBoy.sneakers)                                                     "RUNNING 2016\n"
var superGirl = SuperHero(name: "Super-Girl", birthYear: 2009, sneakers:     SuperHero
    "Jumping Super Girl")
print(superGirl.sneakers)                                                    "JUMPING SUPER GIRL\n"
```

> We can combine a property with the getter and setter methods along with access protection mechanisms and a related property that acts as an underlying field to have absolute control on how values are set to and retrieved from the underlying field.

Understanding property observers

Each superhero has a running speed score that determines how fast he will move when running; therefore, we will add a public `runningSpeedScore` property. We will change the initializer code to set an initial value for the new property. However, this new property has some specific requirements.

Whenever the running speed score is about to change, it will be necessary to trigger a few actions. In addition, we have to trigger other actions after the value for this property changes. We might consider adding code to a setter method combined with a related property, run a code before we set the new value to the related property, and then run a code after we set the new value. However, Swift allows us to take advantage of property observers that make it easier to run code before and after the running speed score changes.

We can define a public `runningSpeedScore` property with both the `willSet` and `didSet` methods. After we create an instance of the new version of the `SuperHero` class and initialize the new property with its initial value, the code in the `willSet` method will be executed when we assign a new value to the property and before Swift sets the new value to the property. Thus, at the time the `willSet` method executes the code, the property still has the previous value, and we can access the new value that will be set by checking the value of the `newValue` implicit parameter.

Then, when Swift changes the value of the property, the `didSet` method will be executed. Thus, at the time the `didSet` method executes the code, the property has the new value.

> The code defined in the `willSet` and/or `didSet` methods only runs when we change the value of the property after its initial value is set. Thus, property observers don't run when the property is initialized.

Encapsulation of Data with Properties

The following lines show the code that defines the new public `runningSpeedScore` property with the property observers and the new code for the initializer. Note that the code for the rest of the class isn't included in order to avoid repeating the previous code:

```
public var runningSpeedScore: Int {
    willSet {
        print("The current value for running speed score is:\
(runningSpeedScore)")
        print("I will set the new value for running speed score to: \
(newValue)")
    }
    didSet {
        print("I have set the new value for running speed score to: \
(runningSpeedScore)")
    }
}

init(name: String, birthYear: Int, sneakers: String,
runningSpeedScore: Int) {
    self.name = name
    self.birthYear = birthYear
    self.runningSpeedScore = runningSpeedScore
    self.sneakers = sneakers
}
```

The `willSet` method prints the current value for `runningSpeedScore` and the new value that will be set to this property and received in the `newValue` implicit parameter. The `didSet` method prints the new value that is set to the `runningSpeedScore` property.

> Swift makes it easy to insert the value of an expression into a string by placing the expression within parentheses after a backslash (\). We took advantage of this syntax in the previous code to print the values of both `runningSpeedScore` and `newValue` as part of a message string.

The initializer for the class added a new argument that provides an initial value for the new `runningSpeedScore` property. The next lines create an instance of the `SuperHero` class and assign a value to the `runningSpeedScore` property. Note that both the `willSet` and `didSet` methods were executed only once because the code didn't run when we initialized the value for the property:

```
var superBoy = SuperHero(name: "Super-Boy", birthYear: 2008, sneakers:
"Running 2016", runningSpeedScore: 5)
```

```
print(superBoy.sneakers)
superBoy.runningSpeedScore = 7
```

The Playground displays a message indicating the current value for the property before the new value that is set, that will be set, and finally, that was set, as shown in the next screenshot:

```
            return components.year
    }
    public var runningSpeedScore: Int {
        willSet {
            print("The current value for running speed score is:\(runningSpeedScore)")
            print("I will set the new value for running speed score to: \(newValue)")
        }
        didSet {
            print("I have set the new value for running speed score to: \
                (runningSpeedScore)")
        }
    }

    init(name: String, birthYear: Int, sneakers: String, runningSpeedScore: Int) {
        self.name = name
        self.birthYear = birthYear
        self.runningSpeedScore = runningSpeedScore
        self.sneakers = sneakers
    }
}

var superBoy = SuperHero(name: "Super-Boy", birthYear: 2008, sneakers: "Running 2016",
    runningSpeedScore: 5)
print(superBoy.sneakers)
superBoy.runningSpeedScore = 7
```

```
RUNNING 2016
The current value for running speed score is:5
I will set the new value for running speed score to: 7
I have set the new value for running speed score to: 7
```

> When we take advantage of property observers, we cannot use getters and/or setters at the same time. Thus, we cannot define getter and/or setter methods when we use the `willSet` and/or `didSet` methods for a property. Swift doesn't make it possible to combine them.

We can use the `didSet` method to keep the value of a property in a valid range. For example, we can define the `runningSpeedScore` property with a `didSet` method that transforms the values lower than 0 to 0 and values higher than 50 to 50. The following code will do the job. We have to replace the previous code that declared the `runningSpeedScore` property with the new code:

```
public var runningSpeedScore: Int {
    didSet {
        if (runningSpeedScore < 0) {
            runningSpeedScore = 0
        } else if (runningSpeedScore > 50) {
            runningSpeedScore = 50
        }
    }
}
```

Encapsulation of Data with Properties

The next lines create an instance of the `SuperHero` class and try to assign different values to the `runningSpeedScore` property. After we specified -5 as the desired value for the `runningSpeedScore` property, we printed its actual value, and the result was 0. After we specified 200, the actual printed value was 50. Finally, after we specified 6, the actual printer value was 6, as shown in the next screenshot. The code in the `didSet` method did its job; we can control all the values accepted for the property. Note that the `didSet` method doesn't execute one more time when we set the new value for the property within the `didSet` method.

```
            return components.year
        }
    public var runningSpeedScore: Int {
        didSet {
            if (runningSpeedScore < 0) {
                runningSpeedScore = 0
            } else if (runningSpeedScore > 50) {
                runningSpeedScore = 50
            }
        }
    }

    init(name: String, birthYear: Int, sneakers: String, runningSpeedScore: Int) {
        self.name = name
        self.birthYear = birthYear
        self.runningSpeedScore = runningSpeedScore
        self.sneakers = sneakers
    }
}

var superBoy = SuperHero(name: "Super-Boy", birthYear: 2008, sneakers: "Running 2016",
    runningSpeedScore: 5)
print(superBoy.runningSpeedScore)
superBoy.runningSpeedScore = -5
print(superBoy.runningSpeedScore)
superBoy.runningSpeedScore = 200
print(superBoy.runningSpeedScore)
superBoy.runningSpeedScore = 6
print(superBoy.runningSpeedScore)
```

SuperHero
SuperHero
SuperHero
"5\n"
SuperHero
"0\n"
SuperHero
"50\n"
SuperHero
"6\n"

We can use the `didSet` method when we want to validate the values accepted for a property after it is initialized. Remember that the `didSet` method isn't executed when the property is initialized. Thus, if we execute the following lines, the printed value will be 135, and the property will be initialized with an invalid value:

```
var superBoy = SuperHero(name: "Super-Boy", birthYear: 2008, sneakers:
"Running 2016", runningSpeedScore: 135)
print(superBoy.runningSpeedScore)
```

Transforming values with setters and getters

We can define a property with a setter method that transforms the values that will be set as valid values for a related property. The getter method would just need to return the value of the related property to generate a property that will always have valid values, even when it is initialized. This way, we can make sure that whenever we require the property value, we will retrieve a valid value.

The following code replaces the previously declared runningSpeedScore property declaration that worked with a property observer—specifically, a didSet method. In this case, the setter transforms the values lower than 0 to 0 and values higher than 50 to 50. The setter stores either the transformed or original value that is in a valid range in the related runningSpeedScoreField property. The getter returns the value of the related runningSpeedScoreField property—that is, the private property that always stores a valid value. We have to replace the previous code that declared the runningSpeedScore property with the new code:

```
private var runningSpeedScoreField: Int = 0
public var runningSpeedScore: Int {
    get {
        return runningSpeedScoreField
    }
    set {
        if (newValue < 0) {
            runningSpeedScoreField = 0
        } else if (newValue > 50) {
            runningSpeedScoreField = 50
        } else {
            runningSpeedScoreField = newValue
        }
    }
}
```

Now, let's execute the following lines in the Playground:

```
var superBoy = SuperHero(name: "Super-Boy", birthYear: 2008, sneakers: "Running 2016", runningSpeedScore: 135)
print(superBoy.runningSpeedScore)
```

Encapsulation of Data with Properties

If we execute the following lines, the printed value will be 50, and the property will be initialized with a valid value because the code defined in the setter method will transform 135 into the maximum accepted value, which is 50, as seen in the following screenshot:

```
        return components.year
    }

    private var runningSpeedScoreField: Int = 0
    public var runningSpeedScore: Int {
        get {
            return runningSpeedScoreField
        }
        set {
            if (newValue < 0) {
                runningSpeedScoreField = 0
            } else if (newValue > 50) {
                runningSpeedScoreField = 50
            } else {
                runningSpeedScoreField = newValue
            }
        }
    }

    init(name: String, birthYear: Int, sneakers: String, runningSpeedScore: Int) {
        self.name = name
        self.birthYear = birthYear
        self.runningSpeedScore = runningSpeedScore
        self.sneakers = sneakers
    }
}

var superBoy = SuperHero(name: "Super-Boy", birthYear: 2008, sneakers: "Running 2016",
    runningSpeedScore: 135)
print(superBoy.runningSpeedScore)
superBoy.runningSpeedScore = -5
print(superBoy.runningSpeedScore)
superBoy.runningSpeedScore = 200
print(superBoy.runningSpeedScore)
superBoy.runningSpeedScore = 6
print(superBoy.runningSpeedScore)
```

> When we initialize a property that has a setter method, Swift calls the setter for the initialization value.

Using type properties to create values shared by all the instances of a class

The `LionSuperHero` class is a blueprint for lions that are superheroes. This class should inherit from the `SuperHero` class, but we will forget about inheritance and other super types of superheroes for a while and use the `LionSuperHero` class to understand the difference between type and instance properties.

We will define the following type properties to store the values that are shared by all the members of the lion superhero group:

- `averageStrength`: This is the average strength for the superhero group.
- `averageRunningSpeed`: This is the average running speed for the superhero group.
- `attackPower`: This is the attack power score for the superhero group.
- `defensePower`: This is the defense power score for the superhero group.
- `warriorScore`: This is the score that combines the previously mentioned values in a single value that determines the warrior score for the superhero group. It is a calculated type property.

The following lines create a `LionSuperHero` class, declare the previously enumerated type properties, and two additional instance public properties, namely `name` and `runningSpeedScore`:

```
public class LionSuperHero {

    public static var averageStrength: Int = 10
    public static var averageRunningSpeed: Int = 9
    public static var attackPower: Int = 10
    public static var defensePower: Int = 6
    public static var warriorScore: Int {
        return (averageStrength * 3) + (attackPower * 3) +
(averageRunningSpeed * 2) + (defensePower * 2)
    }

    public let name: String

    private var runningSpeedScoreField: Int = 0
    public var runningSpeedScore: Int {
        get {
            return runningSpeedScoreField
        }
        set {
            if (newValue < 0) {
                runningSpeedScoreField = 0
            } else if (newValue > 50) {
                runningSpeedScoreField = 50
            } else {
                runningSpeedScoreField = newValue
            }
        }
```

```
        }

        init(name: String, runningSpeedScore: Int) {
            self.name = name
            self.runningSpeedScore = runningSpeedScore
        }
    }
```

The code initializes each type property in the same line that declares the field. The only difference between a type and instance property is the inclusion of the `static` keyword to indicate that we want to create a type property.

The following line prints the value of the previously declared `averageStrength` type property. Note that we didn't create any instance of the `LionSuperHero` class and that we specified the type property name after the class name and a dot:

```
    print(LionSuperHero.averageStrength)
```

Swift doesn't allow us to access a type property from an instance; therefore, we always have to use a class name to access a type property.

You can assign a new value to any type property declared with the `static` and `var` keywords. For example, the following lines assign 9 to the `averageStrength` type property and print the new value:

```
    LionSuperHero.averageStrength = 9
    print(LionSuperHero.averageStrength)
```

The following screenshot shows the results of executing the preceding code in the Playground:

```
public class LionSuperHero {

    public static var averageStrength: Int = 10
    public static var averageRunningSpeed: Int = 9
    public static var attackPower: Int = 10
    public static var defensePower: Int = 6
    public static var warriorScore: Int {
        return (averageStrength * 3) + (attackPower * 3) +                 87
            (averageRunningSpeed * 2) + (defensePower * 2)
    }

    public let name: String

    private var runningSpeedScoreField: Int = 0
    public var runningSpeedScore: Int {
        get {
            return runningSpeedScoreField
        }
        set {
            if (newValue < 0) {
                runningSpeedScoreField = 0
            } else if (newValue > 50) {
                runningSpeedScoreField = 50
            } else {
                runningSpeedScoreField = newValue                           LionSuperHero
            }
        }
    }

    init(name: String, runningSpeedScore: Int) {
        self.name = name
        self.runningSpeedScore = runningSpeedScore
    }
}

print(LionSuperHero.averageStrength)                                        "10\n"

LionSuperHero.averageStrength = 9
print(LionSuperHero.averageStrength)                                        "9\n"
```

We can easily convert a type property into an immutable type property by replacing the `var` keyword with the `let` one. For example, we don't want the class users to change the attack power for the superhero group; therefore, we can change the line that declared the `attackPower` type property with the following line that creates an immutable type property or read-only class constant:

```
public static let attackPower: Int = 10
```

Encapsulation of Data with Properties

The `warriorScore` type property is a calculated type property that only defines a getter method; therefore, it is a read-only calculated type property. Note that the declaration uses the simplified version of a property that has just a getter method and simply returns the calculated value after the type (`Int`):

```
public static var warriorScore: Int {
    return (averageStrength * 3) + (attackPower * 3) + (averageRunningSpeed * 2) + (defensePower * 2)
}
```

The next lines are equivalent to the previous `warriorScore` type property declaration. In this case, the declaration uses the `get` method instead of just returning the calculated value:

```
public static var warriorScore: Int {
    get {
        return (averageStrength * 3) + (attackPower * 3) + (averageRunningSpeed * 2) + (defensePower * 2)
    }
}
```

The following line prints the value for this type property:

```
print(LionSuperHero.warriorScore)
```

The following lines create a new instance of the `LionSuperHero` class and use the value for the `averageRunningSpeed` type property in a sum that specifies the value for the `runningSpeedScore` argument:

```
var superTom = LionSuperHero(name: "Tom", runningSpeedScore: LionSuperHero.averageRunningSpeed + 1)
```

Creating mutable classes

So far, we worked with different type of properties. When we declare stored instance properties with the `var` keyword, we create a mutable instance property, which means that we can change their values for each new instance we create. When we create an instance of a class that defines many public-stored properties, we create a mutable object, which is an object that can change its state.

Chapter 3

For example, let's think about a class named `MutableVector3D` that represents a mutable 3D vector with three public-stored properties: x, y, and z. We can create a new `MutableVector3D` instance and initialize the x, y, and z attributes. Then, we can call the `sum` method with the delta values for x, y, and z as arguments. The delta values specify the difference between the existing and new or desired value. So, for example, if we specify a positive value of 30 in the `deltaX` parameter, it means we want to add 30 to the x value. The following lines declare the `MutableVector3D` class that represents the mutable version of a 3D vector in Swift:

```swift
public class MutableVector3D {
    public var x: Float
    public var y: Float
    public var z: Float

    init(x: Float, y: Float, z: Float) {
        self.x = x
        self.y = y
        self.z = z
    }

    public func sum(deltaX: Float, deltaY: Float, deltaZ: Float) {
        x += deltaX
        y += deltaY
        z += deltaZ
    }

    public func printValues() {
        print("X: \(self.x), Y: \(self.y), Z: \(self.z))")
    }
}
```

Note that the declaration of the `sum` instance method uses the `func` keyword, specifies the arguments with their types enclosed in parentheses, and then declares the body for the method enclosed in curly brackets. The public `sum` instance method receives the delta values for x, y, and z (`deltaX`, `deltaY` and `deltaZ`) and mutates the object, which means that the method changes the values of x, y, and z. The public `printValues` method prints the values of the three instance-stored properties: x, y, and z.

[75]

Encapsulation of Data with Properties

The following lines create a new `MutableVector3D` instance method called `myMutableVector`, initialized with the values for the x, y, and z properties. Then, the code calls the sum method with the delta values for x, y, and z as arguments and finally calls the `printValues` method to check the new values after the object mutated with the call to the sum method:

```
var myMutableVector = MutableVector3D(x: 30, y: 50, z: 70)
myMutableVector.sum(20, deltaY: 30, deltaZ: 15)
myMutableVector.printValues()
```

The results of the execution in the Playground are shown in the following screenshot:

```
public class MutableVector3D {
    public var x: Float
    public var y: Float
    public var z: Float

    init(x: Float, y: Float, z: Float) {
        self.x = x
        self.y = y
        self.z = z
    }

    public func sum(deltaX: Float, deltaY: Float, deltaZ: Float)
    {
        x += deltaX
        y += deltaY
        z += deltaZ
    }

    public func printValues() {
        print("X: \(self.x), Y: \(self.y), Z: \(self.z))")
    }
}

var myMutableVector = MutableVector3D(x: 30, y: 50, z: 70)
myMutableVector.sum(20, deltaY: 30, deltaZ: 15)
myMutableVector.printValues()
```

	"X: 50.0, Y: 80.0, Z: 85.0)\n"
	MutableVector3D
	MutableVector3D
	MutableVector3D

The initial values for the `myMutableVector` fields are 30 for x, 50 for y, and 70 for z. The sum method changes the values of the three instance-stored properties; therefore, the object state mutates as follows:

- `myMutableVector.X` mutates from 30 to 30 + 20 = 50
- `myMutableVector.Y` mutates from 50 to 50 + 30 = 80
- `myMutableVector.Z` mutates from 70 to 70 + 15 = 85

The values for the `myMutableVector` fields after the call to the sum method are 50 for x, 80 for y, and 85 for z. We can say that the method mutated the object's state; therefore, `myMutableVector` is a mutable object and an instance of a mutable class.

It's a very common requirement to generate a 3D vector with all the values initialized to 0 — that is, x = 0, y = 0, and z = 0. A 3D vector with these values is known as an origin vector. We can add a type method to the `MutableVector3D` class named `originVector` to generate a new instance of the class initialized with all the values in 0. Type methods are also known as class or static methods in other object-oriented programming languages. It is necessary to add the `class` keyword before the `func` keyword to generate a type method instead of an instance. The following lines define the `originVector` type method:

```
public class func originVector() -> MutableVector3D {
    return MutableVector3D(x: 0, y: 0, z: 0)
}
```

The preceding method returns a new instance of the `MutableVector3D` class with 0 as the initial value for all the three elements. The following lines call the `originVector` type method to generate a 3D vector, the `sum` method for the generated instance, and finally, the `printValues` method to check the values for the three elements on the Playground:

```
var myMutableVector2 = MutableVector3D.originVector()
myMutableVector2.sum(5, deltaY: 10, deltaZ: 15)
myMutableVector2.printValues()
```

The following screenshot shows the results of executing the preceding code in the Playground:

`public func printValues() {`
`    print("X: \(self.x), Y: \(self.y), Z: \(self.z))")`
`}`
	(2 times)

`public class func originVector() -> MutableVector3D {`
`    return MutableVector3D(x: 0, y: 0, z: 0)`
`}`
`}`
	MutableVector3D

`var myMutableVector = MutableVector3D(x: 30, y: 50, z: 70)`
`myMutableVector.sum(20, deltaY: 30, deltaZ: 15)`
`myMutableVector.printValues()`
	MutableVector3D
	MutableVector3D
	MutableVector3D

`var myMutableVector2 = MutableVector3D.originVector()`
`myMutableVector2.sum(5, deltaY: 10, deltaZ: 15)`
`myMutableVector2.printValues()`
	MutableVector3D
	MutableVector3D
	MutableVector3D

x 5 y 10 z 15	

Encapsulation of Data with Properties

Building immutable classes

Mutability is very important in object-oriented programming. In fact, whenever we expose mutable properties, we create a class that will generate mutable instances. However, sometimes a mutable object can become a problem, and in certain situations, we want to avoid the objects to change their state. For example, when we work with concurrent code, an object that cannot change its state solves many concurrency problems and avoids potential bugs.

For example, we can create an immutable version of the previous `MutableVector3D` class to represent an immutable 3D vector. The new `ImmutableVector3D` class has three immutable instance properties declared with the `let` keyword instead of the previously used `var` keyword: x, y, and z. We can create a new `ImmutableVector3D` instance and initialize the immutable instance properties. Then, we can call the `sum` method with the delta values for x, y, and z as arguments.

The `sum` public instance method receives the delta values for x, y, and z (`deltaX`, `deltaY`, and `deltaZ`), and returns a new instance of the same class with the values of x, y, and z initialized with the results of the sum. The following lines show the code of the `ImmutableVector3D` class:

```
public class ImmutableVector3D {
    public let x: Float
    public let y: Float
    public let z: Float

    init(x: Float, y: Float, z: Float) {
        self.x = x
        self.y = y
        self.z = z
    }

    public func sum(deltaX: Float, deltaY: Float, deltaZ: Float) -> ImmutableVector3D {
        return ImmutableVector3D(x: x + deltaX, y: y + deltaY, z: z + deltaZ)
    }

    public func printValues() {
        print("X: \(self.x), Y: \(self.y), Z: \(self.z)")
    }

    public class func equalElementsVector(initialValue: Float) -> ImmutableVector3D {
```

```
        return ImmutableVector3D(x: initialValue, y: initialValue, z:
initialValue)
    }
    public class func originVector() -> ImmutableVector3D {
        return equalElementsVector(0)
    }
}
```

In the new `ImmutableVector3D` class, the `sum` method returns a new instance of the `ImmutableVector3D` class—that is, the current class. In this case, the `originVector` type method returns the results of calling the `equalElementsVector` type method with 0 as an argument.

The `equalElementsVector` type method receives an `initialValue` argument for all the elements of the 3D vector, creates an instance of the actual class, and initializes all the elements with the received unique value. The `originVector` type method demonstrates how we can call another type method within a type method. Note that both the type methods specify the returned type with -> followed by the type name (`ImmutableVector3D`) after the arguments enclosed in parentheses. The following line shows the declaration for the `equalElementsVector` type method with the specified return type:

```
public class func equalElementsVector(initialValue: Float) ->
ImmutableVector3D {
```

The following lines call the `originVector` type method to generate an immutable 3D vector named `vector0` and the `sum` method for the generated instance and save the returned instance in the new `vector1` variable. The call to the `sum` method generates a new instance and doesn't mutate the existing object:

```
var vector0 = ImmutableVector3D.originVector()
var vector1 = vector0.sum(5, deltaX: 10, deltaY: 15)
vector1.printValues()
```

> The code doesn't allow the users of the `ImmutableVector3D` class to change the values of the x, y, and z properties declared with the `let` keyword. The code doesn't compile if you try to assign a new value to any of these properties after they were initialized. Thus, we can say that the `ImmutableVector3D` class is 100 percent immutable.

Encapsulation of Data with Properties

Finally, the code calls the `printValues` method for the returned instance (`vector1`) to check the values for the three elements on the Playground, as shown in the following screenshot:

```swift
public class ImmutableVector3D {
    public let x: Float
    public let y: Float
    public let z: Float

    init(x: Float, y: Float, z: Float) {
        self.x = x
        self.y = y
        self.z = z
    }

    public func sum(deltaX: Float, deltaY: Float, deltaZ: Float)
        -> ImmutableVector3D {
        return ImmutableVector3D(x: x + deltaX, y: y + deltaY, z:          ImmutableVector3D
            z + deltaZ)
    }

    public func printValues() {
        print("X: \(self.x), Y: \(self.y), Z: \(self.z))")              "X: 5.0, Y: 10.0, Z: 15.0)\n"
    }

    public class func equalElementsVector(initialValue: Float) ->
        ImmutableVector3D {
        return ImmutableVector3D(x: initialValue, y:                    ImmutableVector3D
            initialValue, z: initialValue)
    }
    public class func originVector() -> ImmutableVector3D {
        return equalElementsVector(0)                                   ImmutableVector3D
    }
}
var vector0 = ImmutableVector3D.originVector()                          ImmutableVector3D
var vector1 = vector0.sum(5, deltaY: 10, deltaZ: 15)                    ImmutableVector3D
vector1.printValues()|                                                  ImmutableVector3D

    x 5
    y 10
    z 15
```

[80]

The immutable version adds an overhead compared with the mutable version because it is necessary to create a new instance of the class as a result of calling the `sum` method. The previously analyzed mutable version just changed the values for the attributes, and it wasn't necessary to generate a new instance. Obviously, the immutable version has both a memory and performance overhead. However, when we work with concurrent code, it makes sense to pay for the extra overhead to avoid potential issues caused by mutable objects. We just have to make sure we analyze the advantages and tradeoffs in order to decide which is the most convenient way of coding our specific classes.

Exercises

Now that you understand instance properties, type properties, and methods, it is time to spend some time in the Playground creating new classes and instances:

- **Exercise 1**: Create the mutable versions of the following three classes that we analyzed in *Chapter 1, Objects from the Real World to Playground*:
    - Equilateral triangle (The `EquilateralTriangle` class)
    - Square (The `Square` class)
    - Regular hexagon (The `RegularHexagon` class)

- **Exercise 2**: Create the immutable versions of the previously created classes

Test your knowledge

1. You use the `static var` keywords to declare a:
    1. Type property.
    2. Instance property.
    3. Read-only computed instance property.

2. You use the `static let` keywords to declare a:
    1. Mutable type property.
    2. Immutable instance property.
    3. Immutable type property.

3. An instance-stored property:
    1. Has its own and independent value for each instance of a class.
    2. Has the same value for all the instances of a class.
    3. Has the same value for all the instances of a class, unless it is accessed through the class name followed by dot and the property name.
4. A class that exposes mutable properties will:
    1. Generate immutable instances.
    2. Generate mutable instances.
    3. Generate mutable classes but immutable instances.
5. An instance method:
    1. Cannot access instance properties.
    2. Can access instance properties.
    3. Can access only type properties.

Summary

In this chapter, you learned about the different members of a class or blueprint. We worked with instance properties, type properties, instance methods, and type methods. We worked with stored properties, getters, setters, and property observers, and we took advantage of access modifiers to hide data.

We worked with superheroes and defined the shared properties of a specific type of lion superhero using type properties. We also worked with mutable and immutable versions of a 3D vector. You also understood the difference between mutable and immutable classes.

Now that you have learned to encapsulate data with properties, you are ready to create class hierarchies to abstract and specialize behavior, which is the topic of the next chapter.

4
Inheritance, Abstraction, and Specialization

In this chapter, you will learn about one of the most important topics of object-oriented programming: **inheritance**. We will work with examples on how to create class hierarchies, override methods, overload methods, work with inherited initializers, and overload operators. In addition, you will learn about polymorphism and basic typecasting.

Creating class hierarchies to abstract and specialize behavior

So far, we created classes to generate blueprints for real-life objects. Now, it is time to take advantage of the more advanced features of object-oriented programming and start designing a hierarchy of classes instead of working with isolated classes. First, we will design all the classes that we need based on the requirements, and then, we will use the features available in Swift to code the design.

We worked with classes to represent superheroes. Now, let's imagine that we have to develop a very complex app that requires us to work with hundreds of types of domestic animals. We already know that the app will start working with the following four domestic animal species:

- Dog (*Canis lupus familiaris*)
- Guinea pig (*Cavia porcellus*)
- Domestic canary (*Serinus canaria domestica*)
- Cat (*Felis silvestris catus*)

Inheritance, Abstraction, and Specialization

The previous list provides the scientific name for each domestic animal species. Of course, we will work with the most common name for each species and just have the scientific name as a type property. Thus, we won't have a complex class name, such as `CanipsLupusFamiliaris`, but we will use `Dog` instead.

Initially, we have to work with a limited number of breeds for the previously enumerated four domestic animal species. Additionally, in the future, it will be necessary to work with other members of the listed domestic animal species, other domestic mammals, and even reptiles and birds that don't belong to the domestic animal species. Thus, our object-oriented design must be ready to be expanded for the future requirements. In fact, you will understand how object-oriented programming makes it easy to expand an existing design for future requirements.

Of course, we don't want our object-oriented design to model a complete representation of the animal kingdom and its classification. We just want to create the necessary classes to have a flexible model that can be easily expanded. The animal kingdom is extremely complex, and we will keep our focus in just a few members of this huge family.

> The examples will also allow you to understand that object-oriented programming doesn't sacrifice flexibility. We can start with a simple class hierarchy that can be expanded as the application's complexity increases and we have more information about new requirements.

In this case, we will need many classes to represent a complex classification of animals and their breeds. The following list enumerates the classes that we will create and their descriptions:

- `Animal`: This is a class that generalizes all the members of the animal kingdom. Dogs, guinea pigs, domestic canaries, cats, reptiles, and birds have one thing in common: they are animals. Thus, it makes sense to create a class that will be the baseline for the different classes of animals that we may have to represent in our object-oriented design.

- `Mammal`: This is a class that generalizes all the mammalian animals. Mammals are different from reptiles, amphibians, birds, and insects. As we already know that we will also have to model reptiles and birds, we will create a `Mammal` class at this level.

- `Bird`: This is a class that generalizes all birds. Birds are different from mammals, reptiles, amphibians, and insects. We already know that we will also have to model reptiles and birds. In fact, a domestic canary is a bird, so we will create a `Bird` class at the same level as `Mammal`.

- `DomesticMammal`: This is a subclass of `Mammal`. The tiger (*Panthera tigris*) is the largest and heaviest living species of the cat family. A tiger is a cat, but it is completely different from a domestic cat. The initial requirements tell us that we will work with both domestic and wild animals, so we will create a class that generalizes all domestic mammal animals. In the future, we will have a `WildMammal` subclass that will generalize all the wild mammalian animals.

- `DomesticBird`: The ostrich (*Struthio camelus*) is the largest living bird. However, obviously, an ostrich is completely different from a domestic canary. As we will work with both domestic and wild birds, we will create a class that generalizes all domestic birds. In the future, we will have a `WildBird` class that will generalize all wild birds.

- `Dog`: We could go on specializing the `DomesticMammal` class with additional subclasses until we reach a `Dog` class. For example, we might create a `CanidCarnivorianDomesticMammal` subclass and then make the `Dog` class inherit from it. However, the kind of app we have to develop doesn't require any intermediary class between `DomesticMammal` and `Dog`. At this level we will also have a `Cat` class. The `Dog` class generalizes the properties and methods required for a dog in our application. Subclasses of the `Dog` class will represent the different families of the dog breed. For example, one of the main differences between a dog and a cat in our application domain is that a dog barks and a cat meows.

- `Cat`: The `Cat` class generalizes the properties and methods required for a cat in our application. Subclasses of the `Cat` class will represent the different families of the cat breed. In this case, we create a class to represent domestic cats, so `Cat` is a subclass of `DomesticMammal`.

- `GuineaPig`: The `GuineaPig` class generalizes all the properties and methods required for a guinea pig in our application.

- `TerrierDog`: Each dog breed belongs to a family. We will work with a huge amount of dog breeds, and some profile values determined by their family are very important for our application. Thus, we will create a subclass of `Dog` for each family. In this case, the sample `TerrierDog` class represents the Terrier family.

- `SmoothFoxTerrier`: Finally, a subclass of a dog breed family class will represent a specific dog breed that belongs to the family. Its breed determines the dog's looks and behavior. A dog that belongs to the Smooth Fox Terrier breed is completely different from a dog that belongs to the Tibetan Spaniel breed. Thus, we will create instances of the classes at this level to give life to each dog in our application. In this case, the `SmoothFoxTerrier` class models an animal, a mammal, domestic mammal, dog, and Terrier family dog—specifically, a dog that belongs to the Smooth Fox Terrier breed.
- `DomesticCanary`: The `DomesticCanary` class generalizes the properties and methods required for a domestic canary in our application.

Each class listed in the previous list represents a specialization of the previous class—that is, its superclass, parent class, or superset—as shown in the following table:

Superclass, parent class, or superset	Subclass, child class, or subset
`Animal`	`Mammal`
`Animal`	`Bird`
`Mammal`	`DomesticMammal`
`Bird`	`DomesticBird`
`DomesticMammal`	`Dog`
`DomesticMammal`	`Cat`
`DomesticMammal`	`GuineaPig`
`DomesticBird`	`DomesticCanary`
`Dog`	`TerrierDog`
`TerrierDog`	`SmoothFoxTerrier`

Our application requires many members of the Terrier family, so the `SmoothFoxTerrier` class will not be the only subclass of `TerrierDog`. In the future, we will have the following three additional subclasses of `TerrierDog`:

- `AiredaleTerrier`: This is the Airedale Terrier breed
- `BullTerrier`: This is the Bull Terrier breed
- `CairnTerrier`: This is the Cairn Terrier breed

The following UML diagram shows the previous classes organized in a class hierarchy:

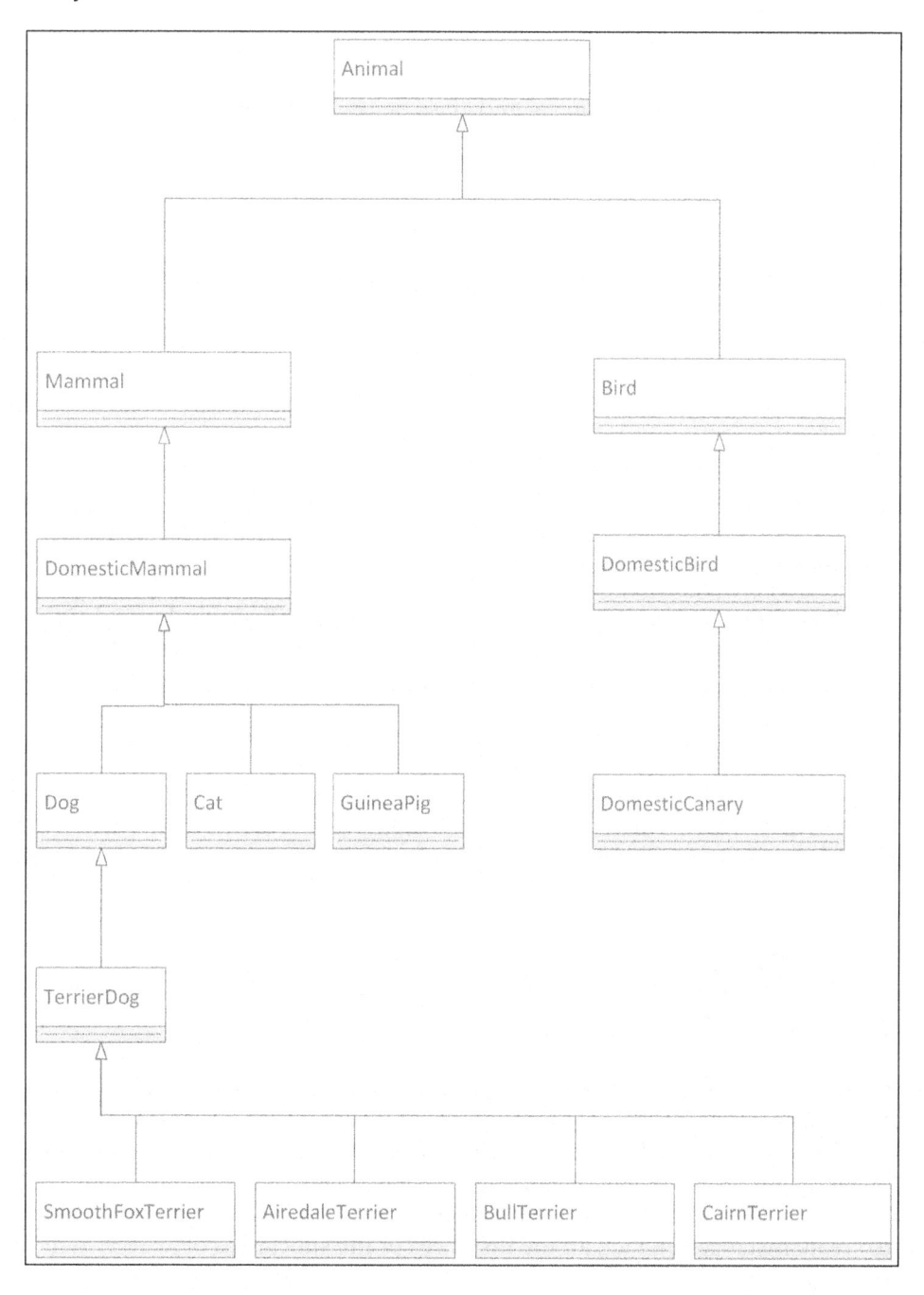

Inheritance, Abstraction, and Specialization

Understanding inheritance

When a class inherits from another class, it inherits all the elements that compose the parent class, which is also known as a superclass. The class that inherits the elements is known as a subclass. For example, the `Mammal` subclass inherits all the properties, instance fields or instance attributes, and class fields or class attributes defined in the `Animal` superclass.

The `Animal` abstract class is the baseline for our class hierarchy. We say that it is an abstract class because we shouldn't create instances of the `Animal` class; instead, we must create instances of the specific subclasses of `Animal`. However, we must take into account that Swift doesn't allow us to declare a class as an abstract class.

We require each `Animal` to specify its age, so we will have to specify the age when we create any `Animal` — that is, any instance of any `Animal` subclass. The class will define an age property and display a message whenever an animal is created. The class defines three type properties that specify the number of legs, the average number of children, and the ability to fly. The first two type properties will be initialized to `0`, and the last one to `false`. The subclasses will have to set appropriate values for these type properties. The `Animal` class defines the following three instance methods:

- **Print legs**: This prints a representation of the specified number of legs. Guinea pigs have legs that are very different from the ones that dogs have.
- **Print children**: This prints a representation of the specific average number of children.
- **Print age**: This prints the animal's age.

In addition, we want to be able to compare the age of the different `Animal` instances using the following operators:

- Less than (<)
- Less than or equal to (<=)
- Greater than (>)
- Greater than or equal to (>=)

We have to print a message whenever we create any `Animal` instance. We won't create instances of the `Animal` class but those of its different subclasses. When we inherit from a class, we also inherit its initializer, so we can call the inherited initializer to run the initialization code for the base class. This way, it is possible to know when an instance of `Animal` is created, even when it is a class that we don't use to create instances. In fact, all the instances of the subclasses of `Animal` will be instances of `Animal` too.

The Mammal class inherits from Animal. We require each Mammal class to specify its age and whether it is pregnant or not when creating an instance. The class inherits the age property from the Animal superclass, so it is only necessary to add a property to specify whether it is pregnant or not. Note that we will not specify the gender at any time in order to keep things simple. If we added gender, we would need a validation to avoid a male being pregnant. Right now, our focus is on inheritance. The class displays a message whenever a mammalian animal is created—that is, whenever its initializer is executed.

> Each class inherits from one class, so each new class we will define has just one superclass. In this case, we will always work with *single inheritance*.

The DomesticMammal class inherits from Mammal. We require each DomesticMammal class to specify its name and favorite toy. Any domestic mammal has a name and it always picks a favorite toy. Sometimes, the favorite toy is not exactly the toy we would like them to pick (our shoes, sneakers, or electronic devices), but let's keep the focus on our classes. It is necessary to add a read-only property to allow access to the name and a read/write property for the favorite toy. You never change the name of a domestic mammal, but you can force it to change its favorite toy. The class displays a message whenever a domestic mammalian animal is created.

The talk instance method will display a message indicating the domestic mammal's name concatenated with the word talk. Each subclass must make the specific domestic mammal talk in a different way. A parrot can really talk, but we will consider a dog's bark and a cat's meow as if they were talking.

The Dog class inherits from DomesticMammal and specifies 4 as the value for the number of legs. The Animal class, that is the Mammal superclass, defined this type attribute with 0 as the value, but Dog overwrites the inherited attribute with 4. The class displays a message whenever a dog is created. The average number of children will be specified in each subclass of Dog that determines a dog breed.

We want the dogs to be able to bark, so we need a bark method. The method has to allow a dog to do the following things:

- Bark happily just once
- Bark happily a specific number of times
- Bark happily at another domestic mammal with a name just once
- Bark happily at another domestic mammal with a name a specific number of times
- Bark angrily just once

- Bark angrily a specific number of times
- Bark angrily at another domestic mammal with a name just once
- Bark angrily at another domestic mammal with a name a specific number of times

We can have just one `bark` method with optional arguments or many `bark` methods. Swift provides many mechanisms to solve the challenges of the different ways in which a dog must be able to bark.

When we call the `talk` method for any dog, we want it to bark happily once. We don't want to display the message defined in the `talk` method introduced in the `DomesticMammal` class. Thus, the `Dog` class must overwrite the inherited `talk` method with its own definition.

We want to know the breed and breed family to which a dog belongs. Thus, we will define both the `breed` and `breed family` type properties. Each subclass of `Dog` must specify the appropriate values for these type properties. In addition, two type methods will allow us to print the dog's breed and breed family.

The `TerrierDog` class inherits from `Dog` and specifies `Terrier` as the value for the breed family. The class displays a message whenever a `TerrierDog` class is created.

Finally, the `SmoothFoxTerrier` class inherits from `TerrierDog` and specifies `Smooth Fox Terrier` as the value for the breed. The class displays a message whenever a `SmoothFoxTerrier` class is created.

First, we will create a base `Animal` class in Swift, and then, we will use simple inheritance to create the subclasses. We will override methods and overload comparison operators to be able to compare different instances of a specific class and its subclasses. We will take advantage of polymorphism, which is a very important feature in object-oriented programming.

Declaring classes that inherit from another class

The following lines show the code for the `Animal` base class in Swift. The class header doesn't specify a base class, so this class will become our base class for the other classes:

```
public class Animal {
    public static var numberOfLegs: Int {
        get {
```

```swift
            return 0;
        
        }
    }
    public static var averageNumberOfChildren: Int {
        get {
            return 0;
        }
    }

    public static var abilityToFly: Bool {
        get {
            return false;
        }
    }

    public var age: Int

    init(age : Int) {
        self.age = age
        print("Animal created")
    }

    public static func printALeg() {
        preconditionFailure("The pringALeg method must be overriden")
    }

    public func printLegs() {
        for _ in 0..<self.dynamicType.numberOfLegs {
            self.dynamicType.printALeg()
        }
        print(String())

    }

    public static func printAChild() {
        preconditionFailure("The printChild method must be overriden")
    }

    public func printChildren() {
        for _ in 0..<self.dynamicType.averageNumberOfChildren {
            self.dynamicType.printAChild()
        }
        print(String())
```

Inheritance, Abstraction, and Specialization

```
    }

    public func printAge() {
        print("I am \(age) years old.")
    }
}
```

The preceding class declares two read-only type-computed properties and both return 0 as their value: `numberOfLegs` and `averageNumberOfChildren`. In addition, the class declares another read-only type computed property that returns `false` as its value: `abilityToFly`. We will be able to return different values for these properties in the different subclasses of `Animal`.

The initializer requires an `age` value to create an instance of the class and prints a message indicating that an animal is created. The class declares an `age` stored instance property. It defines the following three instance methods:

- `printAge`: This displays the age based on the `age` value
- `printALeg`: This uses `preconditionFailure` to indicate that each subclass must override this type method with a specific implementation that prints a single leg for the animal
- `printAChild`: This uses `preconditionFailure` to indicate that each subclass must override this type method with a specific implementation that prints a single child for the animal.

In addition, the class declares the following two type methods:

- `printLegs`: This calls the `printALeg` method the number of times specified in the `numberOfLegs` type property. The method uses the `dynamicType` expression to retrieve the runtime type as a value and access the type property for the specific type that we used to created the instance.
- `printChildren`: This calls the `printAChild` method the number of times specified in the `averageNumberOfChildren` type property. As it happened in the `pringLegs` property, the code uses the `dynamicType` expression to access the necessary type property.

If we execute the following line in the Playground after declaring the `Animal` class, Swift will generate a fatal error and indicate that the `printAChild` type method must be overridden, as shown in the subsequent screenshot:

```
Animal.printAChild()
```

```
    public static var abilityToFly: Bool {
        get {
            return false;
        }
    }

    public var age: Int

    init(age : Int) {
        self.age = age
        print("Animal created")                              "Animal created\n"
    }

    public static func printALeg() {
        preconditionFailure("The pringALeg method must be overriden")
    }

    public func printLegs() {
        for _ in 0..<self.dynamicType.numberOfLegs {
            self.dynamicType.printALeg()
        }
    }

    public static func printAChild() {
        preconditionFailure("The printChild method must be overriden")
    }

    public func printChildren() {
        for _ in 0..<self.dynamicType.averageNumberOfChildren {
            self.dynamicType.printAChild()
        }
    }

    public func printAge() {
        print("I am \(age) years old.")                      "I am 7 years old.\n"
    }
}
Animal.printAChild()
    Execution was interrupted, reason: EXC_BAD_INSTRUCTION (code=EXC_I386_INVOP, subcode=0x0).  Animal
```

We have to add additional functions to allow us to compare the ages of different `Animal` instances using operators. We will add the necessary code to perform this task later.

The following lines show the code for the `Mammal` class that inherits from `Animal`. Note the `class` keyword followed by the class name `Mammal`, a colon (`:`), and `Animal`, which is the superclass from which it inherits, in the class definition:

```
public class Mammal: Animal {
    public var isPregnant: Bool = false

    private func initialize(isPregnant: Bool) {
        self.isPregnant = isPregnant
        print("Mammal created")
    }

    public override init(age: Int) {
```

Inheritance, Abstraction, and Specialization

```
        super.init(age: age)
        initialize(false)
    }

    public init(age: Int, isPregnant: Bool) {
        super.init(age: age)
        initialize(isPregnant)
    }
}
```

The `Mammal` class inherits the members from the previously declared `Animal` class and adds a new `Bool` stored property initialized with the default `false` value. Note that this class declares two initializers. One of the initializers requires an `age` value to create an instance of the class, as it happened with the `Animal` initializer. The other initializer requires the `age` and `isPregnant` values. If we create an instance of this class with just one `age` argument, Swift will use the first initializer. If we create an instance of this class with two arguments—an `Int` value for `age` and a `Bool` value for `isPregnant`—Swift will use the second initializer. Thus, we have overloaded the initializer and provided two different initializers. Of course, we could also take advantage of optional parameters. However, in this case, we want to overload initializers.

The two initializers use the `super` keyword to call the inherited `init` method from the base class or superclass—that is, the `init` method defined in the `Animal` class. Once the superclass' initializer finishes its execution, each initializer calls the `initialize` private method that initializes the `isPregnant` stored property with the value received as an argument or the default `false` value in case it isn't specified.

> We will use `base` to reference the superclass.

One of the initializers uses the `override` keyword to override the initializer with the same declaration that is included in the superclass. We already had an initializer with an `age` argument of type `Int` in the `Animal` superclass. The other initializer doesn't require the override keyword because there is no initializer declared in the `Animal` superclass with the same arguments.

The following lines create an instance of the `Mammal` class in the Playground using the initializer that just requires an `age` argument:

```
var bat = Mammal(age: 3)
bat.printAge()
print(bat.isPregnant)
```

The following lines show the results of the preceding lines. When the superclass initializer is executed, it prints `Animal created`, and after this happens, the initializer defined in the `Mammal` class prints `Mammal created`. The call to the `printAge` method defined in the `Animal` superclass prints the actual value of the age property in this instance of the `Mammal` class. Finally, a line prints the value of the `isPregnant` property that was initialized with `false` because we didn't specify a value for it:

```
Animal created
Mammal created
I am 3 years old.
false
```

The following lines create another instance of the `Mammal` class in the Playground using the initializer that requires two arguments—`age` and `isPregnant`:

```
var cat = Mammal(age: 6, isPregnant: true)
cat.printAge()
print(cat.isPregnant)
```

The following lines show the results of the preceding lines. The last line prints the value of the `isPregnant` property that was initialized with `true` in the initializer defined in the `Mammal` class:

```
Animal created
Mammal created
I am 6 years old.
true
```

The following screenshot shows the results of executing the preceding code in the Playground:

```swift
public class Mammal: Animal {
    public var isPregnant: Bool = false
    
    private func initialize(isPregnant: Bool) {
        self.isPregnant = isPregnant            (2 times)
        print("Mammal created")                 (2 times)
    }
    
    public override init(age: Int) {
        super.init(age: age)
        initialize(false)
    }
    
    public init(age: Int, isPregnant: Bool) {
        super.init(age: age)
        initialize(isPregnant)
    }
}

var bat = Mammal(age: 3)                        Mammal
bat.printAge()                                  Mammal
print(bat.isPregnant)                           "false\n"

var cat = Mammal(age: 6, isPregnant: true)      Mammal
cat.printAge()                                  Mammal
print(cat.isPregnant)                           "true\n"
```

```
Mammal created
I am 3 years old.
false
Animal created
Mammal created
I am 6 years old.
true
```

Overriding and overloading methods

Swift allows us to define a method with the same name many times with different arguments. This feature is known as method overloading. In some cases, as in our previous example, we can overload the initializer. However, it is very important to mention that a similar effect might be achieved with optional parameters or default values for specific arguments.

For example, we can take advantage of method overloading to define multiple versions of the `bark` method that we have to define in the `Dog` class. However, it is very important to avoid code duplication when we overload methods.

Sometimes, we define a method in a class, and we know that a subclass might need to provide a different version of the method. When a subclass provides a different implementation of a method defined in a superclass with the same name, arguments, and return type, we say that we are overriding a method. When we override a method, the implementation in the subclass overwrites the code provided in the superclass.

> It is also possible to override methods related to properties, such as getters and setters, and other members of a class in the subclasses.

The following lines show the code for the `DomesticMammal` class that inherits from `Mammal`. Note the `class` keyword followed by the class name `DomesticMammal`, a colon (`:`), and `Mammal`, which is the superclass from which it inherits, in the class definition:

```
public class DomesticMammal: Mammal {
    public var name = String()
    public var favoriteToy = String()

    private func initialize(name: String, favoriteToy: String) {
        self.name = name
        self.favoriteToy = favoriteToy
        print("DomesticMammal created")
    }

    public init(age: Int, name: String, favoriteToy: String) {
        super.init(age: age)
        initialize(name, favoriteToy: favoriteToy)
    }

    public init(age: Int, isPregnant: Bool, name: String, favoriteToy: String) {
        super.init(age: age, isPregnant: isPregnant)
        initialize(name, favoriteToy: favoriteToy)
    }

    public func talk() {
        print("\(name): talks")
    }
}
```

Inheritance, Abstraction, and Specialization

The preceding class declares two initializers. One of them requires `age`, `name`, and `favoriteToy` to create an instance of a class. The other initializer adds an `isPregnant` argument. As it happened in the `Mammal` class, the code within each initializer uses `super.init` to call the appropriate superclass' initializer. In one case, we just need the `age` value received as an argument, and in the other case, it is also necessary to add the `isPregnant` value. Once the superclass' initializer finishes its execution, the initializers call the `initialize` private method that initializes the `name` and `favoriteToy` properties. After the method finishes initializing the properties, it prints a message indicating that a `DomesticMammal` class is created. The following lines show both initializer declarations:

```
public init(age: Int, name: String, favoriteToy: String) {
public init(age: Int, isPregnant: Bool, name: String, favoriteToy: String) {
```

The class defines two stored properties: `name` and `favoriteToy`. The `talk` instance method displays a message with the `name` value followed by a colon (`:`) and `talks`. Note that we will be able to override this method in any subclass of `DomesticMammal` because each domestic mammal has a different way of talking.

The following lines create an instance of the `DomesticMammal` class in the Playground using the initializer that requires three arguments—`age`, `name`, and `favoriteToy`:

```
var scooby = DomesticMammal(age: 5, name: "Scooby", favoriteToy: "Scarf")
scooby.printAge()
scooby.talk()
print(scooby.favoriteToy)
print(scooby.isPregnant)
```

The following lines show the results of the preceding lines. We can detect the chained execution of the initializers in the base class (`Animal`), the superclass (`Mammal`), and the class (`DomesticMammal`). The first line displays `Animal created`, the second line displays `Mammal created`, and the third line displays `Domestic Mammal created`. The call to the `printAge` method defined in the base class (`Animal`) prints the actual value of the `age` property in this instance of the `DomesticMammal` class. The call to the `talk` method displays the message that starts with the `name` value. A line prints the value of the `favoriteToy` property that is defined in this class, and then, another line prints the value of the inherited `isPregnant` property. In this case, the value of the `isPregnant` property was initialized with `false` because we didn't specify a value for it:

```
Animal created
Mammal created
```

[98]

```
DomesticMammal created
I am 5 years old.
Scooby: talks
Scarf
false
```

The following lines create another instance of the DomesticMammal class in the Playground using the initializer that requires four arguments—age, isPregnant, name, and favoriteToy:

```
var lady = DomesticMammal(age: 6, isPregnant: true, name: "Lady",
favoriteToy: "Teddy")
lady.printAge()
lady.talk()
print(lady.favoriteToy)
print(lady.isPregnant)
```

The following lines show the results of the preceding lines. The last line prints the value of the isPregnant property that was initialized with true in the initializer defined in the Mammal class and called through the initializers' chain:

```
Animal created
Mammal created
DomesticMammal created
I am 6 years old.
Lady: talks
Teddy
true
```

Inheritance, Abstraction, and Specialization

The following screenshot shows the results of executing the preceding code in the Playground:

```swift
    private func initialize(name: String, favoriteToy: String) {
        self.name = name                                            (2 times)
        self.favoriteToy = favoriteToy                              (2 times)
        print("DomesticMammal created")                             (2 times)
    }

    public init(age: Int, name: String, favoriteToy: String) {
        super.init(age: age)
        initialize(name, favoriteToy: favoriteToy)
    }

    public init(age: Int, isPregnant: Bool, name: String, favoriteToy:
        String) {
        super.init(age: age, isPregnant: isPregnant)
        initialize(name, favoriteToy: favoriteToy)
    }

    public func talk() {
        print("\(name): talks")                                     (2 times)
    }
}

var scooby = DomesticMammal(age: 5, name: "Scooby", favoriteToy: "Scarf")   DomesticMammal
scooby.printAge()                                                           DomesticMammal
scooby.talk()                                                               DomesticMammal
print(scooby.favoriteToy)                                                   "Scarf\n"
print(scooby.isPregnant)                                                    "false\n"

var lady = DomesticMammal(age: 6, isPregnant: true, name: "Lady",           DomesticMammal
    favoriteToy: "Teddy")
lady.printAge()                                                             DomesticMammal
lady.talk()                                                                 DomesticMammal
print(lady.favoriteToy)                                                     "Teddy\n"
print(lady.isPregnant)                                                      "true\n"
```

```
Animal created
Mammal created
DomesticMammal created
I am 5 years old.
Scooby: talks
Scarf
false
Animal created
Mammal created
DomesticMammal created
I am 6 years old.
Lady: talks
Teddy
true
```

Dogs are domestic mammals that have four legs, and so far, nobody has discovered a dog breed with the ability to fly. When we define the Dog class that inherits from DomesticMammal, we will want to override the numberOfLegs type property to make its getter return 4 and make sure that the abilityToFly type property will always return false in Dog and any of its subclasses.

Overriding properties

First, we will try to override the `numberOfLegs` type property that the `Dog` class will inherit from the `Animal` base class. We will face an issue and solve it. The following lines show the code for a simplified version of the `Dog` class that inherits from `DomesticMammal` and just tries to override the `numberOfLegs` type property:

```
public class Dog: DomesticMammal {
    public static override var numberOfLegs: Int {
        get {
            return 4;
        }
    }
}
```

After we enter the previous lines in the Playground, we will see the following error message in the line that tries to override the `numberOfLegs` type property: `error: class var overrides a 'final' class var`. The following screenshot shows the error in the Playground:

```
public class Dog: DomesticMammal {
    public static override var numberOfLegs: Int {          Class var overrides a 'final' class var
        get {
            return 4;
        }
    }
}
```

> When we declare either a type property or method with the `static` keyword in a base class, it isn't possible to override it in a subclass. Thus, if we want to enable either a type property or method to be overridden in the subclasses, it is necessary to use the `class` keyword instead of `static` when we declare them in the base class.

We have to change the declaration of the type properties declared in the `Animal` class to use the `class` keyword instead of the `static` keyword. The following lines show the first lines of code of the new version of the `Animal` class that replaces the declaration of the type properties to make it possible to override them in its subclasses. Note that the rest of the code for the class after the declaration of the three type properties remains without changes:

```
public class Animal {
    public class var numberOfLegs: Int {
        get {
            return 0;
```

Inheritance, Abstraction, and Specialization

```
        }
    }
    public class var averageNumberOfChildren: Int {
        get {
            return 0;
        }
    }

    public class var abilityToFly: Bool {
        get {
            return false;
        }
    }

    ...

}
```

After we make the preceding changes to the `Animal` class, we will notice that the Playground will remove the error message in the declaration of the type property we declared in the `Dog` class. In fact, we didn't have to make changes to the type property declaration in the `Dog` class to remove the error. However, we must take into account that the usage of the `static` keyword when declaring the `numberOfLegs` type property in the `Dog` class that overrides the inherited property from the `Animal` class prevents subclasses of `Dog` from overriding this property. When we use `static` for overridden type properties, we are indicating to Swift that we don't want the type property to be overridden any more. In this case, it makes sense because so far, all the dogs that have been discovered have four legs. Thus, any `Dog` subclass won't need to specify a different value for this type property.

The following line prints the value for the overridden type property:

```
print(Dog.numberOfLegs)
```

The next screenshot shows the results of printing the overridden type property in the Playground after we edited the type properties declaration in the `Animal` class:

Code	Output

`public class Dog: DomesticMammal {`
`    public static override var numberOfLegs: Int {`
`        get {`
`            return 4;`
`        }`
`    }`
`}`
`print(Dog.numberOfLegs)`
	4
	
	"4\n"

Controlling whether subclasses can or cannot override members

The following lines show the code for the complete `Dog` class that inherits from `DomesticMammal`. Note that the following code replaces the previous `Dog` class that just declared an overridden type property:

```
public class Dog: DomesticMammal {
    public static override var numberOfLegs: Int {
        get {
            return 4;
        }
    }

    public static override var abilityToFly: Bool {
        get {
            return false;
        }
    }

    public var breed: String {

        get {
            return "Just a dog"
        }
    }

    public var breedFamily: String {

        get {
            return "Dog"
        }
    }

    private func initializeDog() {
        print("Dog created")
    }

    public override init(age: Int, name: String, favoriteToy: String)
{
        super.init(age: age, name: name, favoriteToy: favoriteToy)
```

```swift
        initializeDog()
    }

    public override init(age: Int, isPregnant: Bool, name: String, favoriteToy: String) {
        super.init(age: age, isPregnant: isPregnant, name: name, favoriteToy: favoriteToy)
        initializeDog()
    }

    public final func printBreed() {
        print(breed)
    }

    public final func printBreedFamily() {
        print(breedFamily)
    }

    public func printBark(times: Int, otherDomesticMammal: DomesticMammal?, isAngry: Bool) {
        var bark = "\(name)"
        if let unwrappedOtherDomesticMammal = otherDomesticMammal {
            bark += " to \(unwrappedOtherDomesticMammal.name): "
        } else {
            bark += ": "
        }
        if isAngry {
            bark += "Grr "
        }
        for _ in 0 ..< times {
            bark += "Woof "
        }
        print(bark)
    }

    public func bark() {
        printBark(1, otherDomesticMammal: nil, isAngry: false)
    }

    public func bark(times: Int) {
        printBark(times, otherDomesticMammal: nil, isAngry: false)
    }

    public func bark(times: Int, otherDomesticMammal: DomesticMammal)
    {
```

```
                printBark(times, otherDomesticMammal: otherDomesticMammal,
    isAngry: false)
    }

        public func bark(times: Int, otherDomesticMammal: DomesticMammal,
    isAngry: Bool) {
            printBark(times, otherDomesticMammal: otherDomesticMammal,
    isAngry: isAngry)
    }

    public override func talk() {
        bark()
    }
}
```

The `Dog` class overrides the `talk` method inherited from `DomesticMammal`. As it happened with the overridden properties in other subclasses, we just add the `override` keyword to the method declaration. The method doesn't invoke the method with the same name for its superclass; that is, we don't use the `super` keyword to invoke the `talk` method defined in `DomesticMammal`. The `talk` method in the `Dog` class invokes the `bark` method without parameters because dogs don't talk; they bark.

The `bark` method is overloaded with four declarations with different arguments. The following lines show the four different declarations included within the class body:

```
public func bark()
public func bark(times: Int)
public func bark(times: Int, otherDomesticMammal: DomesticMammal)
public func bark(times: Int, otherDomesticMammal: DomesticMammal,
isAngry: Bool)
```

This way, we can call any of the defined `bark` methods based on the provided arguments. The four methods end up invoking the `printBark` private method with different default values for the arguments not provided in the call to `bark`. The method builds and prints a message according to the specified number of times (`times`), the optional destination domestic mammal (`otherDomesticMammal`), and whether the dog is angry or not (`isAngry`).

The `Dog` class overrides the `abilityToFly` type property with the `static` keyword. This way, subclasses of dog won't be able to override this type property to return a different value because there is no known dog breed that can fly.

Inheritance, Abstraction, and Specialization

The class also declares two read-only computed properties: `breed` and `breedFamily`. We will override their getters in the subclasses of `Dog`. The `printBreed` instance method displays the value of the `breed` computed property, and the `printBreedFamily` instance method displays the value of the `breedFamily` computed property. We won't override these instance methods in the subclasses because we just need to override the values of the properties to achieve our goals; therefore, we declared both methods with the `final` keyword. The following lines show the declarations of both methods with the `final` keyword, which prevents subclasses from overriding these methods:

```
public final func printBreed()
public final func printBreedFamily()
```

If we call these instance methods from an instance of a subclass of `Dog`, they will execute the code specified in the `Dog` class, but the code will use the value of the properties overridden in the subclasses. Thus, we will see the messages displaying the values of the properties as defined in the subclasses.

We want to override both the `printALeg` and `printAChild` type methods inherited from `Animal` in a subclass of `Dog`. We declared both properties with the `static` keyword, so we will only be able to override them if we replace this keyword with `class`. The following lines show the code that replaces the declaration of both properties in the `Animal` class. Note that the rest of the code for the class remains without changes:

```
public class func printALeg() {
    preconditionFailure("The pringALeg method must be overriden")
}

public class func printAChild() {
    preconditionFailure("The printChild method must be overriden")
}
```

The following lines show the code for the `TerrierDog` class that inherits from `Dog`:

```
public class TerrierDog: Dog {
    public override class var averageNumberOfChildren: Int {
        get {
            return 5;
        }
    }

    public override var breed: String {
        get {
```

```swift
            return "Terrier dog"
        }
    }
    
    public override var breedFamily: String {
        get {
            return "Terrier"
        }
    }
    
    private func initializeTerrierDog() {
        print("TerrierDog created")
    }
    
    public override init(age: Int, name: String, favoriteToy: String)
{
        super.init(age: age, name: name, favoriteToy: favoriteToy)
        initializeTerrierDog()
    }
    
    public override init(age: Int, isPregnant: Bool, name: String,
favoriteToy: String) {
        super.init(age: age, isPregnant: isPregnant, name: name,
favoriteToy: favoriteToy)
        initializeTerrierDog()
    }
    
    public override class func printALeg() {
        print("|", terminator: String())
    }
    
    public override class func printAChild() {
        // Print a dog's face emoji
        print(String(UnicodeScalar(0x01f436)), terminator: String())
        
    }
}
```

Inheritance, Abstraction, and Specialization

As it happened in the other subclasses that we coded, we have more than one initializer defined for the class. In this case, one of the initializers requires `age`, `name`, and `favoriteToy` to create an instance of the `TerrierDog` class, and we also have an initializer that adds an `isPregnant` argument. Both initializers invoke the superclass' initializer and then call the private `initializeTerrierDog` method. This method prints a message indicating that a `TerrierDog` class is created. The class overrides the getter methods to return `"Terrier dog"` and `"Terrier"` as the values for the `breed` and `breedFamily` computed properties that were defined in the superclass and overridden in this class.

In addition, the class overrides the getter method for the `averageNumberOfChildren` type property. However, in this case, the overridden type property declaration uses the `class` keyword because we want to enable subclasses of `TerrierDog` to be able to override this type property. The `Terrier` family is huge, and some of the members of this family have different average number of children.

The class also overrides both the `printALeg` and `printAChild` type methods inherited from `Animal`. The `printALeg` method prints a pipe symbol (|), and the `printAChild` method prints a dog's face emoji.

Working with typecasting and polymorphism

We can use the same method — that is, the same name and arguments — to cause different things to happen according to the class on which we invoke the method. In object-oriented programming, this feature is known as *polymorphism*.

For example, consider that we defined a `talk` method in the `Animal` class. The different subclasses of `Animal` must override this method to provide their own implementation of `talk`.

The `Dog` class overrode this method to print the representation of a dog barking — that is, a `Woof` message. On the other hand, a `Cat` class will override this method to print the representation of a cat meowing — that is, a `Meow` message.

Now, let's think about a `CartoonDog` class that represents a dog that can really talk as part of a cartoon. The `CartoonDog` class would override the `talk` method to print a `Hello` message because the dog can really talk.

Thus, depending on the type of the instance, we will see a different result after invoking the same method with the same arguments even when all of them are subclasses of the same base class — that is, the `Animal` class.

The following lines show the code for the `SmoothFoxTerrier` class that inherits from `TerrierDog`:

```
public class SmoothFoxTerrier: TerrierDog {
    public override class var averageNumberOfChildren: Int {
        get {
            return 6;
        }
    }

    public override var breed: String {
        get {
            return "Smooth Fox Terrier dog"
        }
    }


    private func initializeSmoothFoxTerrier() {
        print("SmoothFoxTerrier created")
    }

    public override init(age: Int, name: String, favoriteToy: String)
{
        super.init(age: age, name: name, favoriteToy: favoriteToy)
        initializeSmoothFoxTerrier()
    }

    public override init(age: Int, isPregnant: Bool, name: String,
favoriteToy: String) {
        super.init(age: age, isPregnant: isPregnant, name: name,
favoriteToy: favoriteToy)
        initializeSmoothFoxTerrier()
    }

    public override class func printALeg() {
        print("!", terminator: String())
    }

    public override class func printAChild() {
        // Print Dog's face emoji
        print(String(UnicodeScalar(0x01f415)), terminator: String())
    }
}
```

Inheritance, Abstraction, and Specialization

The class has the same initializers that we coded for its superclass. Both initializers invoke the initializers defined in the superclass and then call the `initializeSmoothFoxTerrier` private method. The method prints a message indicating that a `SmoothFoxTerrier` class is created. The class overrides the getter method to return `"Smooth Fox Terrier"` for the `breed` computed property that was defined in the `Dog` superclass and overridden in the `TerrierDog` superclass and also in this class. In addition, the class overrides the getter method for the `averageNumberOfChildren` type property to return `6`.

The class also overrides both the `printALeg` and `printAChild` type methods inherited from `Animal` and overridden in the `TerrierDog` superclass. The `printALeg` method prints an exclamation mark symbol (`!`) and the `printAChild` method prints a dog emoji different from the dog's face emoji that the method with the same name overrode in the superclass printed.

After we code all the classes, we can write code in the Playground to create instances of both the `TerrierDog` and `SmoothFoxTerrier` classes. The following are the first lines that create an instance of the `SmoothFoxTerrier` class named `tom` and use one of its initializers that doesn't require the `isPregnant` argument:

```
var tom = SmoothFoxTerrier(age: 5, name: "Tom", favoriteToy: "Sneakers")
tom.printBreed()
tom.printBreedFamily()
```

The following lines show the messages displayed in the Playground after we enter the previous code:

```
Animal created
Mammal created
DomesticMammal created
Dog created
TerrierDog created
SmoothFoxTerrier created
Smooth Fox Terrier
Terrier
```

First, the Playground prints the messages displayed by each initializer that is called. Remember that each initializer calls its base class initializer and prints a message indicating that an instance of the class is created. We don't have six different instances; we just have one instance that calls the chained initializers of six different classes to perform all the necessary initialization to create an instance of `SmoothFoxTerrier`. If we execute the following lines in the Playground, all of them will display `true` as a result, because `tom` belongs to the `Animal`, `Mammal`, `DomesticMammal`, `Dog`, `TerrierDog`, and `SmoothFoxTerrier` classes:

```
tom is Animal
tom is Mammal
tom is DomesticMammal
tom is Dog
tom is TerrierDog
tom is SmoothFoxTerrier
```

The following screenshot shows the results of executing the previous lines in the Playground. Note that the Playground uses an icon to let us know that all the `is` tests will always evaluate to `true`:

```
        public override init(age: Int, name: String, favoriteToy: String) {
            super.init(age: age, name: name, favoriteToy: favoriteToy)
            initializeSmoothFoxTerrier()
        }

        public override init(age: Int, isPregnant: Bool, name: String,
            favoriteToy: String) {
            super.init(age: age, isPregnant: isPregnant, name: name,
                favoriteToy: favoriteToy)
            initializeSmoothFoxTerrier()
        }

        public override class func printALeg() {
            print("!", terminator: String())
        }

        public override class func printAChild() {
            // Print Dog's face emoji
            print(String(UnicodeScalar(0x01f415)))
        }
    }

    var tom = SmoothFoxTerrier(age: 5, name: "Tom", favoriteToy: "Sneakers")     SmoothFoxTerrier
    tom.printBreed()                                                              SmoothFoxTerrier
    tom.printBreedFamily()                                                        SmoothFoxTerrier
    tom is Animal                                                                 true
    tom is Mammal                                                                 true
    tom is DomesticMammal                                                         true
    tom is Dog                                                                    true
    tom is TerrierDog                                                             true
    tom is SmoothFoxTerrier                                                       true
```

```
Animal created
Mammal created
DomesticMammal created
Dog created
TerrierDog created
SmoothFoxTerrier created
Smooth Fox Terrier
Terrier
```

Inheritance, Abstraction, and Specialization

We coded the `printBreed` and `printBreedFamily` methods within the `Dog` class, and we didn't override these methods in any of the subclasses. However, we overrode the properties whose content these methods display: `breed` and `breedFamily`. The `TerrierDog` class overrode both properties, and the `SmoothFoxTerrier` class overrode the `breed` property again.

The following line creates an instance of the `TerrierDog` class named `vanessa`. Note that in this case, we will create an instance of the superclass of the `SmoothFoxTerrier` class and use the initializer that requires the `isPregnant` argument:

```
var vanessa = TerrierDog(age: 6, isPregnant: true, name: "Vanessa",
favoriteToy: "Soda bottle")
```

The next lines call the `printLegs` and `printChildren` instance methods for `tom`, the instance of `SmoothFoxTerrier`, and `vanessa`, which is the instance of `TerrierDog`:

```
tom.printLegs()
tom.printChildren()
vanessa.printLegs()
vanessa.printChildren()
```

We coded these methods in the `Animal` class, and we didn't override them in any of its subclasses. Thus, when we call these methods for either `tom` or `vanessa`, Swift will execute the code defined in the `Animal` class. The `printLegs` method calls the `printALeg` type method for the type retrieved from the instance in which we will call it as many times as the value for the `numberOfLegs` type property. The `printChildren` method calls the `printAChild` type method for the type retrieved from the instance in which we will call it as many times as the value for the `averageNumberOfChildren` type property.

Both the `TerrierDog` and `SmoothFoxTerrier` classes overrode the following members: the `printALeg` and `printAChild` type methods and the `averageNumberOfChildren` type property. Thus, our call to the same methods will produce different results. The following screenshot shows the output generated for `tom` and `vanessa`. Note that `tom` prints four exclamation marks (!) to represent its legs, while `vanessa` prints four pipes (|). Regarding children, `tom` prints six dog emoji icons, while `vanessa` prints four dog's face emoji icons. Both instances run the same code for the two type methods that we called. However, each class overrode type properties that provide different values and cause the differences in the output:

```
    var vanessa = TerrierDog(age: 6, isPregnant: true, name: "Vanessa",     TerrierDog
        favoriteToy: "Soda bottle")

    tom.printLegs()                                                          SmoothFoxTerrier
    tom.printChildren()                                                      SmoothFoxTerrier
    vanessa.printLegs()                                                      TerrierDog
    vanessa.printChildren()                                                  TerrierDog
```

```
Animal created
Mammal created
DomesticMammal created
Dog created
TerrierDog created
SmoothFoxTerrier created
Smooth Fox Terrier
Terrier
Animal created
Mammal created
DomesticMammal created
Dog created
TerrierDog created
!!!!
ﰠﰠﰠﰠﰠﰠ
||||
☺☺☺☺☺
```

The following lines call the `bark` method for the instance named `tom` with a different number of arguments. This way, we take advantage of the `bark` method that we overloaded four times with different arguments. Remember that we coded the four `bark` methods in the `Dog` class and the `SmoothFoxTerrier` class inherits the overloaded methods from this superclass through its hierarchy tree:

```
tom.bark()
tom.bark(2)
tom.bark(2, otherDomesticMammal: vanessa)
tom.bark(3, otherDomesticMammal: vanessa, isAngry: true)
```

The following lines show the results of calling the methods with the different arguments:

```
Tom: Woof
Tom: Woof Woof
Tom to Vanessa: Woof Woof
Tom to Vanessa: Grr Woof Woof Woof
```

Inheritance, Abstraction, and Specialization

If we go back to the code that declared the `bark` method in the `Dog` class in the Playground, we will notice that the `SmoothFoxTerrier` class name is displayed on the right-hand side for each method that we used from the `Dog` class:

```
Find ◇          Q▾ bark
        public final func printBreedFamily() {
            print(breedFamily)|                                                 "Terrier\n"
        }

        public func printBark(times: Int, otherDomesticMammal: DomesticMammal?, isAngry:
            Bool) {
            var bark = "\(name)"                                                (4 times)
            if let unwrappedOtherDomesticMammal = otherDomesticMammal {
                bark += " to \(unwrappedOtherDomesticMammal.name): "            (2 times)
            } else {
                bark += ": "                                                    (2 times)
            }
            if isAngry {
                bark += "Grr "                                                  "Tom to Vanessa: Grr "
            }
            for _ in 0 ..< times {
                bark += "Woof "                                                 (8 times)
            }
            print(bark)                                                         (4 times)
        }

        public func bark() {
            printBark(1, otherDomesticMammal: nil, isAngry: false)              SmoothFoxTerrier
        }

        public func bark(times: Int) {
            printBark(times, otherDomesticMammal: nil, isAngry: false)          SmoothFoxTerrier
        }

        public func bark(times: Int, otherDomesticMammal: DomesticMammal) {
            printBark(times, otherDomesticMammal: otherDomesticMammal, isAngry: false)   SmoothFoxTerrier
        }

        public func bark(times: Int, otherDomesticMammal: DomesticMammal, isAngry: Bool)
        {
            printBark(times, otherDomesticMammal: otherDomesticMammal, isAngry: isAngry) SmoothFoxTerrier
        }

        public override func talk() {
            bark()
        }
    }

Tom: Woof
Tom: Woof Woof
Tom to Vanessa: Woof Woof
Tom to Vanessa: Grr Woof Woof Woof
```

The following lines show the code for the `Cat` class that inherits from `DomesticMammal`:

```
public class Cat: DomesticMammal {
    public static override var numberOfLegs: Int {
        get {
            return 4;
        }
```

```swift
    }
    
    public static override var abilityToFly: Bool {
        get {
            return false;
        }
    }
    
    public override class var averageNumberOfChildren: Int {
        get {
            return 6;
        }
    }
    
    private func initializeCat() {
        print("Cat created")
    }
    
    public override init(age: Int, name: String, favoriteToy: String) {
        super.init(age: age, name: name, favoriteToy: favoriteToy)
        initializeCat()
    }
    
    public override init(age: Int, isPregnant: Bool, name: String, favoriteToy: String) {
        super.init(age: age, isPregnant: isPregnant, name: name, favoriteToy: favoriteToy)
        initializeCat()
    }
    
    public func printMeow(times: Int) {
        var meow = "\(name): "
        for _ in 0 ..< times {
            meow += "Meow "
        }
        print(meow)
    }
    
    public override func talk() {
        printMeow(1)
    }
    
    public override class func printALeg() {
```

```
        print("*_*", terminator: String())
    }

    public override class func printAChild() {
        // Print grinning cat face with smiling eyes emoji
        print(String(UnicodeScalar(0x01F638)), terminator: String())
    }
}
```

The `Cat` class overrides the `talk` method inherited from `DomesticMammal`. As it happened with the overridden properties in other subclasses, we just added the `override` keyword to the method declaration. The method doesn't invoke the method with the same name for its superclass; that is, we don't use the `super` keyword to invoke the `talk` method defined in `DomesticMammal`. The `talk` method in the `Cat` class invokes the `meow` method with 1 as the number of times. The `meow` method prints the representation of a cat meowing — that is, a `Meow` message — the number of times specified in its `times` argument.

As it happened with other classes that we analyzed before, the class overrides the getter method for the `averageNumberOfChildren` type property. The class also overrides both the `printALeg` and `printAChild` type methods inherited from `Animal`. The `printALeg` method prints *_*, and the `printAChild` method prints a grinning cat face with a smiling eyes emoji.

The following lines show the code for the `Bird` class that inherits from `Animal`:

```
public class Bird: Animal {
    public var feathersColor: String = String()

    public static override var numberOfLegs: Int {
        get {
            return 2;
        }
    }

    private func initializeBird(feathersColor: String) {
        self.feathersColor = feathersColor
        print("Bird created")
    }

    public override init(age: Int) {
        super.init(age: age)
```

```
            initializeBird("Undefined / Too many colors")
    }

    public init(age: Int, feathersColor: String) {
        super.init(age: age)
        initializeBird(feathersColor)
    }
}
```

The `Bird` class inherits the members from the previously declared `Animal` class and adds a new `String` stored property initialized with the default empty string value. The class overrides the `numberOfLegs` type property to return 2 and disables any subclass' chance to override this type property again using the `static` keyword. Note that this class declares two initializers, as it happened with the `Mammal` class that also inherited from `Animal`. One of the initializers requires an `age` value to create an instance of the class, as it happened with the `Animal` initializer. The other initializer requires the `age` and `feathersColor` values. If we create an instance of this class with just one `age` argument, Swift will use the first initializer. If we create an instance of this class with two arguments, an `Int` value for `age` and a `String` value for `feathersColor`, Swift will use the second initializer. Again, we overloaded the initializer and provided two different initializers.

The two initializers use the `super` keyword to call the inherited `init` method from the base class or superclass—that is, the `init` method defined in the `Animal` class. Once the initialized code in the superclass finishes its execution, each initializer calls the `initializeBird` private method that initializes the `feathersColor` stored property with the value received as an argument or the default `"Undefined / Too many colors"` value in case it isn't specified.

The following lines show the code for the `DomesticBird` class that inherits from `Bird`. The preceding class simply adds a `name` stored property and allows the initializers to specify the desired name for the domestic bird:

```
public class DomesticBird: Bird {
    public var name = String()

    private func initializeDomesticBird(name: String) {
        self.name = name
        print("DomesticBird created")
    }

    public init(age: Int, name: String) {
        super.init(age: age)
```

Inheritance, Abstraction, and Specialization

```
        initializeDomesticBird(name)
    }

    public init(age: Int, feathersColor: String, name: String) {
        super.init(age: age, feathersColor: feathersColor)
        initializeDomesticBird(name)
    }
}
```

The following lines show the code for the DomesticCanary class that inherits from DomesticBird:

```
public class DomesticCanary: DomesticBird {
    public override class var averageNumberOfChildren: Int {
        get {
            return 5;
        }
    }

    private func initializeDomesticCanary() {
        print("DomesticCanary created")
    }

    public override init(age: Int, name: String) {
        super.init(age: age, name: name)
        initializeDomesticCanary()
    }

    public override init(age: Int, feathersColor: String, name: String) {
        super.init(age: age, feathersColor: feathersColor, name: name)
        initializeDomesticCanary()
    }

    public override class func printALeg() {
        print("^", terminator: String())
    }

    public override class func printAChild() {
        // Print bird emoji
        print(String(UnicodeScalar(0x01F426)), terminator: String())
    }
}
```

The class overrides the two initializers declared in the superclass to display a message whenever we create an instance of the `DomesticCanary` class. In addition, the class overrides the `averageNumberOfChildren` type property and the `printALeg` and `printAChild` methods.

After we declare the new classes, we will create the following two functions outside of any class declaration that receives an `Animal` instance as an argument—that is, an `Animal` instance or an instance of any subclass of `Animal`. Each function calls a different instance method defined in the `Animal` class:

```
public func printAnimalChildren(animal: Animal) {
    animal.printChildren()
}

public func printAnimalLegs(animal: Animal) {
    animal.printLegs()
}
```

Then, the following lines create instances of the next classes: `TerrierDog`, `Cat`, and `DomesticCanary`. Then, a few lines call the `printAnimalChildren` and `printAnimalLegs` functions with the instances as arguments:

```
var pluto = TerrierDog(age: 7, name: "Pluto", favoriteToy: "Teddy bear")
var marie = Cat(age: 4, isPregnant: true, name: "Marie", favoriteToy: "Tennis ball")
var tweety = DomesticCanary(age: 2, feathersColor: "Yellow", name: "Tweety")

print("Meet their children")
print(pluto.name)
printAnimalChildren(pluto)
print(marie.name)
printAnimalChildren(marie)
print(tweety.name)
printAnimalChildren(tweety)

print("Look at their legs")
print(pluto.name)
printAnimalLegs(pluto)
print(marie.name)
printAnimalLegs(marie)
print(tweety.name)
printAnimalLegs(tweety)
```

Inheritance, Abstraction, and Specialization

The following screenshot shows the results of executing the previous lines in the Playground. The three instances become an `Animal` argument for the different methods. However, the values used for the properties aren't those declared in the `Animal` class. The call to the `printChildren` and `printLegs` methods take into account all the overridden members because each instance is an instance of a subclass of `Animal`:

> Both the functions can only access the members defined in the `Animal` class for the instances that they receive as arguments because their type within the function is `Animal`. We can unwrap `TerrierDog`, `Cat`, and `DomesticCanary` that are received in the `animal` argument if necessary. However, we will work with these scenarios later as we cover more advanced topics.

```swift
public func printAnimalChildren(animal: Animal) {
    animal.printChildren()                                              (3 times)
}

public func printAnimalLegs(animal: Animal) {
    animal.printLegs()                                                  (3 times)
}

var pluto = TerrierDog(age: 7, name: "Pluto", favoriteToy: "Teddy bear")         TerrierDog
var marie = Cat(age: 4, isPregnant: true, name: "Marie", favoriteToy: "Tennis ball")   Cat
var tweety = DomesticCanary(age: 2, feathersColor: "Yellow", name: "Tweety")     DomesticCanary

print("Meet their children")                                            "Meet their children\n"
print(pluto.name)                                                       "Pluto\n"
printAnimalChildren(pluto)
print(marie.name)                                                       "Marie\n"
printAnimalChildren(marie)
print(tweety.name)                                                      "Tweety\n"
printAnimalChildren(tweety)

print("Look at their legs")                                             "Look at their legs\n"
print(pluto.name)                                                       "Pluto\n"
printAnimalLegs(pluto)
print(marie.name)                                                       "Marie\n"
printAnimalLegs(marie)
print(tweety.name)                                                      "Tweety\n"
printAnimalLegs(tweety)
```

```
Marie
🐱🐱🐱🐱🐱
Tweety
🐤🐤🐤🐤🐤
Look at their legs
Pluto
| | | |
Marie
*_**_**_**_*
Tweety
^^
```

[120]

Now, we will create another function outside of any class declaration that receives a `DomesticMammal` instance as an argument—that is, a `DomesticMammal` instance or an instance of any subclass of `DomesticMammal`. The following function calls the `talk` instance method defined in the `DomesticMammal` class:

```
public func makeDomesticMammalTalk(domesticMammal: DomesticMammal) {
    domesticMammal.talk()
}
```

Then, the following few lines call the `makeDomesticMammalTalk` function with the `TerrierDog` and `Cat` instances as arguments:

```
makeDomesticMammalTalk(pluto)
makeDomesticMammalTalk(marie)
```

The call to the same method for a `DomesticMammal` instance received as an argument produces different results because dogs bark and cats meow. However, both are domestic mammals, and they produce specific sounds instead of talking. We defined the representation of the sounds they produce in the `Dog` and `Cat` classes. The following lines show the results of the two function calls:

```
Pluto: Woof
Marie: Meow
```

Taking advantage of operator overloading

Swift allows us to redefine specific operators to work in a different way based on the classes to which we apply them. For example, we can make comparison operators, such as less than (<) and greater than (>), return the results of comparing the `age` value when they are applied to instances of `Dog`.

> The redefinition of operators to work in a specific way when applied to instances of specific classes is known as operator overloading. Swift allows us to overload operators through the usage of operator functions.

An operator that works in one way when applied to an instance of a class might work differently on instances of another class. We can also redefine the overloaded operators to work on specific subclasses. For example, we can make the comparison operators work in a different way in a superclass and its subclass.

Inheritance, Abstraction, and Specialization

We want to be able to compare the age of the different `Animal` instances using the following binary operators in Swift:

- Less than (<)
- Less than or equal to (<=)
- Greater than (>)
- Greater than or equal to (>=)

We can overload operators in Swift to achieve our goals by declaring operator functions with function names that match the operators to be overloaded and receive `Animal` instances as arguments. In this case, the four operators are binary operators; therefore, all the operator functions receive two input parameters of the `Animal` type and return a `Bool` value. Swift invokes these functions under the hood whenever we use the operators to compare instances of `Animal`. We have to declare operator functions with the following names and specify two `Animal` arguments:

- `<`: This is invoked when we use the less than (<) operator
- `<=`: This is invoked when we use the less than or equal to (<=) operator
- `>`: This is invoked when we use the greater than (>) operator
- `>=`: This is invoked when we use the greater than or equal to (>=) operator

All the operator functions have the same declaration. Swift passes the instance specified on the left-hand side of the operator as the first argument, usually named `left`, and the instance on the right-hand side of the operator as the second argument, which is usually named `right`. Thus, we have `left` and `right` as the arguments for the operator functions, and we must return a `Bool` value with the result of the application of the operator—in our case, with the result of the comparison operator applied to the `age` property of each instance.

Let's consider that we have two instances of `Animal`, or any of its subclasses, named `animal1` and `animal2`. If we enter `print(animal1 < animal2)` in the Playground, Swift will invoke the < operator function with `left` equal to `animal1` and `right` equal to `animal2`. Thus, we must return a `Bool` value indicating whether `left.age < right.age` is equivalent to `animal1.age < animal2.age`.

We must add the following lines to make it possible to compare the age of any animal using the previously specified comparison operators:

```
public func < (left: Animal, right: Animal) -> Bool {
    return left.age < right.age
}

public func <= (left: Animal, right: Animal) -> Bool {
    return left.age <= right.age
}

public func > (left: Animal, right: Animal) -> Bool {
    return left.age > right.age
}

public func >= (left: Animal, right: Animal) -> Bool {
    return left.age >= right.age
}
```

The following lines use the four operators that will work with the `Animal` class and its subclasses: greater than (>), less than (<), greater than or equal to (>=), and less than or equal to (<=). Remember that we created operator functions that Swift invokes under the hood whenever we use the operators. In this case, we will apply the operators on instances of `TerrierDog` and `Cat`. The operators return the results of comparing the `age` value of the different instances:

```
print(tom > pluto)
print(tom < pluto)
print(goofy >= tom)
print(tom <= goofy)
```

Inheritance, Abstraction, and Specialization

The following screenshot shows the four operator functions and the results of their execution in the Playground when we use the operators in instances of `TerrierDog` and `Cat`:

```
public func < (left: Animal, right: Animal) -> Bool {        false
    return left.age < right.age

            false

}
public func <= (left: Animal, right: Animal) -> Bool {       false
    return left.age <= right.age

            false

}
public func > (left: Animal, right: Animal) -> Bool {        true
    return left.age > right.age

            true

}
public func >= (left: Animal, right: Animal) -> Bool {       true
    return left.age >= right.age

            true

}
pluto.printAge()                                             TerrierDog
marie.printAge()                                             Cat
print(pluto > marie)                                         "true\n"
print(pluto < marie)                                         "false\n"
print(pluto >= marie)                                        "true\n"
print(pluto <= marie)                                        "false\n"
```

We also want to be able to increase value of the `age` property of the different `Animal` instances using the following unary operators in Swift:

- **Prefix increment** (++): We will use the operator before the variable to which it is applied (for example, `++pluto`)
- **Postfix increment** (++): We will use the operator after the variable to which it is applied (for example, `pluto++`)

In this case, both the operators use exactly the same characters; therefore, we must use either the `prefix` or `postfix` keywords in each operator's function declaration.

We have to declare operator functions with the following names and specify a single `Animal` argument:

- `prefix ++`: This is invoked when we use the prefix increment (++) operator
- `postfix ++`: This is invoked when we use the postfix increment (++) operator

All the operator functions have the same declaration. For the prefix operator, Swift passes the instance specified on the right-hand side of the operator as the argument. For the postfix operator, Swift passes the instance specified on the left-hand side of the operator as the argument. Let's consider that we have two instances of `Animal` or any of its subclasses named `animal1` and `animal2`. If we enter `++animal1` in the Playground, Swift will invoke the `prefix ++` operator function with the single argument equal to `animal1`. If we enter `animal2++` in the Playground, Swift will invoke the `postfix ++` operator function with the single argument equal to `animal2`.

We must add the following lines to make it possible to use prefix and postfix ++ operators to increase the age of any animal:

```
public prefix func ++ (animal: Animal) {
    ++animal.age
}

public postfix func ++ (animal: Animal) {
    animal.age++
}
```

The following lines print the age for `pluto`—an instance of `TerrierDog`—and then apply the prefix ++ operator, print the new age, apply the postfix ++ operator, and print the new age. Remember that we created operator functions that Swift invokes under the hood whenever we use these operators:

```
pluto.printAge()
pluto++
pluto.printAge()
++pluto
pluto.printAge()
```

The following lines show the output generated by the preceding code:

```
I am 7 years old.
I am 8 years old.
I am 9 years old.
```

Inheritance, Abstraction, and Specialization

The following screenshot shows the two operator functions and their execution in the Playground when we use the operators in the instance of the `TerrierDog` class:

```
public prefix func ++ (animal: Animal) {                         9
    ++animal.age

            9

}
public postfix func ++ (animal: Animal) {                        7
    animal.age++

          7

}
pluto.printAge()                                          TerrierDog
pluto++
pluto.printAge()                                          TerrierDog
++pluto
pluto.printAge()                                          TerrierDog
```

```
false
true
false
I am 7 years old.
I am 8 years old.
I am 9 years old.
```

Declaring operator functions for specific subclasses

We already declared an operator function that allows any instance of Animal or its subclasses to use the postfix increment (++) operator. However, sometimes we want to specify a different behavior for one of the subclasses and its subclasses.

For example, we might want to express the age of dogs in the age value that is equivalent to humans. We can declare an operator function for the postfix increment (++) operator that receives a Dog instance as an argument and increments the age value 7 years instead of just one. The following lines show the code that achieves this goal:

```
public postfix func ++ (dog: Dog) {
    dog.age += 7
}
```

The following lines create an instance of the `SmoothFoxTerrier` class named `goofy`, print the age for `goofy`, apply the postfix `++` operator, and print the new age. Because `SmoothFoxTerrier` is a subclass of `Dog`, Swift invokes the operator function that receives a `Dog` instance instead of invoking the one that receives an `Animal` instance as an argument. As a result of this, the operator function adds 7 to the age value instead of 1:

```
var goofy = SmoothFoxTerrier(age: 7, name: "Goofy", favoriteToy: "Scarf")
goofy.printAge()
goofy++
goofy.printAge()
```

Then, the following code prints the age of a `Cat` instance named `marie`, applies the postfix `++` operator and prints the new age. In this case, `marie` belongs to the `Cat` instance, and `Cat` isn't a subclass of `Dog`. For this reason, Swift invokes the operator function that receives an `Animal` instance as an argument. Thus, the operator function adds just 1 to the age value:

```
marie.printAge()
marie++
marie.printAge()
```

The following lines show the results of the previous lines:

```
Animal created
Mammal created
DomesticMammal created
Dog created
TerrierDog created
SmoothFoxTerrier created
I am 7 years old.
I am 14 years old.
I am 21 years old.
I am 4 years old.
I am 5 years old.
```

Exercises

Create operator functions to allow us to determine whether two `DomesticMammal` instances are equal or not with the `==` and `!=` operators. We will consider the instances to be equal when their `age`, `name`, and `favoriteToy` properties have the same value.

Create the following three new subclasses of the `TerrierDog` class:

- `AiredaleTerrier`: This is an Airedale Terrier breed
- `BullTerrier`: This is a Bull Terrier breed
- `CairnTerrier`: This is a Cairn Terrier breed

Add the necessary code to these classes to print text that represents the children in a different way than we did for the `SmoothFoxTerrier` class. Test the results by creating an instance of each of these classes and calling the `printChildren` method.

Test your knowledge

1. When you use the `static var` keywords to declare a type property:
    1. You cannot override the type property in the subclasses.
    2. You can override the type property in the subclasses.
    3. You can override the type property only in the superclass.

2. When you use the `class var` keywords to declare a type property:
    1. You cannot override the type property in the subclasses.
    2. You can override the type property in the subclasses.
    3. You can override the type property only in the superclass.

3. When you use the `final` keyword to declare an instance method:
    1. You cannot override the instance method in the subclasses.
    2. You can override the instance method in the subclasses.
    3. You can override the instance method only once—that is, in just one subclass.

4. Polymorphism means:
    1. We can call the same method—that is, the same name and arguments—in instances of classes that aren't included in the same hierarchy tree.
    2. We can use the same method—that is, the same name and arguments—to cause different things to happen according to the class on which we invoke the method.
    3. We must declare the same method—that is, the same name and arguments—to enable a class to become a subclass of its superclass.
5. We can redefine specific operators by declaring:
    1. A type method with a name that matches the operator symbols in the appropriate class.
    2. An instance method with a name that matches the operator symbols in the appropriate class.
    3. An operator function with a name that matches the operator symbols.

Summary

In this chapter, you learned how to take advantage of simple inheritance to specialize a base class. We designed many classes from top to bottom using chained initializers, type properties, computed properties, stored properties, and methods. Then, we coded most of these classes in the interactive Playground, taking advantage of different mechanisms provided by Swift.

We took advantage of operator functions to overload operators that we could use with the instances of our classes. We overrode and overloaded initializers, type properties, and methods. We took advantage of one of the most exciting object-oriented features: polymorphism.

Now that we have learned to work with inheritance, abstraction, and specialization, we are ready to work with protocols, which is the topic of the next chapter.

5
Contract Programming with Protocols

In this chapter, we will work with more complex scenarios in which we will have to use instances that belong to more than one blueprint. We use contract programming by taking advantage of protocols.

We will work with examples on how to define protocols, their different kinds of requirements, and then to declare classes that adopt the protocols. We will use the multiple inheritance of protocols and many useful ways of taking advantage of this object-oriented concept, also known as interfaces in other programming languages, such as Java and C#.

Understanding how protocols work in combination with classes

We have to work with two different types of characters: comic and game characters. A comic character has a nickname and must be able to draw speech balloons and thought balloons. The speech balloon might have another comic character as a destination.

A game character has a full name and must be able to perform the following tasks:

- Draw itself in a specific 2D position indicated by the x and y coordinates
- Move itself to a specific 2D position indicated by the x and y coordinates
- Check whether it intersects with another game character

We will work with objects that can be both a comic character and a game character. However, we will also work with objects that will just be either a comic or game character. Neither the game nor the comic character has a generic way of performing the previously described tasks. Thus, each object that declares itself as a comic character must define the tasks related to speech and thought balloons. Each object that declares itself as a game character must define how to draw itself, move, and check whether it intersects with another game character.

An angry dog is a comic character that has a specific way of drawing speech and thought balloons. An angry cat is both a comic and game character, so it defines all the tasks required by both character types.

The angry cat is a very versatile character, and it can use different costumes to participate in either games or comics with different names. An angry cat can also be an alien, a wizard, or a knight:

- An alien has a specific number of eyes and must be able to appear and disappear.
- A wizard has a spell power score and can make an alien disappear.
- A knight has sword power and weight values and can unsheathe his sword. A common task for the knight is to unsheathe his sword and point it to an alien as a target.

We need base blueprints to represent a comic character and a game character. Then, each class that represents any of these types of characters can provide its implementation of the methods. In this case, comic and game characters are very different, and they don't perform similar tasks that might lead to confusion and problems for multiple inheritance. Thus, we can use multiple inheritance to create an angry cat class that implements both comic and game character blueprints. In some cases, multiple inheritance is not convenient because similar blueprints might have methods with the same names, and it can be extremely confusing to use multiple inheritance.

In addition, we can use multiple inheritance to combine the angry cat class with an alien, wizard, and knight. This way, we will have an angry cat alien, an angry cat wizard, and an angry cat knight. We will be able to use any of them, the angry cat alien, angry cat wizard, or angry cat knight, as either a comic or game character.

Our goals are simple, but we face a little problem: Swift doesn't support the multiple inheritance of classes. Instead, we can use multiple inheritance with protocols or combine protocols with classes. So, we will use protocols and classes to fulfill our previous requirements.

Chapter 5

You can think of a *protocol* as a special case of an abstract class that defines the initializers, properties, and methods that a class must implement to be considered a member of the group identified with the protocol name.

> If you have worked with other programming languages, such as Java and C#, you can think of protocols as the Swift version of interfaces.

For example, we can create an `Alien` protocol that specifies the following elements:

- A `numberOfEyes` property
- A parameterless method named `appear`
- A parameterless method named `disappear`

Once we define a protocol, we create a new type; therefore, we can use it to specify the required type for an argument. This way, instead of using classes as types, we will use protocols as types, and we can use an instance of any class that conforms to the specific protocol as an argument. For example, if we use `Alien` as the required type for an argument, we can pass an instance of any class that conforms to the `Alien` protocol as an argument.

However, you must take into account some limitations of the protocols compared with classes. Protocols cannot specify accessibility modifiers in any members. Protocols can declare requirements for the following members:

- Properties
- Methods
- Mutating methods
- Initializers
- Failable initializers

Declaring protocols

Now, it is time to code the protocols in Swift. We will code the following five protocols:

- `ComicCharacter`
- `GameCharacter`
- `Alien`
- `Wizard`
- `Knight`

[133]

Contract Programming with Protocols

The following UML diagram shows the five protocols that we will code in Swift with their required properties and methods included in the diagram:

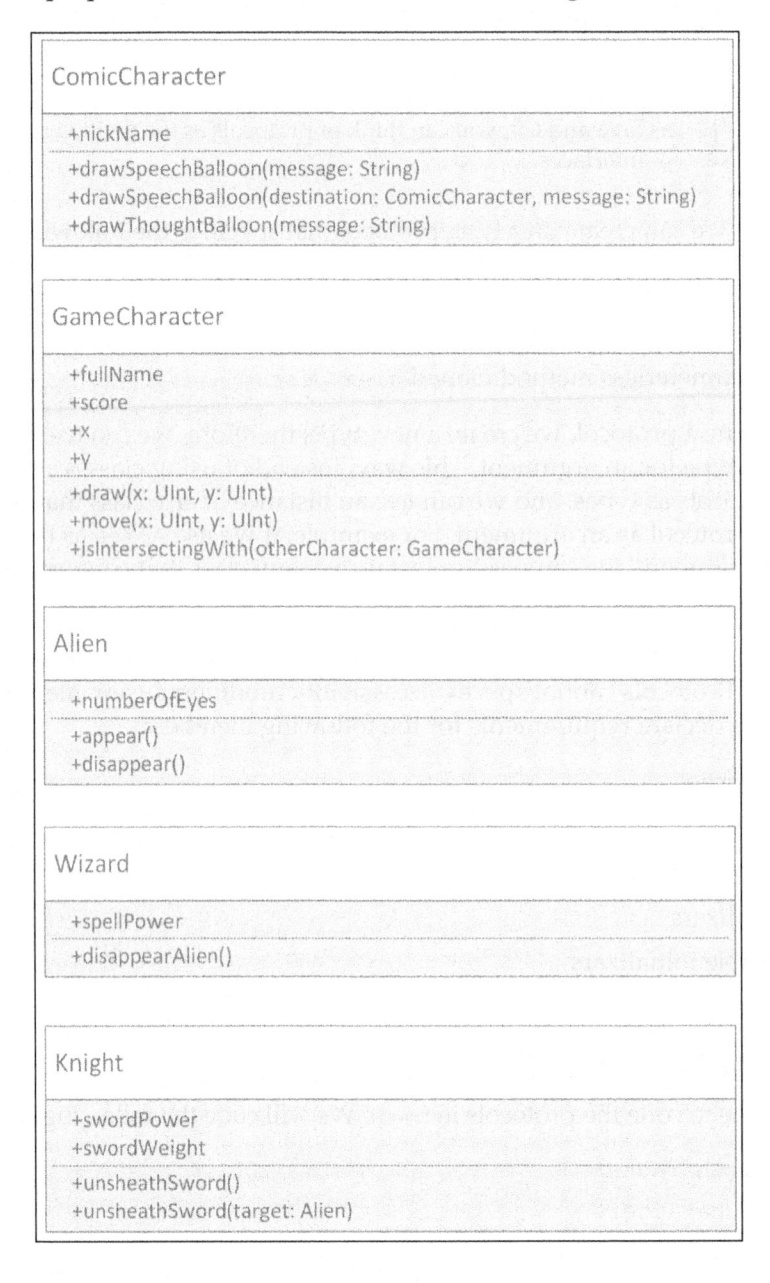

ComicCharacter

+nickName

+drawSpeechBalloon(message: String)
+drawSpeechBalloon(destination: ComicCharacter, message: String)
+drawThoughtBalloon(message: String)

GameCharacter

+fullName
+score
+x
+y

+draw(x: UInt, y: UInt)
+move(x: UInt, y: UInt)
+isIntersectingWith(otherCharacter: GameCharacter)

Alien

+numberOfEyes

+appear()
+disappear()

Wizard

+spellPower

+disappearAlien()

Knight

+swordPower
+swordWeight

+unsheathSword()
+unsheathSword(target: Alien)

Chapter 5

The following lines show the code for the `ComicCharacter` protocol. The `public` modifier followed by the `protocol` keyword and the protocol name, `ComicCharacter`, composes the protocol declaration. As it happens with class declarations, the protocol body is enclosed in curly brackets (`{ }`):

```
public protocol ComicCharacter {
    var nickName: String { get set }

    func drawSpeechBalloon(message: String)
    func drawSpeechBalloon(destination: ComicCharacter, message: String)
    func drawThoughtBalloon(message: String)
}
```

The protocols declare a `nickName` read/write `String` stored property requirement, a `drawSpeechBaloon` method requirement overloaded twice, and a `drawThoughtBalloon` method requirement. The protocol includes only the method declaration because the classes that implement the `ComicCharacter` protocol will be responsible for providing the implementation of the two overloads of the `drawSpeechBalloon` and `drawThoughtBalloon` methods. Note that there is no method body.

The following lines show the code for the `GameCharacter` protocol:

```
public protocol GameCharacter {
    var fullName: String { get set }
    var score: UInt { get set }
    var x: UInt { get set }
    var y: UInt { get set }

    func draw(x: UInt, y: UInt)
    func move(x: UInt, y: UInt)
    func isIntersectingWith(otherCharacter: GameCharacter) -> Bool
}
```

In this case, the protocol declaration includes four read/write stored property requirements: `fullName`, `score`, `x`, and `y`. In addition, the declaration includes three method requirements: `draw`, `move`, and `IsIntersectingWith`. Note that we don't include access modifiers in either the properties or the methods.

> We cannot add access modifiers to the different members of a protocol.

[135]

Contract Programming with Protocols

The following lines show the code for the `Alien` protocol:

```
public protocol Alien {
    var numberOfEyes: Int { get set }

    func appear()
    func disappear()
}
```

In this case, the protocol declaration includes a property requirement, `numberOfEyes`, and two method requirements: `appear` and `disappear`. Note that we don't include the code for either the getter or setter methods of the `numberOfEyes` property. As it happens with the methods, the classes that implement the `Alien` protocol is responsible for providing the implementation of the getter and setter methods for the `numberOfEyes` property. We will create classes that implement the `Alien` protocol later in this chapter.

The following lines show the code for the `Wizard` protocol:

```
public protocol Wizard {
    var spellPower { get set }
    func disappearAlien(alien: Alien)
}
```

In this case, the protocol declaration includes a property requirement, `spellPower`, and a method requirement, `disappearAlien`. As it happened in other method requirement declarations included in the previously declared protocols, we use a protocol name as the type of an argument within a method requirement declaration. In this case, the `alien` argument for the `disappearAlien` method requirement declaration is `Alien`. Thus, we will be able to call the method with any class that conforms to the `Alien` protocol.

The following lines show the code for the `Knight` protocol:

```
public protocol Knight {
    var swordPower: Int { get set }
    var swordWeight: Int { get set }

    func unsheathSword()
    func unsheathSword(target: Alien)
}
```

In this case, the protocol declaration includes two property requirements, `swordPower` and `swordWeight`, and an `unsheathSword` method requirement overloaded twice.

Declaring classes that adopt protocols

Now, we will declare a class that specifies that it conforms to the `ComicCharacter` protocol in its declaration in the Playground. Instead of specifying a superclass, the class declaration includes the name of the previously declared `ComicCharacter` protocol after the class name (`AngryDog`) and the colon (`:`). We can read the class declaration as "the `AngryDog` class conforms to the `ComicCharacter` protocol."

However, the class doesn't implement any of the required properties and methods specified in the protocol, so it doesn't really conform to the `ComicCharacter` protocol, as shown in the following:

```
public class AngryDog: ComicCharacter {

}
```

The Playground execution will fail because the `AngryDog` class doesn't conform to the `ComicCharacter` protocol, so the Swift compiler generates the following errors and notes:

```
error: type 'AngryDog' does not conform to protocol 'ComicCharacter'
public class AngryDog: ComicCharacter {
             ^
note: protocol requires property 'nickName' with type 'String'
    var nickName: String { get set }
        ^
note: protocol requires function 'drawSpeechBalloon' with type
'(String) -> ()'
    func drawSpeechBalloon(message: String)
         ^
note: protocol requires function 'drawSpeechBalloon(_:message:)' with
type '(ComicCharacter, message: String) -> ()'
    func drawSpeechBalloon(destination: ComicCharacter, message:
String)
         ^
note: protocol requires function 'drawThoughtBalloon' with type
'(String) -> ()'
    func drawThoughtBalloon(message: String)
         ^
```

Now, we will replace the previous declaration of the empty `AngryDog` class with a class that tries to conform to the `ComicCharacter` protocol, but it still doesn't achieve its goal. The following lines show the new code for the `AngryDog` class:

```
public class AngryDog: ComicCharacter {
    var nickName: String = String()
```

```swift
    func speak(message: String) {
        print("\(nickName) -> \"\(message)\"")
    }
    
    func think(message: String) {
        print("\(nickName) -> ***\(message)***")
    }
    
    func drawSpeechBalloon(message: String) {
        speak(message);
    }
    
    func drawSpeechBalloon(destination: ComicCharacter, message: String) {
        speak("\(destination.nickName), \(message)")
    }
    
    func drawThoughtBalloon(message: String) {
        think(message)
    }
    
    init (nickName: String) {
        self.nickName = nickName
    }
}
```

The Playground execution will fail because the `AngryDog` class doesn't conform to the `ComicCharacter` protocol; therefore, the Swift compiler generates the following errors and notes:

```
error: property 'nickName' must be declared public because it matches a requirement in public protocol 'ComicCharacter'
    var nickName: String = String()
        ^
    public
error: method 'drawSpeechBalloon' must be declared public because it matches a requirement in public protocol 'ComicCharacter'
    func drawSpeechBalloon(message: String) {
         ^
    public
error: method 'drawSpeechBalloon(_:message:)' must be declared public because it matches a requirement in public protocol 'ComicCharacter'
    func drawSpeechBalloon(destination: ComicCharacter, message: String) {
         ^
```

```
error: method 'drawThoughtBalloon' must be declared public because it
matches a requirement in public protocol 'ComicCharacter'
    func drawThoughtBalloon(message: String) {
         ^
    public
```

The public `ComicCharacter` protocol specifies property and method requirements. Thus, when we declare a class that doesn't declare the required properties and methods as public, the Swift compiler generates errors and indicates that they have to be declared public to match the protocol requirements.

> Whenever we declare a class that specifies that it conforms to a protocol, it must fulfill all the requirements specified in the protocol. If it doesn't, the Swift compiler will throw errors indicating which requirements aren't fulfilled, as it happened in the previous example. When we work with protocols, the Swift compiler makes sure that the requirements specified in protocols are honored in any class that conforms to them.

Finally, we will replace the previous declaration of the `AngryDog` class with a class that really conforms to the `ComicCharacter` protocol. The following lines show the new code for the `AngryDog` class:

```
public class AngryDog: ComicCharacter {
    public var nickName: String = String()
    
    private func speak(message: String) {
        print("\(nickName) -> \"\(message)\"")
    }
    
    private func think(message: String) {
        print("\(nickName) -> ***\(message)***")
    }
    
    public func drawSpeechBalloon(message: String) {
        speak(message);
    }
    
    public func drawSpeechBalloon(destination: ComicCharacter,
message: String) {
        speak("\(destination.nickName), \(message)")
    }
    
    public func drawThoughtBalloon(message: String) {
        think(message)
```

```
        }

        init (nickName: String) {
            self.nickName = nickName
        }
    }
```

The `AngryDog` class declares an initializer that assigns the value of the required `nickName` argument to the `nickName` stored property. In this case, the `ComicCharacter` protocol doesn't include any initializer requirement, so the `AngryDog` class can specify any desired initializer without restrictions.

The class declares the code for the two versions of the `drawSpeechBalloon` method. Both methods call the private `speak` method that prints a message with a specific format that includes the `nickName` value as a prefix. In addition, the class declares the code for the `drawThoughtBalloon` method that invokes the private `think` method that also prints a message including the `nickName` value as a prefix.

The `AngryDog` class implements the property and methods declared in the `ComicCharacter` protocol. However, the class also declares two private members—specifically two private methods.

> As long as we implement all the members declared in the protocol or protocols listed in the class declaration, we can add any desired additional member to the class.

Now, we will declare another class that implements the same protocol that the `AngryDog` class implemented—that is, the `ComicCharacter` protocol. The following lines show the code for the `AngryCat` class:

```
    public class AngryCat: ComicCharacter {
        public var nickName: String = String()

        public var age: UInt = 0

        public func drawSpeechBalloon(message: String) {
            if (age > 5) {
                print("\(nickName) -> \"Meow \(message)\"")
            } else {
                print("\(nickName) -> \"Meeeooow Meeeooow \(message)\"")
            }
        }

        public func drawSpeechBalloon(destination: ComicCharacter,
message: String)
```

```
    {
        print("\(destination.nickName) === \(nickName) ---> \"\
(message)\"")
    }

    public func drawThoughtBalloon(message: String) {
        print("\(nickName) thinks: \(message)")
    }

    init (nickName: String, age: UInt) {
        self.nickName = nickName
        self.age = age
    }
}
```

The `AngryCat` class declares an initializer that assigns the value of the required `nickName` and `age` arguments to the `nickName` and `age` stored properties. The class declares the code for the two versions of the `drawSpeechBalloon` method. The version that requires only a `message` argument uses the value of the `age` property to generate a different message when the `age` value is greater than 5. In addition, the class declares the code for the `drawThoughtBalloon` method.

The `AngryCat` class implements the property and method requirements declared in the `ComicCharacter` protocol. However, the class also declares an additional property, `age`, that isn't required by the protocol.

If we remove the `public` keyword in the line that declares the `nickName` stored property within the `AngryCat` class, the class won't implement all the required members of the `ComicCharacter` protocol as public members; therefore, it won't conform to the protocol:

```
var nickName: String = String()
```

The Playground execution will fail because the `AngryCat` class doesn't conform to the `ComicCharacter` protocol anymore, so the Swift compiler generates the following error:

```
error: property 'nickName' must be declared public because it matches a requirement in public protocol 'ComicCharacter'
    var nickName: String = String()
        ^
    public
```

Thus, the compiler enforces us to implement all the members of a protocol in all the classes that we indicate that conform to a protocol. If we add the `public` keyword again to the line that declares the `nickName` property, we will be able to execute the code in the Playground without compiler errors:

```
public var nickName: String = String()
```

> Protocols in Swift allow us to make sure that the classes that implement them define all the members specified in the protocol. If they don't, the code won't compile.

In this case, the `ComicCharacter` protocol didn't specify any initializer requirements, so each class that conforms to the protocol can define its initializer without any constraint. `AngryDog` and `AngryCat` declare initializers with a different number of arguments.

Taking advantage of the multiple inheritance of protocols

Swift doesn't allow us to declare a class with multiple base classes or superclasses, so there is no support for multiple inheritance of classes. A subclass can inherit just from one class. However, a class can conform to one or more protocols. In addition, we can declare classes that inherit from a superclass and conform to one or more protocols. Thus, we can combine class-based inheritance with protocols.

We want the `AngryCat` class to conform to both the `ComicCharacter` and `GameCharacter` protocols. Thus, we want to use any `AngryCat` instance as both a comic character and a game character. In order to do so, we must change the class declaration and add the `GameCharacter` protocol to the list of protocols that the class conforms to and declare all the members included in this added protocol within the class.

The following lines show the new class declaration that specifies that the `AngryCat` class conforms to both, the `ComicCharacter` and the `GameCharacter` protocols:

```
public class AngryCat: ComicCharacter, GameCharacter {
```

After changing the class declaration, the Playground execution will fail because the `AngryCat` class doesn't implement the members required by the `GameCharacter` protocol. The Swift compiler generates the following errors and notes:

```
error: type 'AngryCat' does not conform to protocol 'GameCharacter'
public class AngryCat: ComicCharacter, GameCharacter {
                      ^
```

```
note: protocol requires property 'fullName' with type 'String'
    var fullName: String { get set }
        ^
note: protocol requires property 'score' with type 'UInt'
    var score: UInt { get set }
        ^
note: protocol requires property 'x' with type 'UInt'
    var x: UInt { get set }
        ^
note: protocol requires property 'y' with type 'UInt'
    var y: UInt { get set }
        ^
note: protocol requires function 'draw(_:y:)' with type '(UInt, y:
UInt) -> ()'
    func draw(x: UInt, y: UInt)
         ^
note: protocol requires function 'move(_:y:)' with type '(UInt, y:
UInt) -> ()'
    func move(x: UInt, y: UInt)
         ^
note: protocol requires function 'isIntersectingWith' with type
'(GameCharacter) -> Bool'
    func isIntersectingWith(otherCharacter: GameCharacter) -> Bool
         ^
```

We have to add the following lines to the body of the `AngryCat` class to implement the stored properties specified in the `GameCharacter` protocol:

```
public var score: UInt = 0
public var fullName: String = String()
public var x: UInt = 0
public var y: UInt = 0
```

We have to add the following lines to the body of the `AngryCat` class to implement the methods specified in the `GameCharacter` protocol:

```
public func draw(x: UInt, y: UInt) {
    self.x = x
    self.y = y
    print("Drawing AngryCat \(fullName) at x: \(x), y: \(y)")
}

public func move(x: UInt, y: UInt) {
    self.x = y
    self.y = y
    print("Moving AngryCat \(fullName) to x: \(x), y: \(y)")
```

Contract Programming with Protocols

```
}

public func isIntersectingWith(otherCharacter: GameCharacter) -> Bool
{
    return ((x == otherCharacter.x) && (y == otherCharacter.y))
}
```

Now, the `AngryCat` class declares the code for the three public methods required to conform to the `GameCharacter` protocol: `draw`, `move`, and `isIntersectingWith`. Finally, it is necessary to replace the previous initializer with a new one that requires additional arguments and sets the initial values of the recently added stored properties. The following lines show the code for the new initializer:

```
init (nickName: String, age: UInt, fullName: String, initialScore:
UInt, x: UInt, y: UInt) {
    self.nickName = nickName
    self.age = age
    self.fullName = fullName
    self.score = initialScore
    self.x = x
    self.y = y
}
```

The new initializer assigns the value of the additional required `fullName`, `initialScore`, x, and y arguments to the `fullName`, `score`, x, and y properties. Thus, we will need to specify more arguments whenever we want to create an instance of the `AngryCat` class.

Combining inheritance and protocols

We can combine class inheritance with protocol conformance. The following lines show the code for a new `AngryCatAlien` class that inherits from the `AngryCat` class and conforms to the `Alien` protocol. Note that the class declaration includes the superclass (`AngryCat`) and the implemented protocol (`Alien`) separated by a comma after the colon (:):

```
public class AngryCatAlien : AngryCat, Alien {
    public var numberOfEyes: Int = 0

    init (nickName: String, age: UInt, fullName: String, initialScore:
UInt, x: UInt, y: UInt, numberOfEyes: Int) {
        super.init(nickName: nickName, age: age, fullName: fullName,
initialScore: initialScore, x: x, y: y)
        self.numberOfEyes = numberOfEyes
    }
```

```
    public func appear() {
        print("I'm \(fullName) and you can see my \(numberOfEyes)
eyes.")
    }

    public func disappear() {
        print("\(fullName) disappears.")
    }
}
```

As a result of the previous code, we have a new class named `AngryCatAlien` that conforms to the following three protocols:

- `ComicCharacter`: This is implemented by the `AngryCat` superclass and inherited by `AngryCatAlien`
- `GameCharacter`: This is implemented by the `AngryCat` superclass and inherited by `AngryCatAlien`
- `Alien`: This is implemented by `AngryCatAlien`

The initializer adds a `numberOfEyes` argument to the argument list defined in the base initializer—that is, the initializer defined in the `AngryCat` superclass. In this case, the initializer calls the base initializer (`self.init`) and then initializes the `numberOfEyes` property with the value received in the `numberOfEyes` argument. The class implements the `appear` and `disappear` methods required by the `Alien` protocol.

The following lines show the code for a new `AngryCatWizard` class that inherits from the `AngryCat` class and implements the `Wizard` protocol. Note that the class declaration includes the superclass (`AngryCat`) and the implemented protocol (`Wizard`) separated by a comma after the colon (`:`):

```
public class AngryCatWizard: AngryCat, Wizard {
    public var spellPower: Int = 0

    public func disappearAlien(alien: Alien) {
        print("\(fullName) uses his \(spellPower) spell power to make
the alien with \(alien.numberOfEyes) eyes disappear.")
    }

    init (nickName: String, age: UInt, fullName: String, initialScore:
UInt, x: UInt, y: UInt, spellPower: Int) {
        super.init(nickName: nickName, age: age, fullName: fullName,
initialScore: initialScore, x: x, y: y)
        self.spellPower = spellPower
    }
}
```

Contract Programming with Protocols

As it happened with the `AngryCatAlien` class, the new `AngryCatWizard` class implements three protocols. Two of these protocols are implemented by the `AngryCat` superclass and inherited by `AngryCatWizard`: `ComicCharacter` and `GameCharacter`. The `AngryCatWizard` class adds the implementation of the `Wizard` protocol.

The initializer adds a `spellPower` argument to the argument list defined in the base constructor (`super.init`), which is the constructor defined in the `AngryCat` superclass. The constructor calls the base constructor and then initializes the `spellPower` property with the value received in the `spellPower` argument. The class implements the `disappearAlien` method required by the `Wizard` protocol.

The `disappearAlien` method receives an `Alien` as an argument. Thus, any instance of `AngryCatAlien` would qualify as an argument for this method—that is, any instance of any class that conforms to the `Alien` protocol.

The following lines show the code for a new `AngryCatKnight` class that inherits from the `AngryCat` class and implements the `Knight` protocol. Note that the class declaration includes the superclass (`AngryCat`) and implemented protocol (`Knight`) separated by a comma after the colon (`:`):

```
public class AngryCatKnight : AngryCat, Knight {
    public var swordPower: Int = 0
    public var swordWeight: Int = 0

    private func writeLinesAboutTheSword() {
        print("\(fullName) unsheaths his sword.")
        print("Sword power: \(swordPower). Sword weight: \(swordWeight).")
    }

    public func unsheathSword() {
        writeLinesAboutTheSword()
    }

    public func unsheathSword(target: Alien) {
        writeLinesAboutTheSword()
        print("The sword targets an alien with \(target.numberOfEyes) eyes.")
    }

    init (nickName: String, age: UInt, fullName: String, initialScore: UInt, x: UInt, y: UInt, swordPower: Int, swordWeight: Int) {
        super.init(nickName: nickName, age: age, fullName: fullName, initialScore: initialScore, x: x, y: y)
```

```
            self.swordPower = swordPower
            self.swordWeight = swordWeight
    }
}
```

As it happened with the two previously coded classes that are inherited from the `AngryCat` class and conformed to protocols, the new `AngryCatKnight` class implements three protocols. Two of these protocols are implemented by the `AngryCat` superclass and inherited by `AngryCatKnight`: `ComicCharacter` and `GameCharacter`. The `AngryCatKnight` class adds the implementation of the `Knight` protocol.

The initializer adds the `swordPower` and `swordWeight` arguments to the argument list defined in the base initializer (`base.init`), which is the constructor defined in the `AngryCat` superclass. The initializer calls the base initializer (`base.init`) and then initializes the `swordPower` and `swordWeight` properties with the values received in the `swordPower` and `swordHeight` arguments.

The class implements the two versions of the `unsheathSword` method required by the `Knight` protocol. Both methods call the private `writeLinesAboutTheSword` method and the overloaded version that receives an `Alien` as an argument prints an additional message about the alien that the sword has as a target—specifically, the number of eyes.

The following table summarizes the list of protocols to which each of the classes we created conform to:

Class name	Conforms to the following protocol(s)
`AngryDog`	`ComicCharacter`
`AngryCat`	`ComicCharacter` and `GameCharacter`
`AngryCatAlien`	`ComicCharacter`, `GameCharacter`, and `Alien`
`AngryCatWizard`	`ComicCharacter`, `GameCharacter`, and `Wizard`
`AngryCatKnight`	`ComicCharacter`, `GameCharacter`, and `Knight`

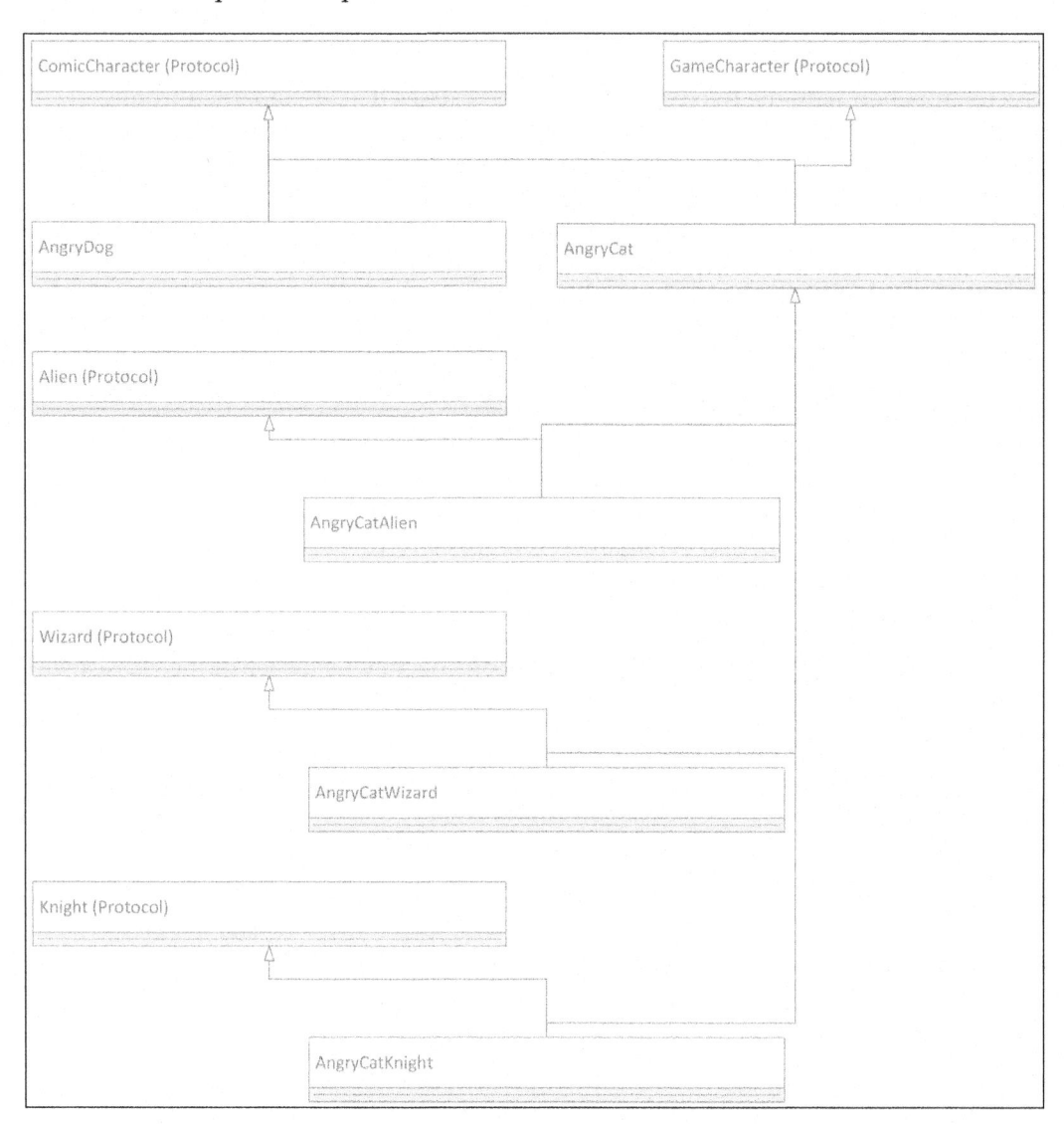

The following simplified UML diagram shows the hierarchy tree for the classes and their relationship with the protocols:

Chapter 5

The following UML diagram shows the protocols and the classes with their properties and methods. We can use the diagram to understand all the things that we will analyze with the next code samples based on the usage of these classes and the previously defined protocols:

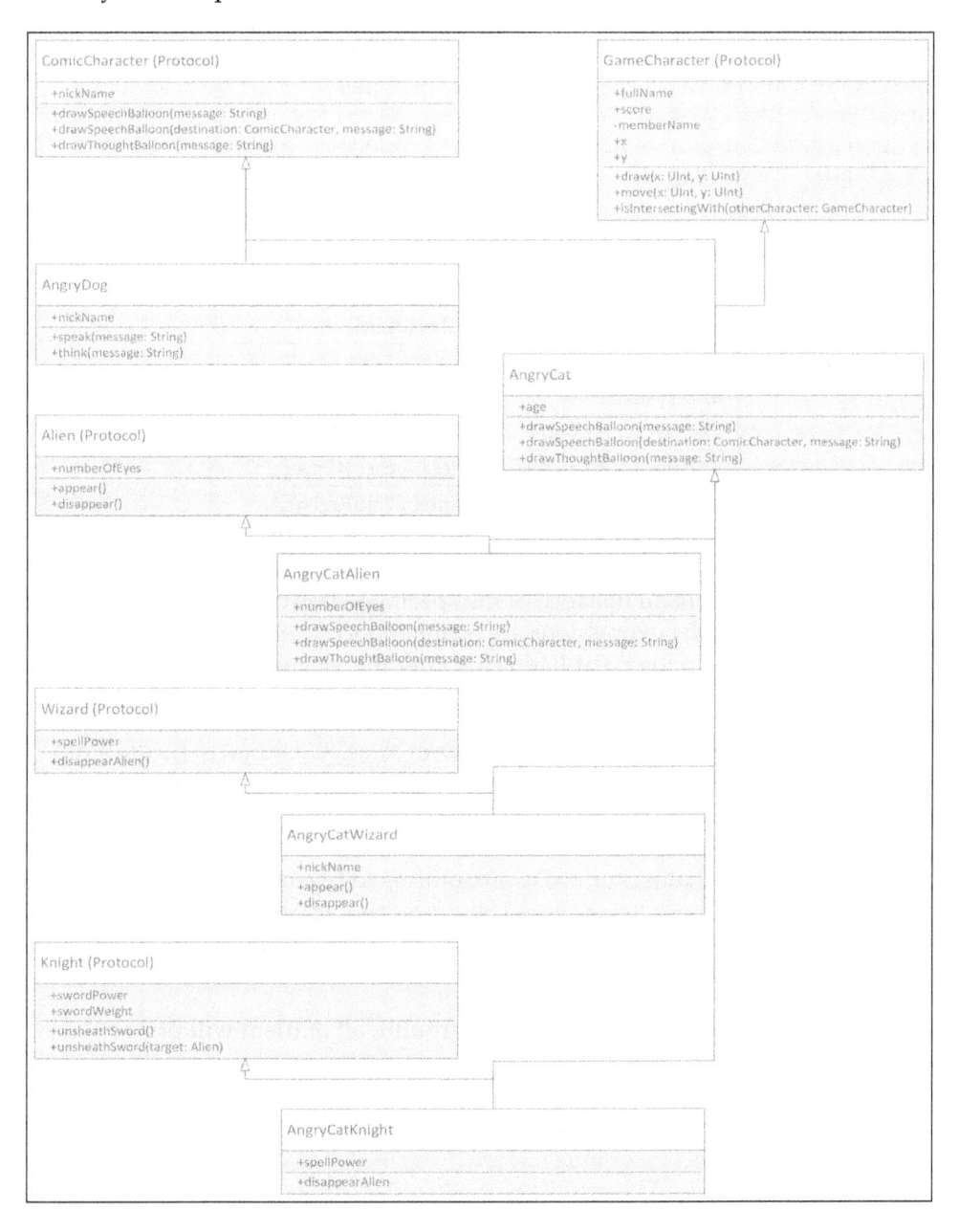

ComicCharacter (Protocol)
+nickName
+drawSpeechBalloon(message: String)
+drawSpeechBalloon(destination: ComicCharacter, message: String)
+drawThoughtBalloon(message: String)

GameCharacter (Protocol)
+fullName
+score
-memberName
+x
+y
+draw(x: UInt, y: UInt)
+move(x: UInt, y: UInt)
+isIntersectingWith(otherCharacter: GameCharacter)

AngryDog
+nickName
+speak(message: String)
+think(message: String)

AngryCat
+age
+drawSpeechBalloon(message: String)
+drawSpeechBalloon(destination: ComicCharacter, message: String)
+drawThoughtBalloon(message: String)

Alien (Protocol)
+numberOfEyes
+appear()
+disappear()

AngryCatAlien
+numberOfEyes
+drawSpeechBalloon(message: String)
+drawSpeechBalloon(destination: ComicCharacter, message: String)
+drawThoughtBalloon(message: String)

Wizard (Protocol)
+spellPower
+disappearAlien()

AngryCatWizard
+nickName
+appear()
+disappear()

Knight (Protocol)
+swordPower
+swordWeight
+unsheathSword()
+unsheathSword(target: Alien)

AngryCatKnight
+spellPower
+disappearAlien

[149]

Contract Programming with Protocols

The following lines create one instance of each of the previously created classes:

```
var angryDog1 = AngryDog(nickName: "Bailey")
var angryCat1 = AngryCat(nickName: "Bella", age: 3, fullName: "Mrs. Bella", initialScore: 20, x: 10, y: 10)
var angryCatAlien1 = AngryCatAlien(nickName: "Lucy", age: 4, fullName: "Mrs. Lucy", initialScore: 50, x: 20, y: 10, numberOfEyes: 3)
var angryCatWizard1 = AngryCatWizard(nickName: "Daisy", age: 4, fullName: "Mrs. Daisy", initialScore: 50, x: 20, y: 10, spellPower: 6)
var angryCatKnight1 = AngryCatKnight(nickName: "Maggie", age: 3, fullName: "Mrs. Maggy", initialScore: 1300, x: 40, y: 10, swordPower: 7, swordWeight: 5)
```

The following table summarizes the instance name and its class name:

Instance name	Class name
angryDog1	AngryDog
angryCat1	AngryCat
angryCatAlien1	AngryCatAlien
angryCatWizard1	AngryCatWizard
angryCatKnight	AngryCatKnight

Now, we will evaluate many expressions that use the `is` keyword to determine whether the instances are an instance of the specified class or conform to a specific protocol. Note that all the expressions are evaluated to `true` because each instance has the type specified on the right-hand side after the `is` keyword as the main class, its superclass, or conforms to the protocol.

For example, `angryCatWizard1` is an instance of `AngryCatWizard`. In addition, `angryCatWizard1` belongs to `AngryCat` because `AngryCat` is the superclass of the `AngryCatWizard` class. It is also true that `angryCatWizard1` conforms to three protocols: `ComicCharacter`, `GameCharacter`, and `Wizard`. The superclass of `AngryCatWizard`—that is, `AngryCat`—conforms to two of these protocols: `ComicCharacter` and `GameCharacter`. Therefore, `AngryCatWizard` inherits the protocol conformance. Finally, the `AngryCatWizard` class not only inherits from `AngryCat`, but also conforms to the `Wizard` protocol.

If we execute the following lines in the Playground, all of them will print `true` as a result:

```
print(angryDog1 is AngryDog)
print(angryDog1 is ComicCharacter)

print(angryCat1 is AngryCat)
print(angryCat1 is ComicCharacter)
```

```
            print(angryCat1 is GameCharacter)

            print(angryCatAlien1 is AngryCat)
            print(angryCatAlien1 is AngryCatAlien)
            print(angryCatAlien1 is ComicCharacter)
            print(angryCatAlien1 is GameCharacter)
            print(angryCatAlien1 is Alien)

            print(angryCatWizard1 is AngryCat)
            print(angryCatWizard1 is AngryCatWizard)
            print(angryCatWizard1 is ComicCharacter)
            print(angryCatWizard1 is GameCharacter)
            print(angryCatWizard1 is Wizard)

            print(angryCatKnight1 is AngryCat)
            print(angryCatKnight1 is AngryCatKnight)
            print(angryCatKnight1 is ComicCharacter)
            print(angryCatKnight1 is GameCharacter)
            print(angryCatKnight1 is Knight)
```

The following screenshot shows the results of executing the previous lines in the Playground. Note that the Playground uses a warning icon to let us know that all the expressions that include the `is` keyword will always be evaluated to `true`. In these cases, the compiler generates a warning:

```
     var angryDog1 = AngryDog(nickName: "Bailey")                                AngryDog
     var angryCat1 = AngryCat(nickName: "Bella", age: 3, fullName: "Mrs. Bella", AngryCat
         initialScore: 20, x: 10, y: 10)
     var angryCatAlien1 = AngryCatAlien(nickName: "Lucy", age: 4, fullName: "Mrs. Lucy",   AngryCatAlien
         initialScore: 50, x: 20, y: 10, numberOfEyes: 3)
     var angryCatWizard1 = AngryCatWizard(nickName: "Daisy", age: 4, fullName: "Mrs.       AngryCatWizard
         Daisy", initialScore: 50, x: 20, y: 10, spellPower: 6)
     var angryCatKnight1 = AngryCatKnight(nickName: "Maggie", age: 3, fullName: "Mrs.      AngryCatKnight
         Maggy", initialScore: 1300, x: 40, y: 10, swordPower: 7, swordWeight: 5)

 ⚠   print(angryDog1 is AngryDog)                                                 "true\n"
 ⚠   print(angryDog1 is ComicCharacter)                                           "true\n"

 ⚠   print(angryCat1 is AngryCat)                                                 "true\n"
 ⚠   print(angryCat1 is ComicCharacter)                                           "true\n"
 ⚠   print(angryCat1 is GameCharacter)                                            "true\n"

 ⚠   print(angryCatAlien1 is AngryCat)                                            "true\n"
     print(angryCatAlien1 is AngryCatAlien)                                       "true\n"
 ⚠   print(angryCatAlien1 is ComicCharacter)                                      "true\n"
 ⚠   print(angryCatAlien1 is GameCharacter)                                       "true\n"
 ⚠   print(angryCatAlien1 is Alien)                                               "true\n"

 ⚠   print(angryCatWizard1 is AngryCat)                                           "true\n"
 ⚠   print(angryCatWizard1 is AngryCatWizard)                                     "true\n"
 ⚠   print(angryCatWizard1 is ComicCharacter)                                     "true\n"
 ⚠   print(angryCatWizard1 is GameCharacter)                                      "true\n"
 ⚠   print(angryCatWizard1 is Wizard)                                             "true\n"

 ⚠   print(angryCatKnight1 is AngryCat)                                           "true\n"
 ⚠   print(angryCatKnight1 is AngryCatKnight)                                     "true\n"
 ⚠   print(angryCatKnight1 is ComicCharacter)                                     "true\n"
 ⚠   print(angryCatKnight1 is GameCharacter)                                      "true\n"
 ⚠   print(angryCatKnight1 is Knight)                                             "true\n"
```

Working with methods that receive protocols as arguments

Now, we will create additional instances of the previous classes and call methods that specified their required arguments with protocol names instead of class names. We will understand what happens under the hood when we use protocols as types.

In the following code, the first two lines of code create two instances of the `AngryDog` class named `brian` and `merlin`. Then, the code calls the two versions of the `drawSpeechBalloon` method for `brian`. The second call to this method passes `merlin` as the `ComicCharacter` argument because `merlin` is an instance of `AngryDog`, which is a class that implements the `ComicCharacter` protocol:

```
var brian = AngryDog(nickName: "Brian")
var merlin = AngryDog(nickName: "Merlin")
brian.drawSpeechBalloon("Hello, my name is \(brian.nickName)")
brian.drawSpeechBalloon(merlin, message: "How do you do?")
merlin.drawThoughtBalloon("Who are you? I think.")
```

> Bear in mind that when we work with protocols, we use them to specify the argument types instead of using class names. Multiple classes might implement a single protocol, so instances of different classes might qualify as an argument of a specific protocol.

The following code creates an instance of the `AngryCat` class named `garfield`. Its `nickName` value is `"Garfield"`. The next line calls the `drawSpeechBalloon` method for the new instance to introduce Garfield in the comic, and then `brian` calls the `drawSpeechBalloon` method and passes `garfield` as the `ComicCharacter` argument because `garfield` is an instance of `AngryCat`, which is a class that implements the `ComicCharacter` protocol. Thus, we can also use instances of `AngryCat` whenever we need a `ComicCharacter` argument:

```
var garfield = AngryCat(nickName: "Garfield", age: 10, fullName: "Mr. Garfield", initialScore: 0, x: 10, y: 20)
garfield.drawSpeechBalloon("Hello, my name is \(garfield.nickName)")
brian.drawSpeechBalloon(garfield, message: "Hello \(garfield.nickName)")
```

The following code creates an instance of the `AngryCatAlien` class named `misterAlien`. Its `nickName` value is `"Alien"`. The next line checks whether the call to the `isIntersectingWith` method with `garfield` as a parameter returns `true`. The method requires a `ComicCharacter` argument, so we can use `garfield`. The method will return `true` because the `x` and `y` properties of both instances have the same value. The line within the `if` block calls the `move` method for `misterAlien`. Then, the code calls the `appear` method:

```
var misterAlien = AngryCatAlien(nickName: "Alien", age: 120, fullName: "Mr. Alien", initialScore: 0, x: 10, y: 20, numberOfEyes: 3)
if (misterAlien.isIntersectingWith(garfield)) {
    misterAlien.move(garfield.X + 20, y: garfield.Y + 20);
}
misterAlien.appear();
```

The following code creates an instance of the `AngryCatWizard` class named `gandalf`. Its `nickName` value is `"Gandalf"`. The next lines call the `draw` method and then the `disappearAlien` method with `misterAlien` as a parameter. The method requires an `Alien` argument, so we can use `misterAlien`, which is the previously created instance of `AngryCatAlien` that implements the `Alien` protocol. Then, a call to the `Appear` method for `misterAlien` makes the alien with three eyes appear again:

```
var gandalf = AngryCatWizard(nickName: "Gandalf", age: 75, fullName: "Mr. Gandalf", initialScore: 10000, x: 30, y: 40, spellPower: 100)
gandalf.draw(gandalf.x, y: gandalf.y)
gandalf.disappearAlien(misterAlien)
misterAlien.appear()
```

The following code creates an instance of the `AngryCatKnight` class named `camelot`. Its `nickName` value is `"Camelot"`. The next lines call the `draw` method and then the `unsheathSword` method with `misterAlien` as a parameter. The method requires an `Alien` argument, so we can use `misterAlien`, the previously created instance of `AngryCatAlien` that implements the `Alien` protocol:

```
var camelot = AngryCatKnight(nickName: "Camelot", age: 35, fullName: "Sir Camelot", initialScore: 5000, x: 50, y: 50, swordPower: 100, swordWeight: 30)
camelot.draw(camelot.x, y: camelot.y)
camelot.unsheathSword(misterAlien)
```

Contract Programming with Protocols

Finally, the code calls the `drawThoughtBalloon` and `drawSpeechBalloon` methods for `misterAlien`. We can do this because `misterAlien` is an instance of `AngryCatAlien`, and this class inherits the conformance to the `ComicCharacter` protocol from its `AngryCat` superclass. The call to the `drawSpeechBalloon` method passes `camelot` as the `ComicCharacter` argument because `camelot` is an instance of `AngryCatKnight`, which is a class that also inherits the conformance to the `ComicCharacter` protocol from its `AngryCat` superclass. Thus, we can also use instances of `AngryCatKnight` whenever we need a `ComicCharacter` argument, as follows:

```
misterAlien.drawThoughtBalloon("I must be friendly or I'm dead...");
misterAlien.drawSpeechBalloon(camelot, message: "Pleased to meet you, Sir.");
```

After you execute the previous lines in the Playground, you will see the following text output:

```
Brian -> "Hello, my name is Brian"
Brian -> "Merlin, How do you do?"
Merlin -> ***Who are you? I think.***
Garfield -> "Meow Hello, my name is Garfield"
Brian -> "Garfield, Hello Garfield"
Moving AngryCat Mr. Alien to x: 30, y: 40
I'm Mr. Alien and you can see my 3 eyes.
Drawing AngryCat Mr. Gandalf at x: 30, y: 40
Mr. Gandalf uses his 100 spell power to make the alien with 3 eyes disappear.
I'm Mr. Alien and you can see my 3 eyes.
Drawing AngryCat Sir Camelot at x: 50, y: 50
Sir Camelot unsheaths his sword.
Sword power: 100. Sword weight: 30.
The sword targets an alien with 3 eyes.
Alien thinks: I must be friendly or I'm dead...
Camelot === Alien ---> "Pleased to meet you, Sir."
```

The next screenshot shows the code and the results of executing it in the Playground:

```
var brian = AngryDog(nickName: "Brian")                                    AngryDog
var merlin = AngryDog(nickName: "Merlin")                                  AngryDog
brian.drawSpeechBalloon("Hello, my name is \(brian.nickName)")             AngryDog
brian.drawSpeechBalloon(merlin, message: "How do you do?")                 AngryDog
merlin.drawThoughtBalloon("Who are you? I think.")                         AngryDog

var garfield = AngryCat(nickName: "Garfield", age: 10, fullName: "Mr. Garfield",   AngryCat
    initialScore: 0, x: 10, y: 20)
garfield.drawSpeechBalloon("Hello, my name is \(garfield.nickName)")       AngryCat
brian.drawSpeechBalloon(garfield, message: "Hello \(garfield.nickName)")   AngryDog

var misterAlien = AngryCatAlien(nickName: "Alien", age: 120, fullName: "Mr. Alien",   AngryCatAlien
    initialScore: 0, x: 10, y: 20, numberOfEyes: 3)
if (misterAlien.isIntersectingWith(garfield)) {
    misterAlien.move(garfield.x + 20, y: garfield.y + 20);                 AngryCatAlien
}
misterAlien.appear();                                                      AngryCatAlien

var gandalf = AngryCatWizard(nickName: "Gandalf", age: 75, fullName: "Mr. Gandalf",
    initialScore: 10000, x: 30, y: 40, spellPower: 100)
gandalf.draw(gandalf.x, y: gandalf.y)                                      AngryCatWizard
gandalf.disappearAlien(misterAlien)                                        AngryCatWizard
misterAlien.appear()                                                       AngryCatAlien

var camelot = AngryCatKnight(nickName: "Camelot", age: 35, fullName: "Sir Camelot",
    initialScore: 5000, x: 50, y: 50, swordPower: 100, swordWeight: 30)
camelot.draw(camelot.x, y: camelot.y)                                      AngryCatKnight
camelot.unsheathSword(misterAlien)                                         AngryCatKnight

misterAlien.drawThoughtBalloon("I must be friendly or I'm dead...");       AngryCatAlien
misterAlien.drawSpeechBalloon(camelot, message: "Pleased to meet you, Sir.");  AngryCatAlien
```

```
Brian -> "Hello, my name is Brian"
Brian -> "Merlin, How do you do?"
Merlin -> ***Who are you? I think.***
Garfield -> "Meow Hello, my name is Garfield"
Brian -> "Garfield, Hello Garfield"
Moving AngryCat Mr. Alien to x: 30, y: 40
I'm Mr. Alien and you can see my 3 eyes.
Drawing AngryCat Mr. Gandalf at x: 30, y: 40
Mr. Gandalf uses his 100 spell power to make the alien with 3 eyes disappear.
I'm Mr. Alien and you can see my 3 eyes.
Drawing AngryCat Sir Camelot at x: 50, y: 50
Sir Camelot unsheaths his sword.
Sword power: 100. Sword weight: 30.
The sword targets an alien with 3 eyes.
Alien thinks: I must be friendly or I'm dead...
Camelot === Alien ---> "Pleased to meet you, Sir."
```

Downcasting with protocols and classes

The `ComicCharacter` protocol defines one of the method requirements for the `drawSpeechBalloon` method with `destination` as an argument of the `ComicCharacter` type, which is the same type that the protocol defined. The following is the first line in our sample code that called this method:

```
brian.drawSpeechBalloon(merlin, message: "How do you do?")
```

We called the method defined within the `AngryDog` class because `brian` is an instance of `AngryDog`. We passed an `AngryDog` instance, `merlin`, to the `destination` argument. The method works with the `destination` argument as an instance that conforms to the `ComicCharacter` protocol; therefore, whenever we reference the destination variable, we will only be able to see what the `ComicCharacter` type defines.

Contract Programming with Protocols

We can easily understand what happens under the hood when Swift downcasts a type from its original type to a target type, such as a protocol to which the class conforms. In this case, `AngryDog` is downcast to `ComicCharacter`. If we enter the following code in the Playground, Xcode will enumerate the members for the `AngryDog` instance named `merlin`:

```
merlin.
```

Xcode will display the following members:

```
Void drawSpeechBalloon(destination: ComicCharacter, message: String)
Void drawSpeechBalloon(message: String)
Void drawThoughtBalloon(message: String)
String nickName
Void speak(message: String)
Void think(message: String)
```

The following screenshot shows the members enumerated in the Playground for `merlin`, which is an `AngryDog` instance:

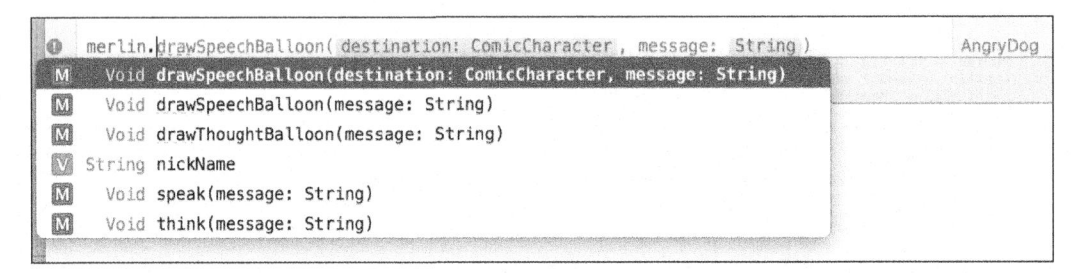

If we enter the following code in the Playground, the `as` downcast operator forces the downcast to the `ComicCharacter` protocol type; therefore, Xcode will only enumerate the members for the `AngryDog` instance named `merlin` that are required members in the `ComicCharacter` protocol:

```
(merlin as ComicCharacter).
```

Xcode will display the following members:

```
Void drawSpeechBalloon(destination: ComicCharacter, message: String)
Void drawSpeechBalloon(message: String)
Void drawThoughtBalloon(message: String)
String nickName
```

[156]

Note that the two methods that are defined in the `AngryDog` class but aren't required in the `ComicCharacter` protocol aren't visible: `speak` and `think`. The following screenshot shows the members enumerated in the Playground for `merlin` downcast to `ComicCharacter`:

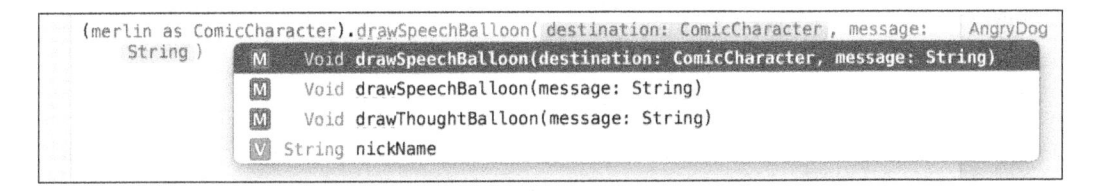

```
(merlin as ComicCharacter).drawSpeechBalloon( destination: ComicCharacter , message:    AngryDog
    String )       M    Void drawSpeechBalloon(destination: ComicCharacter, message: String)
                   M    Void drawSpeechBalloon(message: String)
                   M    Void drawThoughtBalloon(message: String)
                   V    String nickName
```

Now, let's analyze another scenario in which an instance is downcast to one of the protocols to which it conforms. The `GameCharacter` protocol defines a method requirement for the `isIntersectingWith` method with `otherCharacter` as an argument of the `GameCharacter` type, which is the same type that the protocol defined. The following is the first line in our sample code that called this method:

```
if (misterAlien.isIntersectingWith(garfield)) {
```

We called the method defined within the `AngryCat` class because `misterAlien` is an instance of `AngryCatAlien` that inherits the method implementation from the `AngryCat` class. We passed an `AngryCat` instance, `garfield`, to the `otherCharacter` argument. The method works with the `otherCharacter` argument as an instance that conforms to the `GameCharacter` protocol; therefore, whenever we reference the destination variable, we will only be able to see what the `GameCharacter` type defines.

In this case, `AngryCat` is downcast to `GameCharacter`. If we enter the following code in the Playground, Xcode will enumerate the members for the `AngryCat` instance named `garfield`:

```
garfield.
```

Xcode will display the following members:

```
UInt age
Void draw(x: UInt, y: UInt)
Void drawSpeechBalloon(destination: ComicCharacter, message: String)
Void drawSpeechBalloon(message: String)
Void drawThoughtBalloon(message: String)
String fullName
Bool isIntersectingWith(otherCharacter: GameCharacter)
Void move(x: UInt, y: UInt)
String nickName
UInt score
UInt x
UInt y
```

Contract Programming with Protocols

The following screenshot shows the first members enumerated in the Playground for `garfield`, which is an `AngryCat` instance:

```
garfield.age
  V   UInt  age
  M   Void  draw(x: UInt, y: UInt)
  M   Void  drawSpeechBalloon(destination: ComicCharacter, message: String)
  M   Void  drawSpeechBalloon(message: String)
  M   Void  drawThoughtBalloon(message: String)
  V   String fullName
  M   Bool  isIntersectingWith(otherCharacter: GameCharacter)
  M   Void  move(x: UInt, y: UInt)
```

If we enter the following code in the Playground, the `as` downcast operator forces the downcast to the `GameCharacter` protocol type; therefore, Xcode will only enumerate the members for the `AngryCat` instance named `garfield` that are required members in the `GameCharacter` protocol:

```
(garfield as GameCharacter).
```

Xcode will display the following members:

```
Void draw(x: UInt, y: UInt)
String fullName
Bool isIntersectingWith(otherCharacter: GameCharacter)
Void move(x: UInt, y: UInt)
UInt score
UInt x
UInt y
```

Note that the list of members has been reduced to the properties and members required in the `GameCharacter` protocol. The following screenshot shows the members enumerated in the Playground for `garfield` downcast to `GameCharacter`:

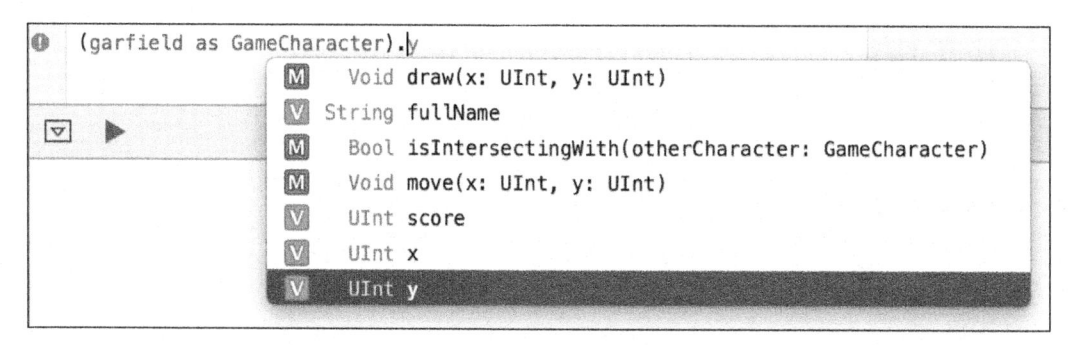

```
(garfield as GameCharacter).y
          M   Void  draw(x: UInt, y: UInt)
          V   String fullName
          M   Bool  isIntersectingWith(otherCharacter: GameCharacter)
          M   Void  move(x: UInt, y: UInt)
          V   UInt  score
          V   UInt  x
          V   UInt  y
```

We can use the `as` operator to force a cast of the previous expression to the original type—that is, to the `AngryCat` type. This way, Xcode will enumerate all the members of the `AngryCat` instance again:

    ((garfield as GameCharacter) as AngryCat).

Xcode will display the following members—that is, all the members that Xcode enumerated when we worked with `garfield`—without any kind of casting:

    UInt age
    Void draw(x: UInt, y: UInt)
    Void drawSpeechBalloon(destination: ComicCharacter, message: String)
    Void drawSpeechBalloon(message: String)
    Void drawThoughtBalloon(message: String)
    String fullName
    Bool isIntersectingWith(otherCharacter: GameCharacter)
    Void move(x: UInt, y: UInt)
    String nickName
    UInt score
    UInt x
    UInt y

The following screenshot shows the first members enumerated in the Playground for `garfield` downcast to `GameCharacter` and then casted back to an `AngryCat` instance:

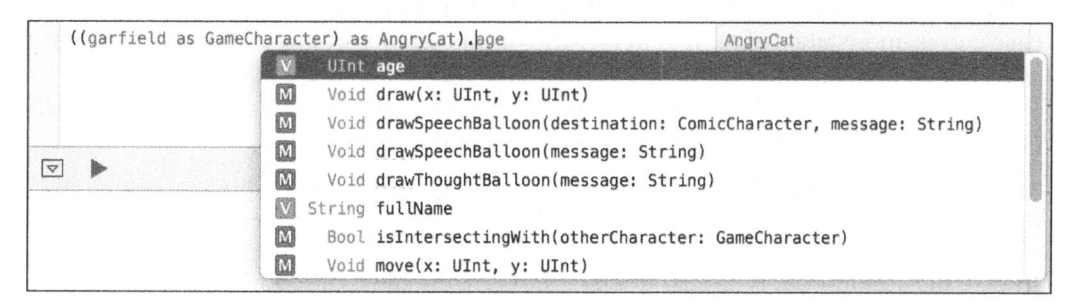

Treating instances of a protocol type as a different subclass

Now, we will take advantage of the possibility that Swift offers us to extend an existing class to add specific members. In this case, we will add an instance method to the previously defined `AngryCat` class. The following lines add the `doSomethingWithAnAngryCat` method to the existing `AngryCat` class:

    public extension AngryCat {
        public func doSomethingWithAnAngryCat(cat: AngryCat) {

Contract Programming with Protocols

```
        if let angryCatAlien = cat as? AngryCatAlien {
            angryCatAlien.appear()
        } else if let angryCatKnight = cat as? AngryCatKnight {
            angryCatKnight.unsheathSword()
        } else if let angryCatWizard = cat as? AngryCatWizard {
            print("My spell power is \(angryCatWizard.spellPower)")
        } else {
            print("This AngryCat doesn't have cool skills.")
        }
    }
}
```

The `doSomethingWithAnAngryCat` method receives an `AngryCat` instance (`cat`) and uses the conditional type casting operator (`as?`) to return an optional value of the type that it tries to cast a subclass of `AngryCat`. In case `cat` is an instance of `AngryCatAlien` or of any potential subclass of `AngryCatAlien`, the first type cast succeeds and the code calls the `appear` method for the `cat` type cast to an `AngryCatAlien` instance, which is saved in the `angryCatAlien` reference constant, as follows:

```
    if let angryCatAlien = cat as? AngryCatAlien {
        angryCatAlien.appear()
```

In case the conditional type cast to `AngryCatAlien` fails, the code uses the conditional type casting operator (`as?`) and tries to cast `cat` to `AngryCatKnight`. In case `cat` is an instance of `AngryCatKnight` or an instance of any potential subclass of `AngryCatKnight`, the conditional type cast succeeds, and the code calls the `unsheathSword` method for the `cat` type cast to an `AngryCatKnight` instance, which is saved in the `angryCatKnight` reference constant:

```
    } else if let angryCatKnight = cat as? AngryCatKnight {
        angryCatKnight.unsheathSword()
```

In case the conditional type cast to `AngryCatKnight` fails, the code uses the conditional type casting operator (`as?`) and tries to cast `cat` to `AngryCatWizard`. In case `cat` is an instance of `AngryCatWizard` or of any potential subclass of `AngryCatWizard`, the conditional type cast succeeds, and the code prints a message indicating the `spellPower` value for the `cat` type cast to an `AngryCatWizard` instance, which is saved in the `angryCatWizard` reference constant, as follows:

```
    } else if let angryCatWizard = cat as? AngryCatWizard {
        print("My spell power is \(angryCatWizard.spellPower)")
```

Finally, if the last conditional type cast to `AngryCatKnight` fails, it means that the `cat` instance just belongs to `AngryCat`, so the code prints a message indicating that `AngryCat` doesn't have cool skills.

> Whenever type casting fails, we must use the conditional form (`as?`) of the type cast operator.

Now, we will take advantage of the instance method added to the `AngryCat` class and call it in instances of `AngryCat` and its subclasses that we created before we declared the extension. We will call the method for the `AngryCat` instance named `garfield` and use it with the following arguments:

- `misterAlien`: This is an instance of the `AngryCatAlien` class
- `camelot`: This is an instance of the `AngryCatKnight` class
- `gandalf`: This is an instance of the `AngryCatWizard` class
- `garfield`: This is an instance of the `AngryCat` class

The following four lines call the `doSomethingWithAnAngryCat` method in the Playground with the previously enumerated arguments:

```
garfield.doSomethingWithAnAngryCat(misterAlien)
garfield.doSomethingWithAnAngryCat(camelot)
garfield.doSomethingWithAnAngryCat(gandalf)
garfield.doSomethingWithAnAngryCat(garfield)
```

The next lines show the output generated in the Playground. Each call triggers a different type cast and calls a method of the type cast instance:

```
I'm Mr. Alien and you can see my 3 eyes.
Sir Camelot unsheaths his sword.
Sword power: 100. Sword weight: 30.
My spell power is 100
This AngryCat doesn't have cool skills.
```

Contract Programming with Protocols

The following screenshot shows that the execution of the four methods generates the `doSomethingWithAnAngryCat` method to execute code in each usage of the conditional type cast operator. Note the values displayed on the right-hand side of each line included within the curly braces after each conditional type cast. The lines that call the methods just display the type cast instance types, `AngryCatAlien` and `AngryCatKnight`, and the lines that call the `print` method display the generated output on the right-hand side.

```
public extension AngryCat {
    public func doSomethingWithAnAngryCat(cat: AngryCat) {
        if let angryCatAlien = cat as? AngryCatAlien {
            angryCatAlien.appear()                                      AngryCatAlien
        } else if let angryCatKnight = cat as? AngryCatKnight {
            angryCatKnight.unsheathSword()                              AngryCatKnight
        } else if let angryCatWizard = cat as? AngryCatWizard {
            print("My spell power is \(angryCatWizard.spellPower)")     "My spell power is 100\n"
        } else {
            print("This AngryCat doesn't have cool skills.")            "This AngryCat doesn't have cool skills.\n"
        }
    }
}

garfield.doSomethingWithAnAngryCat(misterAlien)                         AngryCat
garfield.doSomethingWithAnAngryCat(camelot)                             AngryCat
garfield.doSomethingWithAnAngryCat(gandalf)                             AngryCat
garfield.doSomethingWithAnAngryCat(garfield)                            AngryCat
```

```
I'm Mr. Alien and you can see my 3 eyes.
Sir Camelot unsheaths his sword.
Sword power: 100. Sword weight: 30.
My spell power is 100
This AngryCat doesn't have cool skills.
```

Specifying requirements for properties

In the previous chapter, we worked with simple inheritance to specialize animals. Now, we will go back to this example and refactor it to use protocols that allow us to take advantage of multiple inheritance.

The decision to work with contract-based programming appears with a new requirement, which is the need to make domestic birds and other domestic animals different from domestic mammals which talk and have a favorite toy. We already had a `talk` method and a `favoriteToy` property defined in the `DomesticMammal` class. However, now that we know how to work with protocols, we don't want to introduce duplicate code, and we want to be able to generalize what is required to be domestic, with a specific protocol for this.

We will define the following six protocols and take advantage of inheritance in protocols; that is, we will have protocols that inherit from other protocols, as follows:

- `AbstractAnimal`: This defines the requirements for an animal.
- `AbstractDomestic`: This defines the requirements that make an animal be considered a domestic one. However, it doesn't inherit from `AbstractAnimal`.
- `AbstractMammal`: This defines the requirements for a mammal. The protocol inherits from `AbstractAnimal`.
- `AbstractBird`: This defines the requirements for birds. The protocol inherits from `AbstractAnimal`.
- `AbstractDog`: This defines the requirements for dogs. The protocol inherits from `AbstractMammal`.
- `AbstractCat`: This defines the requirements for cats. The protocol inherits from `AbstracMammal`.

In this case, we will use the `Abstract` prefix to differentiate protocols from classes. All the protocols' names start with `Abstract`. However, take into account that this is not a common convention in Swift. We want to create an `Animal` class, so we cannot have a protocol with the same name.

The following lines show the code that declares the `AbstractAnimal` protocol:

```
public protocol AbstractAnimal {
    static var numberOfLegs: Int { get }
    static var averageNumberOfChildren: Int { get }
    static var abilityToFly: Bool { get }

    var age: Int { get set }

    static func printALeg()
    static func printAChild()

    func printLegs()
    func printChildren()
    func printAge()
}
```

The `AbstractAnimal` protocol requires type properties, stored properties, type methods, and instance methods. First, we will focus on both the type and stored property requirements. The first lines define the type property requirements. We can only use the `static` keyword to specify a type property requirement, but we can use either `static` or `class` when we implement the type property in the class that conforms to the protocol. The usage of the `static` keyword doesn't have the same meaning that this keyword has when we use it in classes; that is, we can still declare type properties that can be overridden in the classes that conform to the protocol. In fact, that is exactly what we will do when we create the class that conforms to the `AbstractAnimal` protocol.

In this case, we want the three type properties to be in a read-only format, so we only include the `get` keyword after the desired type for the type property. The following line shows the type property requirement for `numerOfLegs` with the `get` keyword that makes it a read-only type property:

```
static var numberOfLegs: Int { get }
```

> We always have to specify the required type in each property requirement.

The protocol defines a stored property requirement named `age` with both the `get` and `set` keywords; therefore, this stored property must be a read-write stored property. Each class that conforms to the protocol can decide whether it is convenient to declare explicit getter and setter methods or just declare a stored property without providing these methods. Both cases are valid implementations because the protocol just requires a read/write stored property. The following line shows the stored property requirement for `age`:

```
var age: Int { get set }
```

Specifying requirements for methods

The `AbstractAnimal` protocol requires two type methods: `printALeg` and `printAChild`. As explained with the type property requirements, we can only use the `static` keyword to specify a type method requirement, but we can use either `static` or `class` when we implement the type method in the class that conforms to the protocol. The usage of the `static` keyword doesn't have the same meaning that this keyword has when we use it in classes; that is, we can still declare type methods that can be overridden in the classes that conform to the protocol by declaring them with the `class` keyword in the respective classes. The following line shows the type method requirement for `printALeg`:

```
static func printALeg()
```

The protocol defines three parameterless methods: `printLegs`, `printChildren`, and `printAge`. The method requirements use the `func` keyword followed by the method name and its arguments, as if we were writing the method declaration for a class but without the method body. The following line shows the method requirement for `printLegs`:

```
func printLegs()
```

The following lines show the code that declares the `AbstractDomestic` protocol:

```
public protocol AbstractDomestic {
    var name: String { get set }
    var favoriteToy: String { get set }

    func talk()
}
```

The `AbstractDomestic` protocol requires two read/write stored properties: `name` and `favoriteToy`. In addition, the protocol defines a method requirement for a parameterless `talk` instance method. Note that the `AbstractDomestic` protocol doesn't inherit from the `AbstractAnimal` protocol, so we can combine the conformance to other protocols with `AbstractDomestic` to create a specific domestic version.

The following lines show the code that declares the `AbstractMammal` protocol:

```
public protocol AbstractMammal: AbstractAnimal {
    var isPregnant: Bool { get set }
}
```

The `AbstractMammal` protocol inherits from the `AbstractAnimal` protocol and just adds the requirement for a single read/write stored property: `isPregnant`.

The following lines show the code that declares the `AbstractDog` protocol:

```
public protocol AbstractDog: AbstractMammal {
    var breed: String { get }
    var breedFamily: String { get }

    func printBreed()
    func printBreedFamily()
    func bark()
    func bark(times: Int)
    func bark(times: Int, otherDomestic: AbstractDomestic)
    func bark(times: Int, otherDomestic: AbstractDomestic, isAngry: Bool)
    func printBark(times: Int, otherDomestic: AbstractDomestic?, isAngry: Bool)
}
```

The `AbstractDog` protocol inherits from the `AbstractMammal` protocol and adds two read-only stored properties: `breed` and `breedFamily`. In addition, the protocol adds many method requirements. There are many overloaded method requirements with the same name (`bark`) and different arguments. Thus, the class or classes that implement the `AbstractDog` protocol must implement all the specified overloads for the `bark` method. Note that the `otherDomestic` argument is of a protocol type (`AbstractDomestic`), so any instance of a class that conforms to this protocol can be used as an argument.

The following lines show the code that declares the `AbstractCat` protocol:

```
public protocol AbstractCat: AbstractMammal {
    func printMeow(times: Int)
}
```

The `AbstractCat` protocol inherits from the `AbstractMammal` protocol and adds a `printMeow` method requirement that receives a `times Int` argument.

The following lines show the code that declares the `AbstractBird` protocol:

```
public protocol AbstractBird: AbstractMammal {
    var feathersColor: String { get set }
}
```

The `AbstractBird` protocol inherits from the `AbstractMammal` protocol and adds a `feathersColor` read/write stored property requirement. However, wait; we said that we needed birds to talk and have a favorite toy. The `AbstractBird` class doesn't include a requirement for either a `talk` method or a `favoriteToy` property, and it doesn't inherit. However, we will create a class that implements both the `AbstractBird` and the `AbstractDomestic` protocols, and we will be able to use a domestic bird that talks as an argument in any method that requires `AbstractDomestic`.

Combining class inheritance with protocol inheritance

So far, we have created many protocols for our animals. Some of these protocols inherit from other protocols; therefore, we have a protocol hierarchy tree. Now, it is time to combine class inheritance with protocol inheritance to recreate our animal classes.

The following lines show the new version of the `Animal` class that conforms to the `AbstractAnimal` protocol:

```
public class Animal: AbstractAnimal {
    public class var numberOfLegs: Int {
        get {
            return 0;
        }
    }
    public class var averageNumberOfChildren: Int {
        get {
            return 0;
        }
    }

    public class var abilityToFly: Bool {
        get {
            return false;
        }
    }

    public var age: Int

    init(age : Int) {
        self.age = age
        print("Animal created")
    }

    public class func printALeg() {
        preconditionFailure("The pringALeg method must be overriden")
    }

    public func printLegs() {
        for _ in 0..<self.dynamicType.numberOfLegs {
            self.dynamicType.printALeg()
        }
        print(String())
    }

    public class func printAChild() {
        preconditionFailure("The printChild method must be overriden")
    }

    public func printChildren() {
```

```
        for _ in 0..<self.dynamicType.averageNumberOfChildren {
            self.dynamicType.printAChild()
        }
        print(String())
    }

    public func printAge() {
        print("I am \(age) years old.")
    }
}
```

The following lines show the new version of the `Mammal` class that inherits from the `Animal` class and conforms to the `AbstractMammal` protocol:

```
public class Mammal: Animal, AbstractMammal {
    public var isPregnant: Bool = false

    private func initialize(isPregnant: Bool) {
        self.isPregnant = isPregnant
        print("Mammal created")
    }

    public override init(age: Int) {
        super.init(age: age)
        initialize(false)
    }

    public init(age: Int, isPregnant: Bool) {
        super.init(age: age)
        initialize(isPregnant)
    }
}
```

The following lines show the new version of the `DomesticMammal` class that inherits from the `Mammal` class and conforms to the `AbstractDomestic` protocol. Remember that the `AbstractDomestic` protocol doesn't inherit from any other protocol:

```
public class DomesticMammal: Mammal, AbstractDomestic {
    public var name = String()
    public var favoriteToy = String()

    private func initialize(name: String, favoriteToy: String) {
        self.name = name
        self.favoriteToy = favoriteToy
        print("DomesticMammal created")
```

```
    }

    public init(age: Int, name: String, favoriteToy: String) {
        super.init(age: age)
        initialize(name, favoriteToy: favoriteToy)
    }

    public init(age: Int, isPregnant: Bool, name: String, favoriteToy: String) {
        super.init(age: age, isPregnant: isPregnant)
        initialize(name, favoriteToy: favoriteToy)
    }

    public func talk() {
        print("\(name): talks")
    }
}
```

The following lines show the new version of the `Dog` class that inherits from the `DomesticMammal` class and conforms to the `AbstractDog` protocol:

```
public class Dog: DomesticMammal, AbstractDog {
    public static override var numberOfLegs: Int {
        get {
            return 4;
        }
    }

    public static override var abilityToFly: Bool {
        get {
            return false;
        }
    }

    public var breed: String {
        get {
            return "Just a dog"
        }
    }

    public var breedFamily: String {
        get {
            return "Dog"
        }
    }
```

```swift
    private func initializeDog() {
        print("Dog created")
    }

    public override init(age: Int, name: String, favoriteToy: String) {
        super.init(age: age, name: name, favoriteToy: favoriteToy)
        initializeDog()
    }

    public override init(age: Int, isPregnant: Bool, name: String, favoriteToy: String) {
        super.init(age: age, isPregnant: isPregnant, name: name, favoriteToy: favoriteToy)
        initializeDog()
    }

    public final func printBreed() {
        print(breed)
    }

    public final func printBreedFamily() {
        print(breedFamily)
    }

    public func printBark(times: Int, otherDomestic: AbstractDomestic?, isAngry: Bool) {
        var bark = "\(name)"
        if let unwrappedOtherDomestic = otherDomestic {
            bark += " to \(unwrappedOtherDomestic.name): "
        } else {
            bark += ": "
        }
        if isAngry {
            bark += "Grr "
        }
        for _ in 0 ..< times {
            bark += "Woof "
        }
        print(bark)
    }

    public func bark() {
        printBark(1, otherDomestic: nil, isAngry: false)
    }

    public func bark(times: Int) {
```

```
            printBark(times, otherDomestic: nil, isAngry: false)
    }

    public func bark(times: Int, otherDomestic: AbstractDomestic) {
        printBark(times, otherDomestic: otherDomestic, isAngry: false)
    }

    public func bark(times: Int, otherDomestic: AbstractDomestic,
isAngry: Bool) {
        printBark(times, otherDomestic: otherDomestic, isAngry:
isAngry)
    }

    public override func talk() {
        bark()
    }
}
```

The previous version had overloaded `bark` methods that required an `otherDomesticMammal` argument of the `DomesticMammal` type. The `printBark` method required an optional `otherDomesticMammal` argument of the `DomesticMammal?` type. The new version of the overloaded `bark` methods replaces the `otherDomesticMammal` argument with `otherDomestic` of the `AbstractDomestic` type. This way, it is possible to pass any class that implements the `AbstractDomestic` protocol. The new version of the `printBark` method requires an optional `otherDomestic` argument of the `AbstractDomestic` type. These changes allow dogs to bark at any other domestic animal, such as the domestic bird we will create later. The previous version was only capable of barking at other domestic mammals. However, in real-life scenarios, dogs do bark at birds.

It is not necessary to make any changes to the classes that inherit from `Dog`: `TerrierDog` and `SmoothFoxTerrier`. These classes remain with the same code.

The following lines show the new version of the `Cat` class that inherits from the `DomesticMammal` class and conforms to the `AbstractCat` protocol:

```
public class Cat: DomesticMammal, AbstractCat {
    public static override var numberOfLegs: Int {
        get {
            return 4;
        }
    }

    public static override var abilityToFly: Bool {
        get {
            return false;
```

Contract Programming with Protocols

```swift
        }
    }

    public override class var averageNumberOfChildren: Int {
        get {
            return 6;
        }
    }

    private func initializeCat() {
        print("Cat created")
    }

    public override init(age: Int, name: String, favoriteToy: String) {
        super.init(age: age, name: name, favoriteToy: favoriteToy)
        initializeCat()
    }

    public override init(age: Int, isPregnant: Bool, name: String, favoriteToy: String) {
        super.init(age: age, isPregnant: isPregnant, name: name, favoriteToy: favoriteToy)
        initializeCat()
    }

    public func printMeow(times: Int) {
        var meow = "\(name): "
        for _ in 0 ..< times {
            meow += "Meow "
        }
        print(meow)
    }

    public override func talk() {
        printMeow(1)
    }

    public override class func printALeg() {
        print("*_*", terminator: String())
    }

    public override class func printAChild() {
        // Print grinning cat face with smiling eyes emoji
        print(String(UnicodeScalar(0x01F638)), terminator: String())
    }
}
```

The following lines show the new version of the `Bird` class that inherits from the `Animal` class and conforms to the `AbstractBird` protocol:

```
public class Bird: Animal, AbstractBird {
    public var feathersColor: String = String()

    public static override var numberOfLegs: Int {
        get {
            return 2;
        }
    }

    private func initializeBird(feathersColor: String) {
        self.feathersColor = feathersColor
        print("Bird created")
    }

    public override init(age: Int) {
        super.init(age: age)
        initializeBird("Undefined / Too many colors")
    }

    public init(age: Int, feathersColor: String) {
        super.init(age: age)
        initializeBird(feathersColor)
    }
}
```

The following lines show the new version of the `DomesticBird` class that inherits from the `Bird` class and conforms to the `AbstractDomestic` protocol. Remember that the `AbstractDomestic` protocol doesn't inherit from any other protocol:

```
public class DomesticBird: Bird, AbstractDomestic {
    public var name = String()
    public var favoriteToy = String()

    private func initializeDomesticBird(name: String, favoriteToy:
String) {
        self.name = name
        self.favoriteToy = favoriteToy
        print("DomesticBird created")
    }

    public func talk() {
        print("\(name): Tweet Tweet")
```

[173]

Contract Programming with Protocols

```
    }

    public init(age: Int, name: String, favoriteToy: String) {
        super.init(age: age)
        initializeDomesticBird(name, favoriteToy: favoriteToy)
    }

    public init(age: Int, feathersColor: String, name: String, favoriteToy: String) {
        super.init(age: age, feathersColor: feathersColor)
        initializeDomesticBird(name, favoriteToy: favoriteToy)
    }
}
```

The new `DomesticBird` class adds the `favoriteToy` stored property and talk method to conform to the `AbstractDomestic` protocol. In addition, the initializers add new parameters to make it possible to assign an initial value to `favoriteToy`.

The following lines show the new version of the `DomesticCanary` class that inherits from the `DomesticBird` class:

```
public class DomesticCanary: DomesticBird {
    public override class var averageNumberOfChildren: Int {
        get {
            return 5;
        }
    }

    private func initializeDomesticCanary() {
        print("DomesticCanary created")
    }

    public override init(age: Int, name: String, favoriteToy: String) {
        super.init(age: age, name: name, favoriteToy: favoriteToy)
        initializeDomesticCanary()
    }

    public override init(age: Int, feathersColor: String, name: String, favoriteToy: String) {
        super.init(age: age, feathersColor: feathersColor, name: name, favoriteToy: favoriteToy)
        initializeDomesticCanary()
    }
```

```
    public override class func printALeg() {
        print("^", terminator: String())
    }

    public override class func printAChild() {
        // Print bird emoji
        print(String(UnicodeScalar(0x01F426)), terminator: String())
    }
}
```

The `DomesticCanary` class changes the initializers to match the edits made in its superclass.

The following table summarizes the list of protocols to which each of the new versions of the classes we created conform:

Class name	Conforms to the following protocol(s)
`Animal`	`AbstractAnimal`
`Mammal`	`AbstractAnimal` and `AbstractMammal`
`DomesticMammal`	`AbstractAnimal`, `AbstractMammal`, and `AbstractDomestic`
`Dog`	`AbstractAnimal`, `AbstractMammal`, `AbstractDomestic`, and `AbstractDog`
`TerrierDog`	`AbstractAnimal`, `AbstractMammal`, `AbstractDomestic`, and `AbstractDog`
`SmoothFoxTerrier`	`AbstractAnimal`, `AbstractMammal`, `AbstractDomestic`, and `AbstractDog`
`Cat`	`AbstractAnimal`, `AbstractMammal`, `AbstractDomestic`, and `AbstractCat`
`Bird`	`AbstractAnimal` and `AbstractBird`
`DomesticBird`	`AbstractAnimal`, `AbstractBird`, and `AbstractDomestic`

Contract Programming with Protocols

The following simplified UML diagram shows the hierarchy tree for the protocols and classes and their relationships:

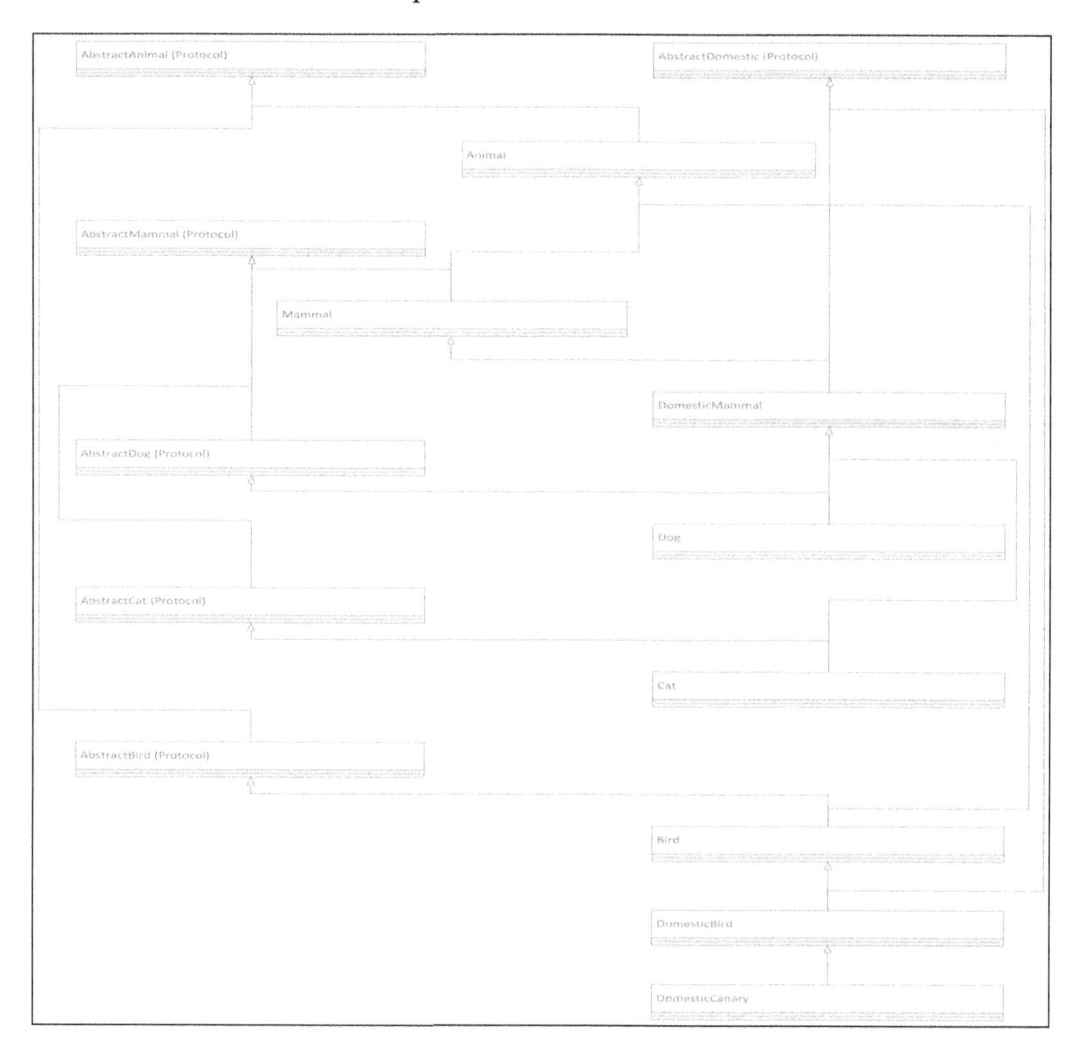

The following lines create an instance of `Dog` named `pluto`, an instance of `Cat` named `marie`, and an instance of `DomesticCanary` named `tweety`. Then, the next lines call the `talk` method for the three instances and make `pluto` bark at `tweety`. It is possible to use `tweety` as the `otherDomestic` argument for the `bark` method because it is an instance of `DomesticCanary`, and it conforms to the `AbstractDomestic` protocol:

```
var pluto = Dog(age: 7, name: "Pluto", favoriteToy: "Teddy bear")
var marie = Cat(age: 4, isPregnant: true, name: "Marie", favoriteToy:
"Tennis ball")
var tweety = DomesticCanary(age: 2, feathersColor: "Yellow", name:
"Tweety", favoriteToy: "Small bell")

tweety.talk()
pluto.bark(3, otherDomestic: tweety)
marie.talk()
pluto.talk()
```

The following lines show the output generated by the last four lines of code:

```
Tweety: Tweet Tweet
Pluto to Tweety: Woof Woof Woof
Marie: Meow
Pluto: Woof
```

If we execute the following lines in the Playground, all of them will display `true` as a result because `tweety` is an instance of a class that conforms to three protocols: `AbstractAnimal`, `AbstractBird`, and `AbstractDomestic`. In addition, `tweety` belongs to `Animal`, `Bird`, `DomesticMammal`, `Dog`, `TerrierDog`, and `SmoothFoxTerrier`.

```
tweety is AbstractAnimal
tweety is AbstractBird
tweety is AbstractDomestic
tweety is Animal
tweety is Bird
tweety is DomesticBird
tweety is DomesticCanary
```

Contract Programming with Protocols

The following screenshot shows the results of executing the previous lines in the Playground. Note that the Playground uses an icon to let us know that all the `is` tests will always be evaluated to `true`:

```
var pluto = Dog(age: 7, name: "Pluto", favoriteToy: "Teddy bear")          Dog
var marie = Cat(age: 4, isPregnant: true, name: "Marie", favoriteToy: "Tennis ball")   Cat
var tweety = DomesticCanary(age: 2, feathersColor: "Yellow", name: "Tweety",   DomesticCanary
    favoriteToy: "Small bell")

tweety.talk()                                                              DomesticCanary
pluto.bark(3, otherDomestic: tweety)                                       Dog
marie.talk()                                                               Cat
pluto.talk()                                                               Dog

tweety is AbstractAnimal                                                   true
tweety is AbstractBird                                                     true
tweety is AbstractDomestic                                                 true
tweety is Animal                                                           true
tweety is Bird                                                             true
tweety is DomesticBird                                                     true
tweety is DomesticCanary                                                   true
```

```
Bird created
DomesticBird created
DomesticCanary created
Tweety: Tweet Tweet
Pluto to Tweety: Woof Woof Woof
Marie: Meow
Pluto: Woof
```

Exercises

Create the following protocols to solve the problem explained in *Chapter 1, Objects from the Real World to Playground*:

- `AbstractShape`
- `AbstractRegularPolygon`
- `AbstractEllipse`
- `AbstractRectangle`
- `AbstractCircle`

After you create the protocols, create the classes that implement them based on the specifications explained in *Chapter 1, Objects from the Real World to Playground*.

The following table summarizes the list of protocols to which each of the classes you must create will conform:

Class name	Conforms to the following protocol(s)
Shape	AbstractShape
Rectangle	AbstractRectangle and AbstractShape
RegularPolygon	AbstractRegularPolygon and AbstractShape
Ellipse	AbstractEllipse and AbstractShape
Circle	AbstractCircle and AbstractShape
EquilateralTriangle	AbstractRegularPolygon and AbstractShape
Square	AbstractRegularPolygon and AbstractShape
RegularHexagon	AbstractRegularPolygon and AbstractShape

Test your knowledge

1. A class can conform to:
    1. Only one protocol.
    2. One or more protocols.
    3. A maximum of two protocols.

2. When a class conforms to a protocol:
    1. It cannot inherit from a class.
    2. It can inherit from an abstract class.
    3. It can also inherit from a class.

3. A protocol:
    1. Can inherit from another protocol.
    2. Can inherit from a class.
    3. Cannot inherit from another protocol.

4. A protocol:
    1. Is a type.
    2. Is a method.
    3. Is the base class for other classes.

5. When we specify a protocol as the type for an argument:
    1. We can use any type method that conforms to the specified protocol as an argument.
    2. We can use any protocol that conforms to the specified protocol as an argument.
    3. We can use any instance of a class that conforms to the specified protocol as an argument.

Summary

In this chapter, you learned about the declaration and combination of multiple blueprints to generate a single instance. We declared protocols with different types of requirements. Then, we created many classes that conformed to these protocols.

We worked with type casting to understand how protocols work as types. Finally, we combined protocols with classes to take advantage of multiple inheritance in Swift. We combined inheritance for protocols and classes.

Now that you have learned about protocols, multiple inheritance, and contract-based programming, we are ready to maximize code reuse with generic code and parametric polymorphism.

6
Maximization of Code Reuse with Generic Code

In this chapter, you will learn about parametric polymorphism and how Swift implements this object-oriented concept through the possibility to write generic code. We will use classes that work with one and two constrained generic types.

In addition, we will learn to combine generic code with inheritance and multiple inheritance to demonstrate the usage of generic code in real-life situations in which the code becomes more complex than the usage of a simple generic class.

Understanding parametric polymorphism and generic code

Let's imagine we want to organize a party of specific animals. We don't want to mix cats with dogs because the party would end up with the dogs chasing cats. We want a party, and we don't want intruders. However, at the same time, we want to take advantage of the procedures we create to organize the party and replicate them with frogs in another party; it would be a party of frogs. We want to reuse the procedures for either dogs or frogs. However, in future, we will probably want to use them with other animals, such as parrots, lions, tigers, and horses.

In the previous chapter, we learned to work with protocols. We can declare a protocol to specify the requirements for an animal and then take advantage of Swift features to write generic code that works with any class that implements the protocol. *Parametric polymorphism* allows us to write generic and reusable code that can work with values without depending on the type while keeping the full static-type safety.

Maximization of Code Reuse with Generic Code

We can take advantage of parametric polymorphism in Swift through generics, also known as generic programming. Once we declare a protocol that specifies the requirements for an animal, we can create a class that works with any instance that conforms to this protocol. This way, we can reuse the code that generates a party of dogs and create a party of frogs, parrots, or any other animal—that is, a party of any instance of a class that conforms to the animal protocol.

> Other strongly typed programming languages, such as C# and Java, allow us to work with parametric polymorphism through generics. In case you worked with these programming languages, you will find that the Swift syntax is very similar. The main difference is that Swift uses protocols instead of interfaces.

Other programming languages work with a different philosophy known as duck typing, where the presence of certain attributes or properties and methods make an object suitable to its usage as a specific animal. With duck typing, if we require animals to have a name property and provide sing and dance methods, we can consider any object an animal as long as it provides the required name property and both the sing and dance methods. Any instance that provides the required property and methods can be used as an animal.

Let's think about the following situation: we see a bird. The bird quacks, swims, and walks like a duck, so we can call this bird a duck. Very similar examples related to a bird and duck generate the *duck typing* name. We don't need additional information to work with the bird as a duck. Python, JavaScript, and Ruby are examples of languages where duck typing is extremely popular.

> We can also work with duck typing in Swift. However, it requires many workarounds, and it is not the most natural way of working in Swift. Thus, we will focus our efforts on writing generic code with parametric polymorphism through generics.

Declaring a protocol to be used as a constraint

We will create an `AnimalProtocol` protocol to specify the requirements that a type must meet in order to be considered an animal. Then, we will create an `Animal` base class that conforms to this protocol, and then, we will specialize this class in three subclasses: `Dog`, `Frog`, and `Lion`. Then, we will create a `Party` class that will be able to work with instances of any class that conforms to the `AnimalProtocol` protocol through generics. We will work with a party of dogs, one of frogs, and another of lions.

Then, we will create a `DeeJayProtocol` protocol and generate a `HorseDeeJay` class that conforms to this new protocol. We will create a subclass of the `Party` class named `PartyWithDeeJay` that will use generics to work with instances of any type that conforms to the `AnimalProtoocol` protocol and instances of any type that conforms to the `DeeJaypProtocol` interface. We will work with a party of dogs with a DJ.

> In this case, we will use the `Protocol` suffix to make it easy to differentiate protocols from classes in our sample code for this chapter. However, take into account that this is not a convention for Swift code. It just makes it easier to understand how generics work.

Now, it is time to code one of the protocols that will be used as a constraint later when we define the class that takes advantage of generics. The following lines show the code for the `AnimalProtocol` protocol. The `public` modifier followed by the `protocol` keyword and the protocol name, `AnimalProtocol`, composes the protocol declaration:

```
public protocol AnimalProtocol {
    var name: String { get }

    init (name: String)

    func dance()
    func say(message: String)
    func sayGoodbye(destination: AnimalProtocol)
    func sayWelcome(destination: AnimalProtocol)
    func sing()
}
```

The protocol declares a read-only `name` String stored property and five method requirements: `dance`, `say`, `sayGoodbye`, `sayWelcome`, and `sing`. As you learned in the previous chapter, the protocol includes only the method declaration because the classes that conform to the `AnimalProtocol` protocol are responsible for providing the implementation of the `name` stored property and the other five methods.

In addition, the protocol specifies an initializer requirement. The initializer requires a `name` argument, so we will make sure that we will be able to create an instance of any class that conforms to this protocol by providing a value to a `name` argument during initialization. The following line specifies the initializer requirement:

```
init (name: String)
```

Declaring a class that conforms to multiple protocols

Now, we will declare a class named `Animal` that conforms to both the previously defined `AnimalProtocol` protocol and the `Equatable` protocol. The latter is a fundamental type in Swift. In order to conform to the `Equatable` protocol, we must implement the `==` operator function for the `Animal` class to determine the equality of the instances after we declare the class. This way, we will be able to determine the equality of instances of classes that implement the `AnimalProtocol` protocol. We can read the class declaration as "the `Animal` class implements both the `AnimalProtocol` and `Equatable` protocols." Take a look at the following code:

```
public class Animal: AnimalProtocol, Equatable {
    public let name: String
    
    public var danceCharacters: String {
        get {
            return String()
        }
    }
    
    public var spelledSound1: String {
        get {
            return String()
        }
    }
    
    public var spelledSound2: String {
        get {
            return String()
```

```swift
        }
    }

    public var spelledSound3: String {
        get {
            return String()
        }
    }

    public required init(name: String) {
        self.name = name
    }

    public func dance() {
        print("\(name) dances \(danceCharacters)")
    }

    public func say(message: String) {
        print("\(name) says: \(message)")
    }

    public func sayGoodbye(destination: AnimalProtocol) {
        print("\(name) says goodbye to \(destination.name): \
(spelledSound1) \(spelledSound2) \(spelledSound3)")
    }

    public func sayWelcome(destination: AnimalProtocol) {
        print("\(name) welcomes \(destination.name): \
(spelledSound2)")
    }

    public func sing() {
        let spelledSingSound = spelledSound1 + " ";
        let separator = ". "
        var song = "\(name) sings: "

        for _ in 1...3 {
            song += spelledSingSound
        }
        song += separator
        for _ in 1...2 {
            song += spelledSingSound
        }
        song += separator
```

```
        song += spelledSingSound
        song += separator

        print(song)
    }
}

public func ==(left: Animal, right: Animal) -> Bool {
    return ((left.dynamicType == right.dynamicType) && (left.name == right.name))
}
```

The `Animal` class declares an initializer that assigns the value of the required `name` argument to the read-only `name` stored property. Note that the initializer declaration uses the `required` keyword because it implements the initializer requirement specified in the `AnimalProtocol` protocol:

```
public required init(name: String) {
```

The class declared the following four `String` computed read-only properties. All of them define a getter method that returns an empty string and that the subclasses will override with the appropriate strings according to the animal:

- danceCharacters
- spelledSound1
- spelledSound2
- spelledSound2

The `dance` method uses the value retrieved from the `danceCharacters` property to print a message indicating that the animal is dancing. The `say` method prints the message received as an argument. Both the `sayWelcome` and `sayGoodbye` methods receive `AnimalProtocol` as an argument that they use to print the name of the destination of the message. The `sayWelcome` method uses a combination of the strings retrieved from `spelledSound1` and `spelledSound3` to say welcome to another animal. The `sayGoodbye` method uses the string retrieved from `spelledSound2` to say goodbye to another animal.

The `==` operator function receives two `Animal` instances as arguments and checks whether the value of the `name` property and type for both instances are the same. In a more complex scenario, we might want to code this method to compare the values of more properties to determine the equality. In our case, we will assume that the same animal with the same name is exactly the same animal. For example, two frogs named Kermit are considered to be one frog. Remember that we needed to write the `==` operator function to make the `Animal` class conform to the `Equatable` protocol.

If we comment out the lines that declare the == operator function, the `Animal` class won't conform to the `Equatable` protocol anymore:

```
/* public func ==(left: Animal, right: Animal) -> Bool {
    return ((left.dynamicType == right.dynamicType) && (left.name == right.name))
} */
```

After we comment out the previous lines, the execution in the Playground will fail, and we will see a long list of errors that include the following ones:

```
error: type 'Animal' does not conform to protocol 'Equatable'
public class Animal: AnimalProtocol, Equatable {

Swift.Equatable:28:8: note: protocol requires function '==' with type '(Animal, Animal) -> Bool'
    func ==(lhs: Self, rhs: Self) -> Bool
```

Swift indicates to us that the class doesn't conform to the `Equatable` protocol and specifies the function that the protocol requires and its declaration. However, the additional generated errors might confuse us.

The following screenshot shows the Playground with the generated errors after we comment out the previous lines that declared the == operator function:

Now that we have checked the results of removing the lines that declared the `==` operator function, we can uncomment it, and the `Animal` class will conform to the `Equatable` protocol again.

Declaring subclasses that inherit the conformance to protocols

We have an `Animal` class that conforms to both, the `AnimalProtocol` and `Equatable` protocols. Now, we will create a subclass of `Animal`, a `Dog` class that overrides the string computed properties defined in the `Animal` class to provide the appropriate values for a dog:

```
public class Dog: Animal {
    public override var spelledSound1: String {
        get {
            return "Woof"
        }
    }
    
    public override var spelledSound2: String {
        get {
            return "Wooooof"
        }
    }
    
    public override var spelledSound3: String {
        get {
            return "Grr"
        }
    }
    
    public override var danceCharacters: String {
        get {
            return "/-\\ \\\\-\\ /-/"
        }
    }
}
```

With just a few additional lines of code, we will create another subclass of `Animal`, which is a `Frog` class that also overrides the string's read-only properties defined in the `Animal` class to provide the appropriate values for a frog, as follows:

```
public class Frog: Animal {
    public override var spelledSound1: String {
        get {
```

```
            return "Ribbit"
        }
    }

    public override var spelledSound2: String {
        get {
            return "Croak"
        }
    }

    public override var spelledSound3: String {
        get {
            return "Croooaaak"
        }
    }

    public override var danceCharacters: String {
        get {
            return "/|\\ \\|/ ^ ^ "
        }
    }
}
```

Finally, we will create another subclass of Animal, which is a Lion class that also overrides the string's read-only properties defined in the Animal class to provide the appropriate values for a lion, as follows:

```
public class Lion: Animal {
    public override var spelledSound1: String {
        get {
            return "Roar"
        }
    }

    public override var spelledSound2: String {
        get {
            return "Rrroarrr"
        }
    }

    public override var spelledSound3: String {
        get {
            return "Rrrrrrroarrrrrr"
        }
    }
```

```
    public override var danceCharacters: String {
        get {
            return "*-* ** *|* ** "
        }
    }
}
```

We have three classes that inherit the conformance to protocols from its base class, which is `Animal`. The following three classes conform to both, the `AnimalProtocol` and `Equatable` protocols, without including the conformance within the class declaration but inheriting it:

- `Dog`
- `Frog`
- `Lion`

Declaring a class that works with a constrained generic type

The following lines declare a `PartyError` enum that conforms to the `ErrorType` protocol. This way, we will be able to throw a specific exception in the next class that we will create:

```
public enum PartyError: ErrorType {
    case InsufficientMembersToRemoveLeader
    case InsufficientMembersToVoteLeader
}
```

The following lines declare a `Party` class that takes advantage of generics to work with many types. The class name is followed by a less than sign (<), a `T` that identifies the generic type parameter, a colon (:), and a protocol name that the `T` generic type parameter must conform to, which is the `AnimalProtocol` protocol. Then, the `where` keyword, followed by `T` (which identified the type) and a colon (:) that indicates that the `T` generic type parameter has to be a type that also conforms to another protocol—that is, the `Equatable` protocol. Finally, the greater than sign (>) ends the type constraints declaration that is included within angle brackets (< >). The following code highlights the lines that use the `T` generic type parameter:

```
public class Party<T: AnimalProtocol where T: Equatable> {
    private var members = [T] ()

    public var leader: T
```

```
init(leader: T) {
    self.leader = leader
    members.append(leader)
}

public func addMember(member: T) {
    members.append(member)
    leader.sayWelcome(member)
}

public func removeMember(member: T) throws -> T? {
    if (member == leader) {
        throw PartyError.InsufficientMembersToRemoveLeader
    }
    if let memberIndex = members.indexOf(member) {
        let removedMember = members.removeAtIndex(memberIndex)
        removedMember.sayGoodbye(leader)
        return removedMember
    } else {
        return T?.None
    }
}

public func dance() {
    for (_, member) in members.enumerate() {
        member.dance()
    }
}

public func sing() {
    for (_, member) in members.enumerate() {
        member.sing()
    }
}

public func voteLeader() throws {
    if (members.count == 1) {
        throw PartyError.InsufficientMembersToVoteLeader
    }
    
    var newLeader = leader
    while (newLeader == leader) {
```

```
            let randomLeaderIndex = Int(arc4random_
uniform(UInt32(members.count)
            newLeader = members[randomLeaderIndex]
        }

        leader.say("\(newLeader.name) has been voted as our new party
leader.")
        newLeader.dance()
        leader = newLeader
    }
}
```

Now, we will analyze many code snippets to understand how the code included in the `Party<T>` class works. The following line starts the class body, declares a private `Array<T>` of the type specified by `T` and initializes it with an empty `Array<T>`. Array uses generics to specify the type of the elements that will be accepted and added to the array. In this case, we will use the array shorthand `[T]` that is equivalent to `Array<T>` — that is, an array of elements whose type is `T` or conforms to the `T` protocol, as follows:

```
private var members = [T]()
```

The previous line is equivalent to the following line:

```
private var members = Array<T>()
```

The following line declares a public `Leader` property whose type is `T`:

```
public var leader: T
```

The following lines declare an initializer that receives a `leader` argument whose type is `T`. The argument specifies the first party leader and also the first member of the party — that is, the first element added of `members Array<T>`:

```
init(leader: T) {
    self.leader = leader
    members.append(leader)
}
```

The following lines declare the `addMember` method that receives a `member` argument whose type is `T`. The code adds the member received as an argument to `members Array<T>` and calls the `leader.sayWelcome` method with `member` as an argument to make the party leader welcome the new member:

```
public func addMember(member: T) {
    members.append(member)
    leader.sayWelcome(member)
}
```

The following lines declare the `removeMember` method that receives a `member` argument whose type is `T`, returns an optional `T` (`T?`), and throws exceptions. The `throws` keyword after the method arguments and before the returned type indicates that the method can throw exceptions. The code checks whether the member to be removed is the party leader. The method throws a `PartyError.InsufficientMembersToRemoveLeader` exception in case the member is the party leader. The code returns an optional `T` (`T?`) that returns the result of calling the `removeAtIndex` method of the members `Array<T>` with the member received as an argument and calls the `sayGoodbye` method for the successfully removed member. This way, the member that leaves the party says goodbye to the party leader. In case the member isn't removed, the method returns `None`—specifically, `T?.None`:

```
public func removeMember(member: T) throws -> T? {
    if (member == leader) {
        throw PartyError.InsufficientMembersToRemoveLeader
    }
    if let memberIndex = members.indexOf(member) {
        let removedMember = members.removeAtIndex(memberIndex)
        removedMember.sayGoodbye(leader)
        return removedMember
    } else {
        return T?.None
    }
}
```

The following lines declare the `dance` method that calls the method with the same name for each member of `members Array<T>`. As we don't use the `final` keyword in the declaration, we will be able to override this method in a future subclass:

```
public func dance() {
    for (_, member) in members.enumerate() {
        member.dance()
    }
}
```

Maximization of Code Reuse with Generic Code

The following lines declare the `sing` method that calls the method with the same name for each member of `members Array<T>`. We will also be able to override this method in a future subclass:

```
public func sing() {
    for (_, member) in members.enumerate() {
        member.sing()
    }
}
```

Finally, the following lines declare the `voteLeader` method that throws exceptions. As it happened in another method, the `throws` keyword after the method arguments indicates that the method can throw exceptions. The code makes sure that there are at least two members in `members Array<T>` when we call this method. In case we just have one member, the method throws a `PartyError.InsufficientMembersToVoteLeader` exception. If we have at least two members, the code generates a new random leader for the party that is different from the existing one. The code calls the `say` method for the actual leader to make it explain to the other party members that another leader is voted. Finally, the code calls the `dance` method for the new leader and sets the new value to the `leader` stored property:

```
public func voteLeader() throws {
    if (members.count == 1) {
        throw PartyError.InsufficientMembersToVoteLeader
    }
    
    var newLeader = leader
    while (newLeader == leader) {
        let randomLeaderIndex = Int(arc4random_uniform(UInt32(members.count)))
        newLeader = members[randomLeaderIndex]
    }
    
    leader.say("\(newLeader.name) has been voted as our new party leader.")
    newLeader.dance()
    leader = newLeader
}
```

Using a generic class for multiple types

We can create instances of the Party<T> class by replacing the T generic type parameter with any type name that conforms to the constraints specified in the declaration of the Party<T> class. So far, we have three concrete classes that implement both the AnimalProtocol and Equatable protocols: Dog, Frog, and Lion. Thus, we can use Dog to create an instance of Party<Dog>—that is, a Party instance of Dog objects.

The following code shows the lines that create four instances of the Dog class: jake, duke, lady, and dakota. Then, the code creates a Party<Dog> instance named dogsParty and passes jake as the leader argument to the initializer. This way, we will create a party of dogs, and Jake is the party leader:

```
var jake = Dog(name: "Jake")
var duke = Dog(name: "Duke")
var lady = Dog(name: "Lady")
var dakota = Dog(name: "Dakota")
var dogsParty = Party<Dog>(leader: jake)
```

The dogsParty instance will only accept a Dog instance for all the arguments in which the class definition uses the generic type parameter named T. The following lines add the previously created three instances of Dog to the dogs' party by calling the addMember method:

```
dogsParty.addMember(duke)
dogsParty.addMember(lady)
dogsParty.addMember(dakota)
```

The following lines call the dance method to make all the dogs dance, remove a member that isn't the party leader, vote a new leader, and finally call the sing method to make all the dogs sing. We will add the try keyword before the calls to removeMember and voteLeader because these methods can throw exceptions. In this case, we don't check the result returned by removeMember:

```
dogsParty.dance()
try dogsParty.removeMember(duke)
try dogsParty.voteLeader()
dogsParty.sing()
```

Maximization of Code Reuse with Generic Code

The following lines create an instance of the `Dog` class named `coby`. Then, the code calls the `removeMember` method and prints a message in case the method returns an instance of `Dog`. If the optional `Dog` (`Dog?`) returned by the method does not contain a value, the code prints a message indicating that the dog isn't removed. Because we haven't added `Coby` to the dog's party, it won't be removed. Then, we will use similar code to remove `lady`. In case she was selected as the random leader, the method will throw an exception. In case she wasn't selected, the code will print a message indicating that `lady` is removed. Remember that the `removeMember` method returns `T?`, which in this case is translated into a `Dog?` return type:

```
var coby = Dog(name: "Coby")
if let removedMember = try dogsParty.removeMember(coby) {
    print("\(removedMember.name) has been removed")
} else {
    print("\(coby.name) hasn't been removed")
}
if let removedMember = try dogsParty.removeMember(lady) {
    print("\(removedMember.name) has been removed")
} else {
    print("\(lady.name) hasn't been removed")
}
```

The following lines show the output after we run the preceding code snippets in the Playground. However, don't forget that there is a random selection of the new leader, and the results will vary in each execution:

```
Jake welcomes Duke: Wooooof
Jake welcomes Lady: Wooooof
Jake welcomes Dakota: Wooooof
Jake dances /-\ \-\ /-/
Duke dances /-\ \-\ /-/
Lady dances /-\ \-\ /-/
Dakota dances /-\ \-\ /-/
Duke says goodbye to Jake: Woof Wooooof Grr
Jake says: Dakota has been voted as our new party leader.
Dakota dances /-\ \-\ /-/
Jake sings: Woof Woof Woof . Woof Woof . Woof .
Lady sings: Woof Woof Woof . Woof Woof . Woof .
Dakota sings: Woof Woof Woof . Woof Woof . Woof .
Coby hasn't been removed
Lady says goodbye to Dakota: Woof Wooooof Grr
Lady has been removed
```

The following screenshot shows the Playground with the execution results:

```
    var jake = Dog(name: "Jake")                                    Dog
    var duke = Dog(name: "Duke")                                    Dog
    var lady = Dog(name: "Lady")                                    Dog
    var dakota = Dog(name: "Dakota")                                Dog
    var dogsParty = Party<Dog>(leader: jake)                        Party<Dog>
    dogsParty.addMember(duke)                                       Party<Dog>
    dogsParty.addMember(lady)                                       Party<Dog>
    dogsParty.addMember(dakota)                                     Party<Dog>
    dogsParty.dance()                                               Party<Dog>
    try dogsParty.removeMember(duke)                                Dog
    try dogsParty.voteLeader()
    dogsParty.sing()                                                Party<Dog>
    var coby = Dog(name: "Coby")                                    Dog
    if let removedMember = try dogsParty.removeMember(coby) {
        print("\(removedMember.name) has been removed")
    } else {
        print("\(coby.name) hasn't been removed")                   "Coby hasn't been removed\n"

        Coby hasn't been removed



    }
    if let removedMember = try dogsParty.removeMember(lady) {
        print("\(removedMember.name) has been removed")             "Lady has been removed\n"

        Lady has been removed



    } else {
        print("\(lady.name) hasn't been removed")
    }
```

```
Jake welcomes Duke: Wooooof
Jake welcomes Lady: Wooooof
Jake welcomes Dakota: Wooooof
Jake dances /-\ \-\ /-/
Duke dances /-\ \-\ /-/
Lady dances /-\ \-\ /-/
Dakota dances /-\ \-\ /-/
Duke says goodbye to Jake: Woof Wooooof Grr
Jake says: Dakota has been voted as our new party leader.
Dakota dances /-\ \-\ /-/
Jake sings: Woof Woof Woof . Woof Woof . Woof .
Lady sings: Woof Woof Woof . Woof Woof . Woof .
Dakota sings: Woof Woof Woof . Woof Woof . Woof .
Coby hasn't been removed
Lady says goodbye to Dakota: Woof Wooooof Grr
Lady has been removed
```

We can use `Frog` to create an instance of `Party<Frog>`. The following code creates four instances of the `Frog` class: `frog1`, `frog2`, `frog3`, and `frog4`. Then, the code creates a `Party<Frog>` instance named `frogsParty` and passes `frog1` as the `leader` argument. This way, we can create a party of frogs, and `Frog #1` is their party leader:

```
var frog1 = Frog(name: "Frog #1")
var frog2 = Frog(name: "Frog #2")
```

Maximization of Code Reuse with Generic Code

```
var frog3 = Frog(name: "Frog #3")
var frog4 = Frog(name: "Frog #4")
var frogsParty = Party<Frog>(leader: frog1)
```

The `frogsParty` instance will only accept a `Frog` instance for all the arguments in which the class definition uses the generic type parameter named T. The following lines add the previously created three instances of `Frog` to the frogs' party by calling the `addMember` method:

```
frogsParty.addMember(frog2)
frogsParty.addMember(frog3)
frogsParty.addMember(frog4)
```

The following lines call the `dance` method to make all the frogs dance, remove a member that isn't the party leader, vote a new leader, and finally call the `sing` method to make all the frogs sing:

```
frogsParty.dance()
try frogsParty.removeMember(frog3)
try frogsParty.voteLeader()
frogsParty.sing()
```

The following lines show the output after we run the preceding code snippets in the Playground. However, don't forget that there is a random selection of the new frog's party leader, and the results will vary in each execution:

```
Frog #1 welcomes Frog #2: Croak
Frog #1 welcomes Frog #3: Croak
Frog #1 welcomes Frog #4: Croak
Frog #1 dances /|\ \|/ ^ ^
Frog #2 dances /|\ \|/ ^ ^
Frog #3 dances /|\ \|/ ^ ^
Frog #4 dances /|\ \|/ ^ ^
Frog #3 says goodbye to Frog #1: Ribbit Croak Croooaaak
Frog #1 says: Frog #2 has been voted as our new party leader.
Frog #2 dances /|\ \|/ ^ ^
Frog #1 sings: Ribbit Ribbit Ribbit . Ribbit Ribbit . Ribbit .
Frog #2 sings: Ribbit Ribbit Ribbit . Ribbit Ribbit . Ribbit .
Frog #4 sings: Ribbit Ribbit Ribbit . Ribbit Ribbit . Ribbit .
```

The following screenshot shows the Playground with the execution results:

```
var frog1 = Frog(name: "Frog #1")                    Frog
var frog2 = Frog(name: "Frog #2")                    Frog
var frog3 = Frog(name: "Frog #3")                    Frog
var frog4 = Frog(name: "Frog #4")                    Frog
var frogsParty = Party<Frog>(leader: frog1)          Party<Frog>
frogsParty.addMember(frog2)                          Party<Frog>
frogsParty.addMember(frog3)                          Party<Frog>
frogsParty.addMember(frog4)                          Party<Frog>
frogsParty.dance()                                   Party<Frog>
try frogsParty.removeMember(frog3)                   Frog
try frogsParty.voteLeader()
frogsParty.sing()                                    Party<Frog>
```

```
Frog #1 welcomes Frog #2: Croak
Frog #1 welcomes Frog #3: Croak
Frog #1 welcomes Frog #4: Croak
Frog #1 dances /|\ \|/ ^ ^
Frog #2 dances /|\ \|/ ^ ^
Frog #3 dances /|\ \|/ ^ ^
Frog #4 dances /|\ \|/ ^ ^
Frog #3 says goodbye to Frog #1: Ribbit Croak Croooaaak
Frog #1 says: Frog #2 has been voted as our new party leader.
Frog #2 dances /|\ \|/ ^ ^
Frog #1 sings: Ribbit Ribbit Ribbit . Ribbit Ribbit . Ribbit .
Frog #2 sings: Ribbit Ribbit Ribbit . Ribbit Ribbit . Ribbit .
Frog #4 sings: Ribbit Ribbit Ribbit . Ribbit Ribbit . Ribbit .
```

We can use `Lion` to create an instance of `Party<Lion>`. The following code creates three instances of the `Lion` class: `simba`, `nala`, and `mufasa`. Then, the code creates a `Party<Lion>` instance named `lionsParty` and passes `simba` as the `leader` argument. This way, we can create a party of lions, and Simba is the party leader:

```
var simba = Lion(name: "Simba")
var nala = Lion(name: "Nala")
var mufasa = Lion(name: "Mufasa")
var lionsParty = Party<Lion>(leader: simba)
```

The `lionsParty` instance will only accept a `Lion` instance for all the arguments in which the class definition uses the generic type parameter named `T`. The following lines add the previously created two instances of `Lion` to the lions' party by calling the `addMember` method:

```
lionsParty.addMember(nala)
lionsParty.addMember(mufasa)
```

The following lines call the `sing` method and then the `dance` method to make all the lions sing and dance. Then, the code calls the `voteLeader` method to select a new random leader and finally tries to remove `nala` from the party by calling the `removeMember` method:

```
lionsParty.sing()
lionsParty.dance()
try lionsParty.voteLeader()
try lionsParty.removeMember(nala)
```

The following lines show the output after we run the preceding code snippets in the Playground:

```
Simba welcomes Nala: Rrroarrr
Simba welcomes Mufasa: Rrroarrr
Simba sings: Roar Roar Roar . Roar Roar . Roar .
Nala sings: Roar Roar Roar . Roar Roar . Roar .
Mufasa sings: Roar Roar Roar . Roar Roar . Roar .
Simba dances *-* ** *|* **
Nala dances *-* ** *|* **
Mufasa dances *-* ** *|* **
Simba says: Mufasa has been voted as our new party leader.
Mufasa dances *-* ** *|* **
Nala says goodbye to Mufasa: Roar Rrroarrr Rrrrrrroarrrrrr
```

The following screenshot shows the Playground with the execution results:

```
var simba = Lion(name: "Simba")                          Lion
var nala = Lion(name: "Nala")                            Lion
var mufasa = Lion(name: "Mufasa")                        Lion
var lionsParty = Party<Lion>(leader: simba)              Party<Lion>
lionsParty.addMember(nala)                               Party<Lion>
lionsParty.addMember(mufasa)                             Party<Lion>
lionsParty.sing()                                        Party<Lion>
lionsParty.dance()                                       Party<Lion>
try lionsParty.voteLeader()
try lionsParty.removeMember(nala)                        Lion
```

```
Simba welcomes Nala: Rrroarrr
Simba welcomes Mufasa: Rrroarrr
Simba sings: Roar Roar Roar . Roar Roar . Roar .
Nala sings: Roar Roar Roar . Roar Roar . Roar .
Mufasa sings: Roar Roar Roar . Roar Roar . Roar .
Simba dances *-* ** *|* **
Nala dances *-* ** *|* **
Mufasa dances *-* ** *|* **
Simba says: Mufasa has been voted as our new party leader.
Mufasa dances *-* ** *|* **
Nala says goodbye to Mufasa: Roar Rrroarrr Rrrrrrroarrrrrr
```

If we try to call the `addMember` method with the wrong type for an instance of `Party<Lion>`, the code won't compile because Swift cannot convert an instance of `Dog` to the required argument type (`Lion`). Thus, the following line won't be executed in the Playground because `lady` is an instance of `Dog`:

```
lionsParty.addMember(lady)
```

Combining initializer requirements in protocols with generic types

We included an initializer requirement when we declared the `AnimalProtocol` protocol, so we know the necessary arguments to create an instance of any class that conforms to this protocol. We will add a new method that creates an instance of the generic type `T` and adds it to the party members in `Party<T>` class.

Maximization of Code Reuse with Generic Code

The following lines show the code for the new `createAndAddMember` method that receives a `name` `String` argument and returns an instance of the generic type `T`. We add the method to the body after the `Party<T: AnimalProtocol where T: Equatable> {` public class declaration:

```
public func createAndAddMember(name: String) -> T {
    let newMember = T(name: name)
    addMember(newMember)

    return newMember
}
```

The method uses the generic type `T` and passes the `name` argument to create a new instance called `newMember`. Then, the code calls the `addMember` method with `newMember` as an argument and finally returns the recently created instance.

The following lines call the recently added `createAndAddMember` method to create and add a new `Lion` instance with the name initialized to `King` to the `lionsParty Party<Lion>` instance. Then, the next line calls the `say` method for the returned instance:

```
let king = lionsParty.createAndAddMember("King")
king.say("My name is King")
```

The next lines show the output generated when we enter the previous lines at the end of our Playground:

```
Simba welcomes King: Rrroarrr
King says: My name is King
```

Declaring associated types in protocols

Now, we want to declare a `PartyProtocol` protocol and make the generic `Party<T>` class conform to this new protocol. The main challenge is to specify the type for both the method arguments and returned values. In the generic class, we will use the generic type parameter, but protocols don't allow us to use them.

Associated types allow us to solve the problem. We can declare one or more associated types as part of the protocol definition. In this case, we just need one associated type to provide us with a placeholder name — also known as alias — to a type that we will use as part of the protocol and that will be specified during the protocol implementation — that is, when we declare a class that conforms to the protocol. It is just necessary to use the `typealias` keyword followed by the desired name for the associated type, and then, we can use the name in our requirements' declarations.

The following lines show the declaration of the `PartyProtocol` protocol. We must declare the protocol before the `public class Party<T: AnimalProtocol where T: Equatable>: PartyProtocol {` line that starts the declaration of the `Party<T>` class that we want to edit to make it conform to this new protocol:

```
public protocol PartyProtocol {
    typealias MemberType
    
    init(leader: MemberType)
    
    func createAndAddMember(name: String) -> MemberType
    func addMember(member: MemberType)
    func removeMember(member: MemberType) throws -> MemberType?
    func dance()
    func sing()
    func voteLeader() throws
}
```

The first line within the protocol body declares an associated type named `MemberType`. Then, the initializer and method requirements use `MemberType` to specify the type that the generic class that conforms to this protocol will replace with the generic type parameter name.

The following code shows the first lines of the new declaration of the `Party<T>` class that conforms to the recently created `PartyProtocol`. After the type constraints included within angle brackets (< >), the class declaration adds a colon (:) followed by the protocol to which the generic class conforms: `PartyProtocol`. As we specified an initializer requirement in the `PartyProtocol` protocol, we have to add `public required` as a prefix before the `init` declaration. The rest of the code for the class remains without changes:

```
public class Party<T: AnimalProtocol where T: Equatable>:
PartyProtocol {
    private var members = [T]()
    
    public var leader: T
    
    public required init(leader: T) {
        self.leader = leader
        members.append(leader)
    }
    
    /* The rest of the code for the class remains without changes */
    
}
```

> The usage of an associated type in the protocol declaration allows us to create a protocol that can be implemented with a class that uses generics.

Creating shortcuts with subscripts

We want to create a shortcut to access the members of the party. Subscripts are very useful to generate shortcuts to access members of any array, collection, list, or sequence. Subscripts can define getter and/or setter methods that receive the argument specified in the subscript declaration. In this case, we will add a read-only subscript to allow us to retrieve a member of the party through its index value. Thus, the subscript will only define a getter method.

We will use `UInt` as the type for the `index` argument because we don't want negative integer values, and the getter for the subscript will return an optional type. In case the index value received is an invalid value, the getter will return `None`.

First, we will add the following line to the `PartyProtocol` protocol body:

```
subscript(index: UInt) -> MemberType? { get }
```

We included the `subscript` keyword followed by the argument name and its required type—which is the returned type, `MemberType?`—and the requirement for just a getter method, `get`. The requirements for the getter and/or setter methods are included with the same syntax we used for properties' requirements in protocols. Remember that `MemberType` is the associated type we added to the `PartyProtocol` protocol.

Now, we have to add the code that implements the previously defined subscript in the `Party<T>` class. We must add the following code after the `public class Party<T: AnimalProtocol where T: Equatable>: PartyProtocol {` line that starts the declaration of the `Party<T>` class that we want to edit to make it conform to the changes in the `PartyProtocol` protocol:

```
public subscript(index: UInt) -> T? {
    get {
        if (index <= UInt(members.count - 1)) {
            return members[Int(index)]
        } else {
            return T?.None
        }
    }
}
```

After making the preceding changes, we can specify an `UInt` value enclosed in square brackets after an instance of `Party<T>` to retrieve an instance of T — specifically T? — from the party. The following lines show examples of its usage with the `Party<Lion>` instance named `lionsParty`. The first two lines retrieve a `Lion` instance and print the value for its `name` property because the array has a member both at index 0 and index 1. However, the array doesn't have a member at index 50, so the `else` condition will be executed in this case:

```
if let lion = lionsParty[0] {
    print(lion.name)
}
if let lion = lionsParty[1] {
    print(lion.name)
}
if let lion = lionsParty[50] {
    print(lion.name)
} else {
    print("There is no lion with that index value")
}
```

The following lines show the output generated in the Playground after making the changes to the `PartyProtocol` protocol and the `Party<T>` class and executing the preceding code:

```
Simba
Nala
There is no lion with that index value
```

The following screenshot shows the Playground with the execution results:

```
    let king = lionsParty.createAndAddMember("King")         Lion
    king.say("My name is King")                              Lion

    if let lion = lionsParty[0] {
        print(lion.name)                                     "Simba\n"
    }
    if let lion = lionsParty[1] {
        print(lion.name)                                     "Nala\n"
    }
    if let lion = lionsParty[50] {
        print(lion.name)
    } else {
        print("There is no lion with that index value")      "There is no lion with that index value\n"
    }
```

```
Mufasa dances *-* ** *|* **
Simba welcomes King: Rrroarrr
King says: My name is King
Simba
Nala
There is no lion with that index value
```

Declaring a class that works with two constrained generic types

Now, it is time to code another protocol that will be used as a constraint later when we define another class that takes advantage of generics with two constrained generic types. The following lines show the code for the `DeeJayProtocol` protocol. The `public` modifier followed by the `protocol` keyword and the protocol name, `DeeJayProtocol`, composes the protocol declaration, as follows:

```
public protocol DeeJayProtocol {
    var name: String { get }

    init(name: String)

    func playMusicToDance()
    func playMusicToSing()
}
```

The protocol declares a `name String` read-only stored property and two method requirements: `playMusicToDance` and `playMusicToSing`. As you learned in the previous chapter, the protocol includes only the method declaration because the classes that conform to the `DeejayProtocol` protocol will be responsible for providing the implementation of the `name` stored property and the other two methods.

In addition, the protocol specifies an initializer requirement. The initializer requires a `name` argument; therefore, we will make sure that we will be able to create an instance of any class that conforms to this protocol by providing a value to a `name` argument during the initialization.

Now, we will declare a class named `HorseDeeJay` that conforms to the previously defined `DeeJayProtocol` protocol. We can read the class declaration as "the `HorseDeeJay` class implements the `DeeJayProtocol` protocol." Take a look at the following code:

```
public class HorseDeeJay: DeeJayProtocol {
    public let name: String

    public required init(name: String) {
        self.name = name
    }

    public func playMusicToDance() {
        print("My name is \(name). Let's Dance.")
        // Multiple musical notes emoji icon
```

```
            print(String(UnicodeScalar(0x01F3B6)))
            // Dancer emoji icon
            print(String(UnicodeScalar(0x01F483)))
        }

        public func playMusicToSing() {
            print("Time to sing!")
            // Guitar emoji icon
            print(String(UnicodeScalar(0x01F3B8)))
        }
    }
```

The `HorseDeeJay` class declares an initializer that assigns the value of the required `name` argument to the `name` read-only stored property. The class declares a name read-only stored property.

The `playMusicToDance` method prints a message that displays the horse DJ name and invites the party members to dance. Then, it prints the multiple musical notes and dancer emoji icons. The `playMusicToSing` method prints a message that invites the party members to sing. Then, it prints a guitar emoji icon.

The following lines declare a subclass of the previously created `Party<T>` class that takes advantage of generics to work with two constrained types. The type constraints declaration is included within angle brackets (< >). In this case, we have two generic type parameters: `T` and `K`. The generic type parameter named `T` must conform to the `AnimalProtocol` protocol and also the `Equatable` protocol, as it happened in the `Party<T>` superclass. The generic type parameter named `T` must conform to the `DeeJayProtocol` protocol. The `where` keyword allows us to add a second constraint to the generic type parameter named `T`. This way, the class specifies constraints for both the `T` and `K` generic type parameters. Don't forget that we are talking about a subclass of `Party<T>`. The following code highlights the lines that use the `K` generic type parameter:

```
    public class PartyWithDeeJay<T: AnimalProtocol, K: DeeJayProtocol
    where T: Equatable>: Party<T> {
        public var deeJay: K

        init(leader: T, deeJay: K) {
            self.deeJay = deeJay
            super.init(leader: leader)
        }

        public override func dance() {
            deeJay.playMusicToDance()
            super.dance()
```

```
    }

    public override func sing() {
        deeJay.playMusicToSing()
        super.sing()
    }
}
```

Now, we will analyze many code snippets to understand how the code included in the `PartyWithDeeJay<T, K>` class works. The following line starts the class body and declares a public `deeJay` stored property of the type specified by `K`:

```
public var deeJay: K
```

The following lines declare an initializer that receives two arguments—`leader` and `deeJay`—whose types are `T` and `K`. The arguments specify the first party leader, the first member of the party, and the DJ that will make the party members dance and sing. Note that the initializer calls the initializer defined in its superclass—that is, the `Party<T>` `init` method—with `leader` as an argument:

```
init(leader: T, deeJay: K) {
    self.deeJay = deeJay
    super.init(leader: leader)
}
```

The following lines declare a `dance` method that overrides the method with the same declaration included in the superclass. The code calls the `deeJay.playMusicToDance` method and then the `super.dance` method—that is, the `dance` method defined in the `Party<T>` superclass:

```
public override func dance() {
    deeJay.playMusicToDance()
    super.dance()
}
```

Finally, the following lines declare a `sing` method that overrides the method with the same declaration included in the superclass. The code calls the `deeJay.PlayMusicToSing` method and then calls the `super.sing` method—that is, the `sing` method defined in the `Party<T>` superclass:

```
public override func sing() {
    deeJay.playMusicToSing()
    super.sing()
}
```

Using a generic class with two generic type parameters

We can create instances of the `PartyWithDeeJay<T, K>` class by replacing both the T and K generic type parameters with any type names that conform to the constraints specified in the declaration of the `PartyWithDeeJay<T, K>` class. We have three concrete classes that implement both the `AnimalProtocol` and `Equatable` protocols: `Dog`, `Frog`, and `Lion`. We have one class that conforms to the `DeeJayProtocol` protocol: `HorseDeeJay`. Thus, we can use `Dog` and `HorseDeeJay` to create an instance of `PartyWithDeeJay<Dog, HorseDeeJay>`.

The following lines create a `HorseDeeJay` instance named `silver`. Then, the code creates a `PartyWithDeeJay<Dog, HorseDeeJay>` instance named `silverParty` and passes `jake` and `silver` as arguments. This way, we can create a party of dogs with a horse DJ, where Jake is the party leader, and Silver is the DJ:

```
var silver = HorseDeeJay(name: "Silver")
var silverParty = PartyWithDeeJay<Dog, HorseDeeJay>(leader: jake,
deeJay: silver)
```

The `silverParty` instance will only accept a `Dog` instance for all the arguments in which the class definition uses the generic type parameter named T. The following lines add the previously created three instances of `Dog` to the party by calling the `addMember` method:

```
silverParty.addMember(duke)
silverParty.addMember(lady)
silverParty.addMember(dakota)
```

The following lines call the `dance` method to make the DJ invite all the dogs to dance and then make them dance. Then, the code removes a member that isn't the party leader, votes on a new leader, and finally calls the `sing` method to make the DJ invite all the dogs to sing and then make them sing:

```
silverParty.dance()
try silverParty.removeMember(duke)
try silverParty.voteLeader()
silverParty.sing()
```

The following lines show the generated output after we run the added code. The lines don't include the emoji icons:

```
Jake welcomes Duke: Wooooof
Jake welcomes Lady: Wooooof
Jake welcomes Dakota: Wooooof
My name is Silver. Let's Dance.
Jake dances /-\ \-\ /-/
Duke dances /-\ \-\ /-/
Lady dances /-\ \-\ /-/
Dakota dances /-\ \-\ /-/
Duke says goodbye to Jake: Woof Wooooof Grr
Jake says: Lady has been voted as our new party leader.
Lady dances /-\ \-\ /-/
Time to sing!
Jake sings: Woof Woof Woof . Woof Woof . Woof .
Lady sings: Woof Woof Woof . Woof Woof . Woof .
Dakota sings: Woof Woof Woof . Woof Woof . Woof .
My name is Silver. Let's Dance.
Jake dances /-\ \-\ /-/
Duke dances /-\ \-\ /-/
Lady dances /-\ \-\ /-/
Dakota dances /-\ \-\ /-/
Duke says goodbye to Jake: Woof Grr Woof
Jake says: Lady has been voted as our new party leader.
Lady dances /-\ \-\ /-/
Time to sing!
Jake sings: Woof Woof Woof . Woof Woof . Woof .
Lady sings: Woof Woof Woof . Woof Woof . Woof .
Dakota sings: Woof Woof Woof . Woof Woof . Woof .
```

The following screenshot shows the Playground with the execution results, including the emoji icons:

```
    public override func dance() {
        deeJay.playMusicToDance()                           HorseDeeJay
        super.dance()
    }

    public override func sing() {
        deeJay.playMusicToSing()                            HorseDeeJay
        super.sing()
    }
}
var silver = HorseDeeJay(name: "Silver")                    HorseDeeJay
var silverParty = PartyWithDeeJay<Dog, HorseDeeJay>(leader: jake,   PartyWithDeeJay<Dog, HorseDeeJay>
    deeJay: silver)

silverParty.addMember(duke)                                 PartyWithDeeJay<Dog, HorseDeeJay>
silverParty.addMember(lady)                                 PartyWithDeeJay<Dog, HorseDeeJay>
silverParty.addMember(dakota)                               PartyWithDeeJay<Dog, HorseDeeJay>

silverParty.dance()                                         PartyWithDeeJay<Dog, HorseDeeJay>
try silverParty.removeMember(duke)                          Dog
try silverParty.voteLeader()
silverParty.sing()                                          PartyWithDeeJay<Dog, HorseDeeJay>
```

```
My name is Silver. Let's Dance.
🎵
🐎
Jake dances /-\ \-\ /-/
Duke dances /-\ \-\ /-/
Lady dances /-\ \-\ /-/
Dakota dances /-\ \-\ /-/
Duke says goodbye to Jake: Woof Wooooof Grr
Jake says: Lady has been voted as our new party leader.
Lady dances /-\ \-\ /-/
Time to sing!
🎸
Jake sings: Woof Woof Woof . Woof Woof . Woof .
Lady sings: Woof Woof Woof . Woof Woof . Woof .
Dakota sings: Woof Woof Woof . Woof Woof . Woof .
```

The following lines create a `PartyWithDeeJay<Frog, HorseDeeJay>` instance named `silverAndFrogsParty` and passes `frog1` and `silver` as arguments. This way, we can create a party of frogs with a horse DJ, where `Frog #1` is the party leader, and Silver is the DJ:

```
var silverAndFrogsParty = PartyWithDeeJay<Frog, HorseDeeJay>(leader: frog1, deeJay: silver)
```

Maximization of Code Reuse with Generic Code

The `silverAndFrogsParty` instance will only accept a `Frog` instance for all the arguments in which the class definition uses the generic type parameter named T. The following lines add the previously created two instances of `Frog` to the party by calling the `addMember` method:

```
silverAndFrogsParty.addMember(frog2)
silverAndFrogsParty.addMember(frog3)
```

The following lines call the `dance` method to make the DJ invite all the dogs to dance and then make them dance. Finally, the code calls the `sing` method to make the DJ invite all the dogs to sing and then make them sing:

```
silverAndFrogsParty.dance()
silverAndFrogsParty.sing()
```

The following lines show the generated output after we run the added code. The lines don't include the emoji icons:

```
Frog #1 welcomes Frog #2: Croak
Frog #1 welcomes Frog #3: Croak
My name is Silver. Let's Dance.
Frog #1 dances /|\ \|/ ^ ^
Frog #2 dances /|\ \|/ ^ ^
Frog #3 dances /|\ \|/ ^ ^
Time to sing!
Frog #1 sings: Ribbit Ribbit Ribbit . Ribbit Ribbit . Ribbit .
Frog #2 sings: Ribbit Ribbit Ribbit . Ribbit Ribbit . Ribbit .
Frog #3 sings: Ribbit Ribbit Ribbit . Ribbit Ribbit . Ribbit .
```

The following screenshot shows the Playground with the execution results, including the emoji icons:

Inheriting and adding associated types in protocols

Now, we want to declare a `PartyWithDeeJayProtocol` protocol and make the generic `PartyWithDeeJay<T, K>` class conform to this new protocol. We will make this protocol inherit from the previously created `PartyProtocol` that defined a `MemberType` associated type. Thus, the `PartyWithDeeJayProtocol` protocol will inherit this associated type. We have to specify another associated type that will be specified during the protocol implementation—that is, when we declare the class that conforms to the new protocol.

The following lines show the declaration of the `PartyWithDeeJayProtocol` protocol that inherits from the `PartyProtocol` protocol. We must declare the protocol before the `public class PartyWithDeeJay<T: AnimalProtocol, K: DeeJayProtocol where T: Equatable>: Party<T>` line that starts the declaration of the `Party<T, K>` class that we want to edit to make it conform to this new protocol:

```
public protocol PartyWithDeeJayProtocol: PartyProtocol {
    typealias DeeJayType

    init(leader: MemberType, deeJay: DeeJayType)
}
```

The first line within the protocol body declares an associated type named `DeeJayType`. Then, the initializer requirement uses the inherited `MemberType` type `typealias` and the new `DeeJayType` `typealias` to specify the types that the generic class that conforms to this protocol will replace with the generic type parameter names.

The following code shows the first lines of the new declaration of the `Party<T, K>` class that conforms to the recently created `PartyWithDeeJayProtocol` protocol. After the type constraints included within angle brackets (< >) and the colon (:) followed by the class from which the class inherits, `Party<T>`, the class declaration adds a comma (,), followed by the protocol to which the generic class conforms: `PartyWithDeeJayProtocol`. As we specified an initializer requirement in the `PartyWithDeeJayProtocol` protocol, we have to add `public required` as a prefix before the `init` declaration. The rest of the code for the class remains without changes:

```
public class PartyWithDeeJay<T: AnimalProtocol, K: DeeJayProtocol
where T: Equatable>: Party<T>, PartyWithDeeJayProtocol {
    public var deeJay: K

    public required init(leader: T, deeJay: K) {
        self.deeJay = deeJay
        super.init(leader: leader)
```

```
    }

    public override func dance() {
        deeJay.playMusicToDance()
        super.dance()
    }

    public override func sing() {
        deeJay.playMusicToSing()
        super.sing()
    }
}
```

Generalizing existing classes with generics

In *Chapter 3, Encapsulation of Data with Properties*, we created a class to represent a mutable 3D vector named `MutableVector3D` and a class to represent an immutable version of a 3D vector named `ImmutableVector3D`.

Both versions were capable of working with 3D vectors with `Float` values for x, y, and z. We now realize that we also have to work with 3D vectors with `Double` values for x, y, and z in both classes. We definitely don't want to create two new classes, such as `MutableDoubleVector3D` and `ImmutableDoubleVector3D`. We can take advantage of generics to create two classes capable of working with elements of any floating point type supported in Swift—that is, either `Float`, `Float80`, or `Double`.

We want to create the following two classes:

- `MutableVector3D<T>`
- `ImmutableVector3D<T>`

It seems to be a pretty simple task. We just have to replace `Float` with the generic type parameter, `T`, and change the class declaration to include the generic type constraint. However, we face a big problem: we don't have protocols that allow us to easily build the generic type constraint.

The three floating point types supported in Swift conform to `FloatingPointType`; therefore, our first approach might be to include this protocol name in the generic type constraint. This solution won't work in either the `MutableVector3D<T>` or `ImmutableVector3D<T>` class. However, it is important to understand why it doesn't work.

The following lines show the code for the new `MutableVector3D<T>` class that will generate an error that we will solve later. Note that the code doesn't work, and the highlighted lines within the `sum` method will generate errors:

```
public class MutableVector3D<T: FloatingPointType> {
    public var x: T
    public var y: T
    public var z: T

    init(x: T, y: T, z: T) {
        self.x = x
        self.y = y
        self.z = z
    }

    public func sum(deltaX: T, deltaY: T, deltaZ: T) {
        x += deltaX
        y += deltaY
        z += deltaZ
    }

    public func printValues() {
        print("X: \(self.x), Y: \(self.y), Z: \(self.z))")
    }
}
```

After we enter the previous code in the Playground, it will generate the following errors:

```
error: binary operator '+=' cannot be applied to two 'T' operands
        x += deltaX
        ~ ^ ~~~~~~
error: binary operator '+=' cannot be applied to two 'T' operands
        y += deltaY
        ~ ^ ~~~~~~
error: binary operator '+=' cannot be applied to two 'T' operands
        z += deltaZ
        ~ ^ ~~~~~~
```

Maximization of Code Reuse with Generic Code

The following screenshot shows the Playground with the generated errors:

```
public class MutableVector3D<T: FloatingPointType> {
    public var x: T
    public var y: T
    public var z: T

    init(x: T, y: T, z: T) {
        self.x = x
        self.y = y
        self.z = z
    }

    public func sum(deltaX: T, deltaY: T, deltaZ: T) {
        x += deltaX         Binary operator '+=' cannot be applied to two 'T' operands
        y += deltaY         Binary operator '+=' cannot be applied to two 'T' operands
        z += deltaZ         Binary operator '+=' cannot be applied to two 'T' operands
    }

    public func printValues() {
        print("X: \(self.x), Y: \(self.y), Z: \(self.z)")
    }
}
```

```
Playground execution failed: /var/folders/kv/5mbg_v3x6_l7ysvkvtvq5yxm0000gn/T/./lldb/3904/playground79.swift:110:11: error: binary operator
'+=' cannot be applied to two 'T' operands
    x += deltaX
    ~ ^  ~~~~~~
/var/folders/kv/5mbg_v3x6_l7ysvkvtvq5yxm0000gn/T/./lldb/3904/playground79.swift:111:11: error: binary operator '+=' cannot be applied to two
'T' operands
    y += deltaY
    ~ ^  ~~~~~~
/var/folders/kv/5mbg_v3x6_l7ysvkvtvq5yxm0000gn/T/./lldb/3904/playground79.swift:112:11: error: binary operator '+=' cannot be applied to two
'T' operands
    z += deltaZ
    ~ ^  ~~~~~~
```

The generated errors make it easy to understand the problem. The `FloatingPointType` protocol doesn't require the `+=` operator, so we cannot apply the `+=` operator to the `T` operands that just conform to this protocol.

Now, let's try to generate the `ImmutableVector3D<T>` class and check whether it works with a similar approach. The following lines show the code for the new `ImmutableVector3D<T>` class that will generate a different error that we will solve later. Note that the code doesn't work, and the highlighted line will generate an error:

```
public class ImmutableVector3D<T: FloatingPointType> {
    public let x: T
    public let y: T
    public let z: T

    init(x: T, y: T, z: T) {
        self.x = x
        self.y = y
        self.z = z
    }

    public func sum(deltaX: T, deltaY: T, deltaZ: T) -> ImmutableVector3D<T> {
        return ImmutableVector3D<T>(x: x + deltaX, y: y + deltaY, z: z + deltaZ)
```

```
    }

    public func printValues() {
        print("X: \(self.x), Y: \(self.y), Z: \(self.z))")
    }

    public class func equalElementsVector(initialValue: T) -> 
ImmutableVector3D<T> {
        return ImmutableVector3D<T>(x: initialValue, y: initialValue, 
z: initialValue)
    }
    public class func originVector() -> ImmutableVector3D<T> {
        return equalElementsVector(T(0))
    }
}
```

After we enter the previous code in the Playground, it will generate the following error:

```
error: binary operator '+' cannot be applied to two 'T' operands
        return ImmutableVector3D<T>(x: x + deltaX, y: y + deltaY, z: z 
+ deltaZ)
                                       ~ ^ ~~~~~~
```

The following screenshot shows the Playground with the generated error:

Maximization of Code Reuse with Generic Code

As in the previous case, the generated error makes it easy to understand the problem. The `FloatingPointType` protocol doesn't require the + operator, so we cannot apply the + operator to the T operands that just conform to this protocol.

Basically, we need all the floating point types to do the following:

- Provide an initializer that creates an instance initialized to zero
- Implement the + operator
- Implement the += operator

We just need to create a protocol that specifies these requirements and extends all the floating point types we want to be used as types in our `MutableVector3D<T>` and `ImmutableVector3D<T>` classes. We must extend these types to conform to the new protocol.

The following lines show the code that declares the new `NumericForVector` protocol:

```
public protocol NumericForVector {
    init()

    func +(lhs: Self, rhs: Self) -> Self
    func +=(inout lhs: Self, rhs: Self)
}
```

The protocol declares an initializer without arguments. All the numeric types provide an initializer without arguments to generate a value of the type initialized to zero. It is exactly what we need to initialize our `Immutable3DVector` to an origin vector.

Then, the protocol declares the + function that represents the + operator. The function requires two arguments, `lhs` and `rhs`, which are acronyms for left-hand side and right-hand side, to specify the values on the left-hand side and right-hand side of the operator. Both arguments are of the `Self` type.

> In protocols, `Self` means the actual type that implements the protocol, and it is different from `self` with a lowercase s that we use in methods and that refers to the actual instance. The + function returns `Self`, so the implementation of this function in Double receives two Double arguments and returns a Double argument with the result of the sum of the two received values. The implementation of this function in Float receives two Float arguments and returns a Float argument with the result of the sum of the the two received values.

Finally, the protocol declares the += function that represents the += operator. The function requires two arguments: lhs and rhs. In this case, the first argument is an in/out parameter as it includes the inout keyword at the start of the parameter definition. Thus, Swift passes the value of lhs and the function can modify it and pass it back out of the function to replace the original value. Both arguments are of the Self type and the += function returns Self.

Now, we have to extend all the floating point types we want to be used as types in our MutableVector3D<T> and ImmutableVector3D<T> classes to make it conform to the recently created NumericForVector protocol, as follows:

```swift
extension Double: NumericForVector { }
extension Float: NumericForVector { }
extension Float80: NumericForVector { }
```

We don't need to add code to make Double, Float, and Float80 conform to the new NumericForVector protocol because the three types already implement the necessary actions to conform to the protocol. We need to have a protocol that groups all the requirements to use it as a type constraint for the generic type in our two classes.

The following lines show the code for the new MutableVector3D<T> class that works as expected:

```swift
public class MutableVector3D<T: NumericForVector> {
    public var x: T
    public var y: T
    public var z: T
    
    init(x: T, y: T, z: T) {
        self.x = x
        self.y = y
        self.z = z
    }
    
    public func sum(deltaX: T, deltaY: T, deltaZ: T) {
        x += deltaX
        y += deltaY
        z += deltaZ
    }
    
    public func printValues() {
        print("X: \(self.x), Y: \(self.y), Z: \(self.z)")
    }
}
```

The class name is followed by a less than sign (<), a T that identifies the generic type parameter, a colon (:), and a protocol name that the T generic type parameter must conform to—that is, the NumericForVector protocol. The protocol specifies the requirement for a += function; therefore, the sum method can apply this operator to the stored properties (x, y, and z) and delta arguments (deltaX, deltaY, and deltaZ), all of them of the T type.

The following lines show the code for the new ImmutableVector3D<T> class that works as expected:

```swift
public class ImmutableVector3D<T: NumericForVector> {
    public let x: T
    public let y: T
    public let z: T

    init(x: T, y: T, z: T) {
        self.x = x
        self.y = y
        self.z = z
    }

    public func sum(deltaX: T, deltaY: T, deltaZ: T) -> ImmutableVector3D<T> {
        return ImmutableVector3D<T>(x: x + deltaX, y: y + deltaY, z: z + deltaZ)
    }

    public func printValues() {
        print("X: \(self.x), Y: \(self.y), Z: \(self.z)")
    }

    public class func equalElementsVector(initialValue: T) -> ImmutableVector3D<T> {
        return ImmutableVector3D<T>(x: initialValue, y: initialValue, z: initialValue)
    }

    public class func originVector() -> ImmutableVector3D<T> {
        let zero = T()
        return equalElementsVector(zero)
    }
}
```

The class name is followed by a less than sign (<), a T that identifies the generic type parameter, a colon (:), and a protocol name that the T generic type parameter must conform to—that is, the NumericForVector protocol. The protocol specifies the requirement for a + function, so the sum method can apply this operator to the stored properties (x, y, and z) and delta arguments (deltaX, deltaY, and deltaZ) to use the results as arguments to create a new instance of ImmutableVector3D<T>.

The originVector type method calls the initializer without arguments to create a value of the T type initialized to zero. We can use this initializer because we specified it as a requirement in the NumericForVector protocol.

Now, we can create instances of any of the following:

- MutableVector3D<Double>
- MutableVector3D<Float>
- MutableVector3D<Float80>
- ImmutableVector3D<Double>
- ImmutableVector3D<Float>
- ImmutableVector3D<Float80>

The following lines create instances of the previously enumerated—that is, both MutableVector3D and ImmutableVector3D—with the generic type parameter set to Double, Float, and Float80. The code also calls the sum and printValues methods for each instance:

```
let mutableVector0 = MutableVector3D<Double>(x: 10.1, y: 10.2, z: 10.3)
mutableVector0.sum(3.4, deltaY: 4.52, deltaZ: 3.32)
mutableVector0.printValues()

let mutableVector1 = MutableVector3D<Float>(x: 3.456, y: 9.231, z: 3.324)
mutableVector1.sum(3.411, deltaY: 4.232, deltaZ: 3.465)
mutableVector1.printValues()

let mutableVector2 = MutableVector3D<Float80>(x: 7.2345, y: 2.3489, z: 1.3485)
mutableVector2.sum(3.4113, deltaY: 1.2332, deltaZ: 1.3482)
mutableVector2.printValues()

let immutableVector0 = ImmutableVector3D<Double>(x: 10.1, y: 10.2, z: 10.3)
let immutableVector1 = immutableVector0.sum(3.4, deltaY: 4.52, deltaZ: 3.32)
```

```
immutableVector1.printValues()

let immutableVector2 = ImmutableVector3D<Float>(x: 3.456, y: 9.231, z:
3.324)
let immutableVector3 = immutableVector2.sum(3.411, deltaY: 4.232,
deltaZ: 3.465)
immutableVector3.printValues()

let immutableVector4 = ImmutableVector3D<Float80>(x: 7.2345, y:
2.3489, z: 1.3485)
let immutableVector5 = immutableVector4.sum(3.4113, deltaY: 1.2332,
deltaZ: 1.3482)
immutableVector5.printValues()
```

The following lines show the output generated by the preceding code:

```
X: 13.5, Y: 14.72, Z: 13.62)
X: 6.867, Y: 13.463, Z: 6.789)
X: 10.6458, Y: 3.5821, Z: 2.6967)
X: 13.5, Y: 14.72, Z: 13.62
X: 6.867, Y: 13.463, Z: 6.789
X: 10.6458, Y: 3.5821, Z: 2.6967
```

The following screenshot shows the Playground with the types generated in each line specified on the right-hand side:

[222]

Extending base types to conform to custom protocols

Now, we want to be able to use any of the integer types as types in our `MutableVector3D<T>` and `ImmutableVector3D<T>` classes. We just need to extend the desired types to make them conform to the previously created `NumericForVector` protocol.

We want to make the two classes capable of working with elements of any integer type supported in Swift—that is, any of the following types:

- `Int`
- `Int16`
- `Int32`
- `Int64`
- `Int8`
- `UInt`
- `UInt16`
- `UInt32`
- `UInt64`
- `UInt8`

The following lines extend the previously enumerated types to conform to the `NumericForVector` protocol:

```
// Signed integers
extension Int: NumericForVector { }
extension UInt: NumericForVector { }
extension Int16: NumericForVector { }
extension Int32: NumericForVector { }
extension Int64: NumericForVector { }
extension Int8: NumericForVector { }

// Unsigned integers
extension UInt16: NumericForVector { }
extension UInt32: NumericForVector { }
extension UInt64: NumericForVector { }
extension UInt8: NumericForVector { }
```

Maximization of Code Reuse with Generic Code

As it happened when we extended `Double`, `Float`, and `Float80` to conform to the `NumericForVector` protocol, we don't need to add any code to these new supported types because they already implement the necessary actions to conform to the protocol. Now, the two classes are capable of working with the integer types supported by Swift apart from the floating point types.

The following lines create instances of `MutableVector3D` and `ImmutableVector3D` with the generic type parameter set to `Int` and `UInt`. The code also calls the `sum` and `printValues` methods for each instance:

```
let mutableVector4 = MutableVector3D<Int>(x: -10, y: -11, z: -12)
mutableVector4.sum(7, deltaY: 8, deltaZ: 9)
mutableVector4.printValues()

let mutableVector5 = MutableVector3D<UInt>(x: 10, y: 11, z: 12)
mutableVector5.sum(7, deltaY: 8, deltaZ: 9)
mutableVector5.printValues()

let immutableVector6 = ImmutableVector3D<Int>(x: -7, y: -2, z: -1)
let immutableVector7 = immutableVector6.sum(3, deltaY: 12, deltaZ: 14)
immutableVector7.printValues()

let immutableVector8 = ImmutableVector3D<UInt>(x: 7, y: 2, z: 1)
let immutableVector9 = immutableVector8.sum(3, deltaY: 12, deltaZ: 14)
immutableVector9.printValues()
```

The following lines show the output generated by the preceding code:

```
X: -3, Y: -3, Z: -3)
X: 17, Y: 19, Z: 21)
X: -4, Y: 10, Z: 13
X: 10, Y: 14, Z: 15
```

The following screenshot shows the Playground with the types generated in each line specified on the right-hand side:

```
// Signed integers
extension Int: NumericForVector { }
extension Int16: NumericForVector { }
extension Int32: NumericForVector { }
extension Int64: NumericForVector { }
extension Int8: NumericForVector { }

// Unsigned integers
extension UInt: NumericForVector { }
extension UInt16: NumericForVector { }
extension UInt32: NumericForVector { }
extension UInt64: NumericForVector { }
extension UInt8: NumericForVector { }

let mutableVector4 = MutableVector3D<Int>(x: -10, y: -11, z: -12)     MutableVector3D<Int>
mutableVector4.sum(7, deltaY: 8, deltaZ: 9)                           MutableVector3D<Int>
mutableVector4.printValues()                                          MutableVector3D<Int>

let mutableVector5 = MutableVector3D<UInt>(x: 10, y: 11, z: 12)       MutableVector3D<UInt>
mutableVector5.sum(7, deltaY: 8, deltaZ: 9)                           MutableVector3D<UInt>
mutableVector5.printValues()                                          MutableVector3D<UInt>

let immutableVector6 = ImmutableVector3D<Int>(x: -7, y: -2, z: -1)    ImmutableVector3D<Int>
let immutableVector7 = immutableVector6.sum(3, deltaY: 12, deltaZ: 14) ImmutableVector3D<Int>
immutableVector7.printValues()                                        ImmutableVector3D<Int>

let immutableVector8 = ImmutableVector3D<UInt>(x: 7, y: 2, z: 1)      ImmutableVector3D<UInt>
let immutableVector9 = immutableVector8.sum(3, deltaY: 12, deltaZ: 14) ImmutableVector3D<UInt>
immutableVector9.printValues()                                        ImmutableVector3D<UInt>
```

```
X: -3, Y: -3, Z: -3)
X: 17, Y: 19, Z: 21)
X: -4, Y: 10, Z: 13
X: 10, Y: 14, Z: 15
```

Test your knowledge

1. When we declare protocols, the `Self` keyword signifies:
    1. The type that implements the protocol.
    2. The instance of a class that conforms to the protocol.
    3. The instance of a struct that conforms to the protocol.

2. Generics allow us to declare a class that:
    1. Can use a generic type only as the type for stored and type properties.
    2. Can use a genric type only as an argument for its initializers.
    3. Can work with many generic types.

3. The `public class ImmutableVector3D<T: FloatingPointType>` line means:
    1. The generic type constraint specifies that T must conform to the `ImmutableVector3D` protocol or belong to the `ImmutableVector3D` class hierarchy.
    2. The generic type constraint specifies that T must conform to the `FloatingPointType` protocol or belong to the `FloatingPointType` class hierarchy.
    3. The class is a subclass of `FloatingPointType`.
4. The `public class Party<T: AnimalProtocol where T: Equatable>` line means:
    1. The generic type constraint specifies that T must conform to both the `AnimalProtocol` and `Equatable` protocols.
    2. The generic type constraint specifies that T must conform to either the `AnimalProtocol` or `Equatable` protocol.
    3. The class is a subclass of both the `AnimalProtocol` and `Equatable` classes.
5. The `typealias` keyword followed by the desired name allows us to declare:
    1. The generic type constraints, which is equivalent to the `where` keyword.
    2. An associated type for a protocol.
    3. An alias name for the protocol name.

Exercises

Add the following operators to work with both `MutableVector3D<T>` and `ImmutableVector3D<T>`:

- `==`: This determines whether all the elements that compose a 3D vector (x, y, and z) are equal.
- `+`: This sums each element that composes a 3D vector and saves the result in each element or in the new returned instance according to the class version (mutable or immutable). The new x must have the result of the left-hand side x + right-hand side x, the new y must be that of left-hand side y + right-hand side y, and the new z must be that of left-hand side z + right-hand side z.

In *Chapter 4, Inheritance, Abstraction, and Specialization* we created an `Animal` class and then defined specific operator functions to allow us to use operators with instances of this class. Redefine this class to conform to both the `Comparable` and `Equatable` protocols.

The following lines show the source code for the `Equatable` protocol:

```
public protocol Equatable {
    @warn_unused_result
    public func ==(lhs: Self, rhs: Self) -> Bool
}
```

The following lines show the source code for the `Comparable` protocol, which inherits from the `Equatable` protocol.

```
public protocol Comparable : Equatable {
    @warn_unused_result
    public func <(lhs: Self, rhs: Self) -> Bool
    @warn_unused_result
    public func <=(lhs: Self, rhs: Self) -> Bool
    @warn_unused_result
    public func >=(lhs: Self, rhs: Self) -> Bool
    @warn_unused_result
    public func >(lhs: Self, rhs: Self) -> Bool
}
```

Implement all the necessary operator functions to make the `Animal` class conform to both the protocols.

Summary

In this chapter, you learned how to maximize code reuse by writing code capable of working with objects of different types—that is, instances of classes that conform to specific protocols or whose class hierarchy includes specific superclasses. We worked with protocols and generics. We created classes capable of working with one or two constrained generic types.

We combined inheritance, protocols, and extensions to maximize the reusability of code. We could make classes work with many different types.

Now that we have learned about parametric polymorphism and generics, we are ready to combine object-oriented programming and functional programming, which is the topic of the next chapter.

7
Object-Oriented Programming and Functional Programming

In this chapter, we will refactor an existing code that doesn't use an object-oriented programming approach and make it easier to understand, expand, and maintain. We will discuss functional programming and how Swift implements many functional programming concepts. We will work with many examples of how to mix functional programming with object-oriented programming.

Refactoring code to take advantage of object-oriented programming

Sometimes, we are extremely lucky and have the possibility to follow best practices as we kick off a project. If we start writing object-oriented code from scratch, we can take advantage of all the features that we used in our examples throughout the book. As the requirements evolve, we might need to further generalize or specialize the blueprints. However, as we started our project with an object-oriented approach and by organizing our code, it is easier to make adjustments to the code.

Most of the time, we aren't extremely lucky and have to work on projects that don't follow best practices, and we, in the name of agility, generate pieces of code that perform similar tasks but without decent organization. Instead of following the same bad practices that generate error-prone, repetitive, and difficult-to-maintain code, we can use the features provided by Xcode and additional helper tools to refactor existing code and generate object-oriented code that promotes code reuse and allows us to reduce maintenance headaches.

Object-Oriented Programming and Functional Programming

For example, imagine that we have to develop a universal app that allows us to work with 3D models and render them on the device screen. The requirements specify that the first 3D models that we will have to render are two: a sphere and a cube. The application must allow us to change the parameters of a perspective camera that allows us to see a specific part of the 3D world rendered on a 2D screen (refer to Figure 1 and Figure 2):

- The X, Y, and Z positions
- The X, Y, and Z directions
- The X, Y, and Z up vectors

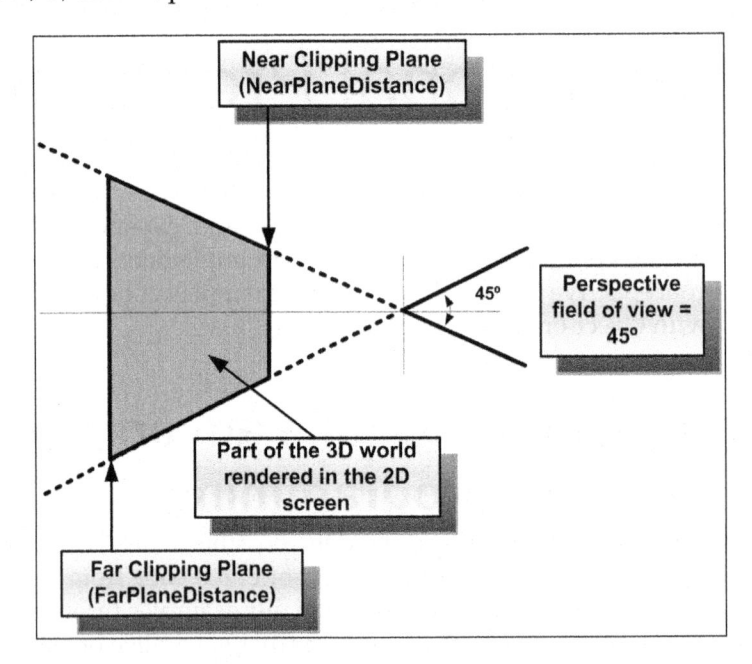

In addition, the application must allow us to change the values for the following parameters:

- **The perspective field of view in degrees**: This value determines the angle for the perspective camera's lens. A low value for this angle narrows the view. Thus, the models will appear larger in the lens with a perspective field of view of 45 degrees. A high value for this angle widens the view, so the models appear smaller in the visible part of the 3D world.

- **The near clipping plane**: The 3D region, which is visible on the 2D screen, is formed by a clipped pyramid called a frustum. This value controls the position of the plane that slices the top of the pyramid and determines the nearest part of the 3D world that the camera will render on the 2D screen. As the value is expressed taking into account the Z-axis, it is a good idea to add code to check whether we are entering a valid value for this parameter.
- **The far clipping plane**: This value controls the position of the plane that slices the back of the pyramid and determines the more distant part of the 3D world that the camera will render on the 2D screen. The value is also expressed taking into account the Z -axis; therefore, it is a good idea to add code to check whether we are entering a valid value for this parameter.

In addition, we can change the color of a directional light—that is, one that casts light in a specific direction, similar to sunlight.

Imagine that other developers started working on the project and generated a single Swift file with a class wrapper that declares many type methods that render a cube and a sphere. These functions receive all the necessary parameters to render each 3D figure—including the **X**, **Y**, and **Z** positions—determine the 3D figure's size, and configure the camera and directional light:

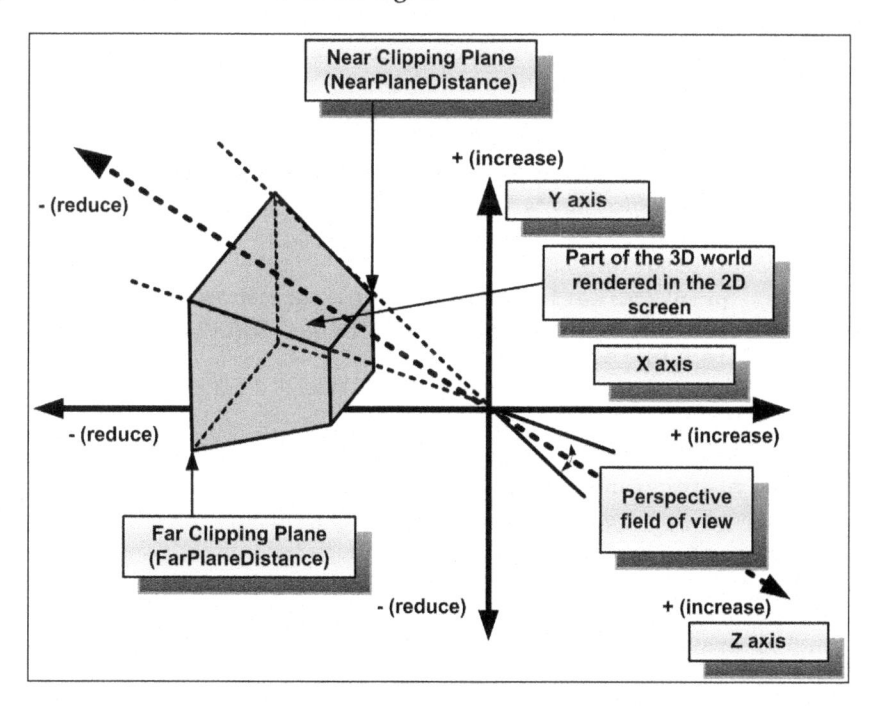

Object-Oriented Programming and Functional Programming

The following lines show an example of the declaration of a `SphereAndCube` class with two type methods: `renderSphere` and `renderCube`. As we might guess from the type method names, the first one renders a sphere, and the second one renders a cube:

```
public class SphereAndCube {
    public static func renderSphere(
        x: Int, y: Int, z: Int, radius: Int,
        cameraX: Int, cameraY: Int, cameraZ: Int,
        cameraDirectionX: Int, cameraDirectionY: Int,
cameraDirectionZ: Int,
        cameraVectorX: Int, cameraVectorY: Int, cameraVectorZ: Int,
        cameraPerspectiveFieldOfView: Int,
        cameraNearClippingPlane: Int,
        cameraFarClippingPlane: Int,
        directionalLightX: Int, directionalLightY: Int,
directionalLightZ: Int,
        directionalLightColor: Int) {
            print("Creating camera at X:\(cameraX), Y:\(cameraY), Z:\
(cameraZ)")
            print("Setting camera direction to X:\(cameraDirectionX),
Y:\(cameraDirectionY), Z:\(cameraDirectionZ)")
            print("Setting camera vector to X:\(cameraVectorX), Y:\
(cameraVectorY), Z:\(cameraVectorZ)")
            print("Setting camera perspective field of view to: \
(cameraPerspectiveFieldOfView)")
            print("Setting camera near clipping plane to: \
(cameraNearClippingPlane)")
            print("Setting camera far clipping plane to: \
(cameraFarClippingPlane)")
            print("Creating directional light at X:\
(directionalLightX), Y:\(directionalLightY), Z:\(directionalLightZ).
Light color is \(directionalLightColor)")
            print("Drawing sphere at X:\(x), Y:\(y), Z:\(z)")
    }

    public static func renderCube(
        x: Int, y: Int, z: Int, edgeLength: Int,
        cameraX: Int, cameraY: Int, cameraZ: Int,
        cameraDirectionX: Int, cameraDirectionY: Int,
cameraDirectionZ: Int,
        cameraVectorX: Int, cameraVectorY: Int, cameraVectorZ: Int,
        cameraPerspectiveFieldOfView: Int,
        cameraNearClippingPlane: Int,
        cameraFarClippingPlane: Int,
```

```
        directionalLightX: Int, directionalLightY: Int,
directionalLightZ: Int,
        directionalLightColor: Int) {
            print("Creating camera at X:\(cameraX), Y:\(cameraY), Z:\
(cameraZ)")
            print("Setting camera direction to X:\(cameraDirectionX),
Y:\(cameraDirectionY), Z:\(cameraDirectionZ)")
            print("Setting camera vector to X:\(cameraVectorX), Y:\
(cameraVectorY), Z:\(cameraVectorZ)")
            print("Setting camera perspective field of view to: \
(cameraPerspectiveFieldOfView)")
            print("Setting camera near clipping plane to: \
(cameraNearClippingPlane)")
            print("Setting camera far clipping plane to: \
(cameraFarClippingPlane)")
            print("Creating directional light at X:\
(directionalLightX), Y:\(directionalLightY), Z:\(directionalLightZ).
Light color is \(directionalLightColor)")
            print("Drawing cube at X:\(x), Y:\(y), Z:\(z)")
    }
}
```

Each type method requires a huge number of parameters. Let's imagine that we have the requirement to add code to render additional shapes and add different types of cameras and lights. The code can easily become a really big mess, repetitive, and difficult to maintain.

In *Chapter 3, Encapsulation of Data with Properties,* we worked with both mutable and immutable versions of a class that represented a 3D vector. Then, we learned to overload operators and take advantage of generics. We created an improved version of both the mutable and immutable versions of the 3D vector in *Chapter 6, Maximization of Code Reuse with Generic Code.*

The first change we can make is to work with `MutableVector3D<Int>` instead of working with separate *X*, *Y*, and *Z* values. However, we won't use the same code we created in the previous chapter because we want a different behavior. We will create a new version of the `NumericForVector` protocol that will allow us to specify all the requirements that any numeric type must implement in order to use it as the generic type parameter for the new `MutableVector3D` class. In this case, we will just include a parameterless initializer. However, we will need to add many operators as we expand the `ImmutableVector3D` class. Therefore, in this case, we will just include the protocol to have our code ready for future requirements.

Object-Oriented Programming and Functional Programming

The following lines show the code that declares the new `NumericForVector` protocol:

```
public protocol NumericForVector {
    init()
}
```

Now, we have to extend the existing `Int` type that we want to use for our `ImmutableVector3D<T>` class to make it conform to the recently created `NumericForVector` protocol:

```
extension Int: NumericForVector { }
```

The following lines show the code for the new `ImmutableVector3D<T>` class:

```
public class MutableVector3D<T: NumericForVector> {
    public var x: T
    public var y: T
    public var z: T

    public var stringRepresentation: String {
        get {
            return String("X: \(self.x), Y: \(self.y), Z: \(self.z)")
        }
    }

    init(x: T, y: T, z: T) {
        self.x = x
        self.y = y
        self.z = z
    }

    public class func equalElementsVector(initialValue: T) -> MutableVector3D<T> {
        return MutableVector3D<T>(x: initialValue, y: initialValue, z: initialValue)
    }

    public class func originVector() -> MutableVector3D<T> {
        let zero = T()
        return equalElementsVector(zero)
    }
}
```

[234]

The code doesn't overload operators because we want to keep our focus on the refactoring process. The class declares a `stringRepresentation` read-only computed property of the `String` type that returns a string with the values for the x, y, and z constants. The `SphereAndCube.renderSphere` and `SphereAndCube.renderCube` type methods print the values for the x, y, and z coordinates of many elements that compose the scene. We will generalize the generation of the string representation that will allow us to print the values.

We will create a simple protocol named `SceneElementProtocol` to specify the requirements for scene elements, as follows:

```
public protocol SceneElementProtocol {
    var location: MutableVector3D<Int> { get set }

    init(location: MutableVector3D<Int>)
}
```

The following lines declare the `SceneElement` class that adopts the previously defined `SceneElementProtocol` protocol. The class represents a 3D element that is part of a scene and has a location specified with `MutableVector3D<Int>`. It is the base class for all the scene elements that require a location in the 3D space:

```
public class SceneElement: SceneElementProtocol {
    public var location: MutableVector3D<Int>
}
```

The following lines declare another abstract class named `Light` that is a subclass of the previously defined `SceneElement` class. The class represents a 3D light and is the base class for all the lights that might be included in a scene. In this case, the class declaration is empty, and we only declare it because we know that there will be many types of lights, and we want to be able to generalize the common requirements for all types of lights in the future. We are preparing the code for further enhancements:

```
public class Light: SceneElement {

}
```

The following lines declare a subclass of `Light` named `DirectionalLight`. The class represents a directional light and adds a `color` stored property. In this case, we don't add validations for the property setters just to make the example simple. However, we already know how to do it:

```
public class DirectionalLight: Light
{
```

Object-Oriented Programming and Functional Programming

```
    public var color: Int

    init(location: MutableVector3D<Int>, color: Int) {
        self.color = color
        super.init(location: location)
    }
}
```

The following lines declare a class named `Camera` that inherits from `SceneElement`. The class represents a 3D camera. It is the base class for all cameras. In this case, the class declaration is empty, and we only declare it because we know that there will be many types of cameras. Also, we want to be able to generalize the common requirements for all types of cameras in the future as we did for the lights:

```
public class Camera: SceneElement {

}
```

The following lines declare a subclass of `Camera` named `PerspectiveCamera`. The class represents a perspective camera and adds the following `ImmutableVector3D<Int>` stored properties: `direction` and `vector`. In addition, the class adds the following three stored properties: `fieldOfView`, `nearClippingPlane`, and `farClippingPlane`:

```
public class PerspectiveCamera: Camera {
    public var direction: MutableVector3D<Int>
    public var vector: MutableVector3D<Int>
    public var fieldOfView: Int
    public var nearClippingPlane: Int
    public var farClippingPlane: Int

    init(location: MutableVector3D<Int>, direction: MutableVector3D<Int>, vector: MutableVector3D<Int>, fieldOfView: Int, nearClippingPlane: Int, farClippingPlane: Int) {
        self.direction = direction
        self.vector = vector
        self.fieldOfView = fieldOfView
        self.nearClippingPlane = nearClippingPlane
        self.farClippingPlane = farClippingPlane
        super.init(location: location)
    }
}
```

Chapter 7

The following lines declare a class named `Shape` that inherits from `SceneElement`. The class represents a 3D shape and is the base class for all the 3D shapes. The class defines a `render` method that receives a `Camera` instance and an array of `Light` instances. Each subclass that implements a specific shape will be able to override the empty `render` method to render a specific shape:

```
public class Shape: SceneElement
{
    public func render(camera: Camera, lights: [Light]) {

    }
}
```

The following lines declare a `Sphere` class, a subclass of `Shape` that adds a `radius` property and overrides the `render` method defined in its superclass to render a sphere:

```
public class Sphere: Shape {
    public var radius: Int

    init(location: MutableVector3D<Int>, radius: Int) {
        self.radius = radius
        super.init(location: location)
    }

    public override func render(camera: Camera, lights: [Light]) {
        print("Drawing sphere at \(location.stringRepresentation)")
    }
}
```

The following lines declare a `Cube` class, a subclass of `Shape` that adds an `edgeLength` property and overrides the `render` method defined in its superclass to render a cube:

```
public class Cube: Shape {
    public var edgeLength: Int

    init(location: MutableVector3D<Int>, edgeLength: Int) {
        self.edgeLength = edgeLength
        super.init(location: location)
    }

    public override func render(camera: Camera, lights: [Light]) {
        print("Drawing cube at \(location.stringRepresentation)")
    }
}
```

Object-Oriented Programming and Functional Programming

Finally, the following lines declare the `Scene` class that represents the scene to be rendered. The class defines an `activeCamera` private stored property that holds a `Camera` instance. The `lights` private stored property is an array of `Light` instances, and the `shapes` private stored property is an array of `Shape` instances that compose the scene. The `addLight` method adds a `Light` instance to the `lights` array. The `addShape` method adds a `Shape` instance to the `shapes` array. Finally, the `render` method prints some details about the scene that is set up based on the types of camera and lights. Then, this method calls the `render` method for each of the `Shape` instances included in the `shapes` array and passes the `activeCamera` and `lights` arrays as arguments:

```
public class Scene {
    private var lights = [Light]()
    private var shapes = [Shape]()
    private var activeCamera: Camera

    init(initialCamera: Camera) {
        activeCamera = initialCamera
    }

    public func addLight(light: Light) {
        lights.append(light)
    }

    public func addShape(shape: Shape) {
        shapes.append(shape)
    }

    public func render() {
        print("Creating camera at \(activeCamera.location.stringRepresentation)")
        if let perspectiveCamera = activeCamera as? PerspectiveCamera {
            print("Setting camera direction to \(perspectiveCamera.direction.stringRepresentation)")
            print("Setting camera vector to \(perspectiveCamera.vector.stringRepresentation)")
            print("Setting camera perspective field of view to: \(perspectiveCamera.fieldOfView)")
            print("Setting camera near clipping plane to: \(perspectiveCamera.nearClippingPlane)")
            print("Setting camera far clipping plane to: \(perspectiveCamera.farClippingPlane)")
        }
        for light in lights {
            if let directionalLight = light as? DirectionalLight {
```

```
            print("Creating directional light at \
(directionalLight.location.stringRepresentation). Light color is \
(directionalLight.color)")
        } else {
            print("Creating light at \(light.location.
stringRepresentation)")
        }
    }

    for shape in shapes {
        shape.render(activeCamera, lights: lights)
    }
  }
}
```

After we create the previously shown classes, we can enter the following code in the Playground:

```
var camera = PerspectiveCamera(location: MutableVector3D<Int>.
equalElementsVector(30),
    direction: MutableVector3D<Int>(x: 50, y: 0, z: 0),
    vector: MutableVector3D<Int>(x: 4, y: 5, z: 2),
    fieldOfView: 90, nearClippingPlane: 20, farClippingPlane: 40)
var sphere = Sphere(location: MutableVector3D<Int>(x: 20, y: 20, z:
20), radius: 8)
var cube = Cube(location: MutableVector3D<Int>.
equalElementsVector(10), edgeLength: 5)
var light = DirectionalLight(location: MutableVector3D<Int>(x: 2, y:
2, z: 5), color: 235)

var scene = Scene(initialCamera: camera)
scene.addShape(sphere)
scene.addShape(cube)
scene.addLight(light)

scene.render()
```

The code is very easy to understand and read. We will create a `PerspectiveCamera` instance with the necessary parameters and then create two shapes: `Sphere` and `Cube`. Finally, we will create `DirectionalLight` with all the necessary parameters and `Scene` with the previously created `PerspectiveCamera` as the initial camera. Then, we will add the shapes and light to the scene and call the `render` method to render the scene. The following lines show the generated output:

```
Creating camera at X: 30, Y: 30, Z: 30
Setting camera direction to X: 50, Y: 0, Z: 0
Setting camera vector to X: 4, Y: 5, Z: 2
Setting camera perspective field of view to: 90
```

Object-Oriented Programming and Functional Programming

```
Setting camera near clipping plane to: 20
Setting camera far clipping plane to: 40
Creating directional light at X: 2, Y: 2, Z: 5. Light color is 235
Drawing sphere at X: 20, Y: 20, Z: 20
Drawing cube at X: 10, Y: 10, Z: 10
```

Now, compare the previous code with the following lines that call the `SphereAndCube.renderSphere` and `SphereAndCube.renderCube` methods with more than a dozen parameters:

```
SphereAndCube.renderCube(10, y: 20, z: 30, edgeLength: 50,
cameraX: 25, cameraY: 25, cameraZ: 70, cameraDirectionX: 30,
cameraDirectionY: 20, cameraDirectionZ: 35, cameraVectorX: 11,
cameraVectorY: 15, cameraVectorZ: 25, cameraPerspectiveFieldOfView:
140, cameraNearClippingPlane: 150, cameraFarClippingPlane: 160,
directionalLightX: 30, directionalLightY: 30, directionalLightZ: 25,
directionalLightColor: 156)

SphereAndCube.renderSphere(10, y: 15, z: 25, radius: 32,
cameraX: 25, cameraY: 35, cameraZ: 10, cameraDirectionX: 30,
cameraDirectionY: 35, cameraDirectionZ: 10, cameraVectorX: 62,
cameraVectorY: 5, cameraVectorZ: 2, cameraPerspectiveFieldOfView:
7, cameraNearClippingPlane: 20, cameraFarClippingPlane: 30,
directionalLightX: 5, directionalLightY: 4, directionalLightZ: 7,
directionalLightColor: 232)
```

The following screenshot shows the object-oriented version and the call to the two type methods. The object-oriented version is definitely easier to read and understand. In addition, there is almost always a lot less code duplication:

```
var camera = PerspectiveCamera(location: MutableVector3D<Int>.equalElementsVector(30),    PerspectiveCamera
    direction: MutableVector3D<Int>(x: 50, y: 0, z: 0),
    vector: MutableVector3D<Int>(x: 4, y: 5, z: 2),
    fieldOfView: 90, nearClippingPlane: 20, farClippingPlane: 40)
var sphere = Sphere(location: MutableVector3D<Int>(x: 20, y: 20, z: 20), radius: 8)       Sphere
var cube = Cube(location: MutableVector3D<Int>.equalElementsVector(10), edgeLength: 5)    Cube
var light = DirectionalLight(location: MutableVector3D<Int>(x: 2, y: 2, z: 5), color: 235)  DirectionalLight
var scene = Scene(initialCamera: camera)                                                  Scene
scene.addShape(sphere)                                                                    Scene
scene.addShape(cube)                                                                      Scene
scene.addLight(light)                                                                     Scene
scene.render()                                                                            Scene

SphereAndCube.renderCube(10, y: 20, z: 30, edgeLength: 50, cameraX: 25, cameraY: 25,
    cameraZ: 70, cameraDirectionX: 30, cameraDirectionY: 20, cameraDirectionZ: 35,
    cameraVectorX: 11, cameraVectorY: 15, cameraVectorZ: 25, cameraPerspectiveFieldOfView:
    140, cameraNearClippingPlane: 150, cameraFarClippingPlane: 160, directionalLightX: 30,
    directionalLightY: 30, directionalLightZ: 25, directionalLightColor: 156)

SphereAndCube.renderSphere(10, y: 15, z: 25, radius: 32, cameraX: 25, cameraY: 35, cameraZ:
    10, cameraDirectionX: 30, cameraDirectionY: 35, cameraDirectionZ: 10, cameraVectorX:
    62, cameraVectorY: 5, cameraVectorZ: 2, cameraPerspectiveFieldOfView: 7,
    cameraNearClippingPlane: 20, cameraFarClippingPlane: 30, directionalLightX: 5,
    directionalLightY: 4, directionalLightZ: 7, directionalLightColor: 232)
```

```
Setting camera direction to X:30, Y:35, Z:10
Setting camera vector to X:62, Y:5, Z:2
Setting camera perspective field of view to: 7
Setting camera near clipping plane to: 20
Setting camera far clipping plane to: 30
Creating directional light at X:5, Y:4, Z:7. Light color is 232
Drawing sphere at X:10, Y:15, Z:25
```

The object-oriented version requires a higher amount of code. However, it is easier to understand and expand based on future requirements. In addition, the object-oriented version reuses many pieces of code. If you need to add a new type of light, shape, or camera, you know where to add the pieces of code, which classes to create, and which methods to change.

Understanding functions as first-class citizens

Swift is a multiparadigm programming language, and one of its supported programming paradigms is functional programming. Functional programming favors immutable data and, therefore, avoids state changes. The code written with a functional programming style is as declarative as possible, and it is focused on what it does instead of how it must do it.

As it happens in many modern programming languages, functions are first-class citizens in Swift. You can use functions as arguments for other functions or methods. We can easily understand this concept with a simple example: array filtering. However, take into account that we will start by writing imperative code with functions as first-class citizens, and then, we will create a new version for this code that uses a functional approach in Swift through a filter operation.

The following lines declare the `applyFunctionToNumbers` function that receives an array of `Int` and numbers and a function type, `condition`. The function type specifies the parameter types and the return types for the function. In this case, `condition` specifies a function type that receives `Int` and returns a `Bool` value. The function executes the received function, `condition`, for each element in the input array and adds the element to an output array whenever the result of the called function is true. This way, only the elements that meet the specified condition will appear in the resulting array of `Int`:

```
func applyFunctionToNumbers(numbers: [Int], condition: Int -> Bool) -> [Int] {
    var returnNumbers = [Int]()
    for number in numbers {
        if condition(number) {
            returnNumbers.append(number)
        }
    }
    
    return returnNumbers
}
```

Object-Oriented Programming and Functional Programming

The following line declares a `divisibleBy5` function that receives `Int` and returns `Bool`, indicating whether the received number is divisible by 5 or not:

```
func divisibleBy5(number: Int) -> Bool {
    return number % 5 == 0
}
```

The function type for the `divisibleBy5` function is equal to the function type specified in the `condition` argument for the `applyFunctionToNumbers` function. The following lines show the function type specified in the `condition` argument followed by the `divisibleBy5` function declaration. The function type specified in the `condition` argument matches the function type for the `divisibleBy5` function:

```
condition: Int -> Bool
func divisibleBy5(number: Int) -> Bool
```

The following two lines declare an array of `Int` initialized with 10 numbers and call the `applyFunctionToNumbers` function with the array of `Int` and the `divisibleBy5` function as the arguments. The `divisibleBy5Numbers` array of `Int` will have the following values after the `applyFunctionToNumber` function runs: [10, 20, 30, 40, 50, 60].

```
var numbers = [10, 20, 30, 40, 50, 60, 63, 73, 43, 89]
var divisibleBy5Numbers = applyFunction(numbers, divisibleBy10)
```

The following screenshot shows the results of executing the previous lines in the Playground:

```
func applyFunctionToNumbers(numbers: [Int], condition: Int -> Bool) ->
    [Int] {
    var returnNumbers = [Int]()                                              []
    for number in numbers {
        if condition(number) {                                               (6 times)
            returnNumbers.append(number)
        }
    }
    return returnNumbers                                                     [10, 20, 30, 40, 50, 60]
}

func divisibleBy5(number: Int) -> Bool {
    return number % 5 == 0                                                   (10 times)
}

var numbers = [10, 20, 30, 40, 50, 60, 63, 73, 43, 89]                       [10, 20, 30, 40, 50, 60, 63, 73, 43, 89]
var divisibleBy5Numbers = applyFunctionToNumbers(numbers, condition:         [10, 20, 30, 40, 50, 60]
    divisibleBy5)

    [0] 10
    [1] 20
    [2] 30
    [3] 40
    [4] 50
    [5] 60
```

Working with function types within classes

The following lines declare a `myFunction` variable with a function type—specifically, a function that receives an `Int` argument and returns a `Bool` value. The variable works in the same way as an argument that specifies a function type for a function:

```
var myFunction: (Int -> Bool)
myFunction = divisibleBy5
let myNumber = 20
print("Is \(myNumber) divisible by 5: \(myFunction(myNumber))")
```

Then, the code assigns the `divisibleBy5` function to `myFunction`. It is very important to understand that the line doesn't call the `divisibleBy5` function and save the result of this call in the `myFunction` variable. Instead, it just assigns the function to the variable that has a function type. The lack of a parenthesis after the function name makes the difference.

Then, the code prints whether the `Int` value specified in the `myNumber` constant is divisible by 5 or not using the `myFunction` variable to call the referenced function with `myNumber` as an argument.

The following screenshot shows the results of executing the previous lines in the Playground. Note that the result of executing `myFunction = divisibleBy5` displays an `Int -> Bool` type on the right-hand side:

```
var myFunction: (Int -> Bool)
myFunction = divisibleBy5                                   Int -> Bool

    Int -> Bool


let myNumber = 20                                           20
print("Is \(myNumber) divisible by 5: \            "Is 20 divisible by 5: true\n"
    (myFunction(myNumber))")

    Is 20 divisible by 5: true
```

Type inference also works with functions, so we might replace the two lines that declared the `myFunction` variable and assigned the `divisibleBy5` function with the following single line:

```
var myFunction = divisibleBy5
```

Object-Oriented Programming and Functional Programming

So far, we worked with function types in functions. We can definitely take advantage of function types in object-oriented code. For example, the following lines show the code for a new `NumberWorker` class that declares the `applyFunctionToNumbers` method with a function type as a parameter type:

```
public class NumbersWorker {
    private var numbers = [Int]()

    init(numbers: [Int]) {
        self.numbers = numbers
    }

    public func applyFunctionToNumbers(condition: Int -> Bool) -> [Int] {
        var returnNumbers = [Int]()
        for number in numbers {
            if condition(number) {
                returnNumbers.append(number)
            }
        }

        return returnNumbers
    }
}
```

The following lines show the code for the `NumberFunctions` class that defines the `isNumberDivisibleBy5` type method. We will use this type method as an argument when we call the `applyFunctionToNumbers` method:

```
public class NumberFunctions {
    public static func isNumberDivisibleBy5(number: Int) -> Bool {
        return number % 5 == 0
    }
}
```

The next lines create a `numbersList` array of `Int` and then pass it as an argument to the initializer of the `NumbersWorker` class. The last line calls the `worker.applyFunctionToNumbers` method with the `NumberFunctions.isNumberDivisibleBy5` type method as an argument:

```
var numbersList = [-60, -59, -48, -35, -25, -10, 11, 12, 13, 14, 15]
var worker = NumbersWorker(numbers: numbersList)
worker.applyFunctionToNumbers(NumberFunctions.isNumberDivisibleBy5)
```

> In this case, we used a type method as the argument for a method that specified a function type as a parameter type. We can also use an instance method as an argument that requires a function type.

The following screenshot shows the result of executing the previous lines in the Playground:

Code	Output
| ```swift
public class NumbersWorker {
    private var numbers = [Int]()

    init(numbers: [Int]) {
        self.numbers = numbers
    }

    public func applyFunctionToNumbers(condition: Int -> Bool) -> [Int]
    {
        var returnNumbers = [Int]()
        for number in numbers {
            if condition(number) {
                returnNumbers.append(number)
            }
        }
        return returnNumbers
    }

    public func filterNumbersByCondition(condition: Int -> Bool) ->
      [Int] {
        return numbersList.filter({
            (number: Int) -> Bool in
            return condition(number)
        })
    }
}
public class NumberFunctions {
    public static func isNumberDivisibleBy5(number: Int) -> Bool {
        return number % 5 == 0
    }
}
var numbersList = [-60, -59, -48, -35, -25, -10, 11, 12, 13, 14, 15]
var worker = NumbersWorker(numbers: numbersList)
worker.applyFunctionToNumbers(NumberFunctions.isNumberDivisibleBy5)
``` | []<br><br>(5 times)<br><br>[-60, -35, -25, -10, 15]<br><br><br><br><br><br><br>(11 times)<br><br>[-60, -59, -48, -35, -25, -10, 11, 12, 13, 14, 15]<br>NumbersWorker<br>[-60, -35, -25, -10, 15] |

Creating a functional version of array filtering

The collections included in Swift allow us the use of higher order functions—that is, functions that take other functions and use them to perform transformations on datasets. For example, an array provides us with the `filter`, `map`, and `reduce` methods.

[245]
```

Object-Oriented Programming and Functional Programming

As previously explained, the preceding code represents an imperative version of array filtering. We can achieve the same goal with a functional approach using the `filter` method included in all the types that conform to the `SequenceType` protocol. The `Array<Element>` struct conforms to the `SequenceType` protocol and many other protocols.

> As it happens in most modern languages, Swift supports closures, which are also known as anonymous functions. Closures are self-contained blocks of functionality that we can pass around and use within our code as functions without names. Closures automatically capture everything we reference, such as variables and functions that aren't defined within the closure. Closures in Swift are similar to blocks in Objective-C.

The following lines use a closure as an argument for the `filter` method to generate the array with the numbers divisible by 5. The closure is the code surrounded with braces (`{}`) and uses the `in` keyword to separate the argument (`number: Int`) and the return type (`Bool`) for the closure from its body:

```
var filteredNumers = numbersList.filter({
    (number: Int) -> Bool in
    return NumberFunctions.isNumberDivisibleBy5(number)
})
```

The code calls the `filter` method for the previously defined `numbersList` `Array<Int>`. This method creates and returns a new `Array<Int>` that contains only the elements of `numbersList` `Array<Int>` for which the `Bool` value returned by the specified closure returns `true`. In this case, the closure receives a `number` value of the `Int` type and returns the result of calling the `NumberFunctions.isNumberDivisibleBy5` type method with `number` as an argument.

The following lines add a new `filterNumbersByCondition` method to the existing `NumbersWorker` class. The method specifies a function type for the `condition` argument and then uses the function type within the closure that the `filter` method calls. This way, we are able to call this method with the function name that we want to receive an `Int` value and return `Bool` to evaluate which members of the original array are returned in the resulting array:

```
public func filterNumbersByCondition(condition: Int -> Bool) -> [Int]
{
    return numbersList.filter({
        (number: Int) -> Bool in
        return condition(number)
    })
}
```

The next lines create a `numbersList2` array of `Int` and then pass it as an argument to the initializer of the `NumbersWorker` class. The last line calls the `worker2.applyFunctionToNumbers` method with the `NumberFunctions.isNumberDivisibleBy5` type method as an argument:

```
var numbersList2 = [-30, -29, -47, 10, 30, 50, 80]
var worker2 = NumbersWorker(numbers: numbersList)
worker2.applyFunctionToNumbers(NumberFunctions.isNumberDivisibleBy5)
```

The following screenshot shows the results of executing the previous lines in the Playground:

```
var filteredNumbers = numbersList.filter({        [-60, -35, -25, -10, 15]

    [0] -60
    [1] -35
    [2] -25
    [3] -10
    [4] 15

    (number: Int) -> Bool in
        return NumberFunctions.isNumberDivisibleBy5(number)    (11 times)
})
var numbersList2 = [-30, -29, -47, 10, 30, 50, 80]             [-30, -29, -47, 10, 30, 50, 80]
var worker2 = NumbersWorker(numbers: numbersList2)             NumbersWorker
worker2.applyFunctionToNumbers(NumberFunctions.isNumberDivisibleBy5)   [-30, 10, 30, 50, 80]

    [0] -30
    [1] 10
    [2] 30
    [3] 50
    [4] 80
```

Writing equivalent closures with simplified code

It is possible to omit the type for the closure's parameter and return type. The following lines show a simplified version of the previously shown code that generates the same result. Note that the closure code is really simplified and doesn't even include the return statement because it uses an implicit return. Swift evaluates the code we write after the `in` keyword and returns its evaluation as if we included the return statement before the expression. Swift infers the return type:

```
public func filterNumbersByCondition(condition: Int -> Bool) -> [Int]
{
    return numbersList.filter({
        (number) in condition(number)
    })
}
```

We can go a step further and use the argument shorthand notation. This way, the closure omits the type for the parameters and its return type, takes advantage of implicit returns, and also uses the argument shorthand notation. The dollar sign followed by the argument number identifies each of the arguments for the closure. In this case, there is only one argument, so we will use $0 to reference it. Obviously, $1 would reference a second argument, $2 would reference a third argument, and so on:

```
public func filterNumbersByCondition(condition: Int -> Bool) -> [Int]
{
    return numbersList.filter({ condition($0) })
}
```

The following three pieces of code are equivalent and produce the same results. The first two versions make it easier to understand that the closure receives a number argument because we use a specific name for it:

```
return numbersList.filter({
    (number: Int) -> Bool in
    return condition(number)
})

return numbersList.filter({
    (number) in condition(number)
})

return numbersList.filter({
    return condition($0)
})
```

Creating a data repository with generics and protocols

Now, we want to create a repository that provides us with entities so that we can apply the functional programming features included in Swift to retrieve and process data from these entities. First, we will create an EntityProtocol protocol that defines the requirements for an entity. We want any class that conforms to this protocol to have a read-only id property of the Int type to provide a unique identifier for the entity:

```
public protocol EntityProtocol {
    var id: Int { get }
}
```

Chapter 7

The next lines create a `Repository<T>` generic class that specifies that `T` must conform to the recently created `EntityProtocol` protocol in the generic type constraint. The class declares a `getAll` method that we will override in the subclasses:

```
public class Repository<T: EntityProtocol> {
    public func getAll() -> [T] {
        return [T]()
    }
}
```

The next lines create the `Entity` class, which is the base class for all the entities. The class conforms to the `EntityProtocol` protocol and defines a read-only `id` property of the `Int` type:

```
public class Entity: EntityProtocol {
    public let id: Int

    init(id: Int) {
        self.id = id
    }
}
```

The next lines create the `Game` class, which is a subclass of `Entity` that conforms to the `CustomStringConvertible` protocol. The class adds the following stored properties: `name`, `highestScore`, and `playedCount`. The `CustomStringConvertible` protocol requires the class to implement a `description` calculated property that Swift uses whenever we write values to the output string. This way, whenever we use print and specify an instance of the `Game` class, Swift will print the value for the description calculated property:

```
public class Game: Entity, CustomStringConvertible {
    public var name: String
    public var highestScore: Int
    public var playedCount: Int

    public var description: String {
        get {
            return "id: \(id), name: \"\(name)\", highestScore: \(highestScore), playedCount: \(playedCount)"
        }
    }

    init(id: Int, name: String, highestScore: Int, playedCount: Int) {
        self.name = name
        self.highestScore = highestScore
        self.playedCount = playedCount
```

[249]

Object-Oriented Programming and Functional Programming

```
        super.init(id: id)
    }
}
```

The following lines create the `GameRepository` class, a subclass of `Repository<Game>`. The class overrides the `getAll` method declared in the generic superclass — that is, in the `Repository<T>` class. In this case, the method returns an array of Game, `Array<Game>` specified with the `[Game]` shortcut. The overridden method creates 10 Game instances and appends them to an array of Game that the method returns as a result. Note that we use underscores as separators to make it easier to read integer numbers. For example, instead of writing `3050`, we write `3_050`, and it is equivalent to `3050`. This way, we can easily realize that it is three thousand and fifty:

```
public class GameRepository: Repository<Game> {
    public override func getAll() -> [Game] {
        var gamesList = [Game]()

        gamesList.append(Game(id: 1, name: "Invaders 2016", highestScore: 1050, playedCount: 3_050))

        gamesList.append(Game(id: 2, name: "Minecraft", highestScore: 3741050, playedCount: 780_009_992))

        gamesList.append(Game(id: 3, name: "Minecraft Story Mode", highestScore: 67881050, playedCount: 304_506_506))

        gamesList.append(Game(id: 4, name: "Soccer Warriors", highestScore: 10_025, playedCount: 320_450))

        gamesList.append(Game(id: 5, name: "The Walking Dead Stories", highestScore: 1_450_708, playedCount: 75_405_350))

        gamesList.append(Game(id: 6, name: "Once Upon a Time in Wonderland", highestScore: 1_050_320, playedCount: 7_052))

        gamesList.append(Game(id: 7, name: "Cars Forever", highestScore: 6_705_203, playedCount: 850_021))

        gamesList.append(Game(id: 8, name: "Jake & Peter Pan", highestScore: 4_023_134, playedCount: 350_230))

        gamesList.append(Game(id: 9, name: "Kong Strikes Back", highestScore: 1_050_230, playedCount: 450_050))
```

```
        gamesList.append(Game(id: 10, name: "Mario Kart 2016",
highestScore: 10_572_340, playedCount: 3_760_879))

        return gamesList
    }
}
```

The following lines create an instance of `GameRepository` and call the `forEach` method for the array of `Game` returned by the `getAll` method. The `forEach` method calls a body on each element in the array, as is done in a `for in` loop. The closure specified as an argument for the `forEach` method calls the print method with the `Game` instance as an argument. This way, Swift uses the `description` computed property to generate a String representation for each `Game` instance:

```
var gameRepository = GameRepository()
gameRepository.getAll().forEach({ (game) in print(game) })
```

The following lines show the output generated by the preceding code:

```
id: 1, name: "Invaders 2016", highestScore: 1050, playedCount: 3050
id: 2, name: "Minecraft", highestScore: 3741050, playedCount:
780009992
id: 3, name: "Minecraft Story Mode", highestScore: 67881050,
playedCount: 304506506
id: 4, name: "Soccer Warriors", highestScore: 10025, playedCount:
320450
id: 5, name: "The Walking Dead Stories", highestScore: 1450708,
playedCount: 75405350
id: 6, name: "Once Upon a Time in Wonderland", highestScore: 1050320,
playedCount: 7052
id: 7, name: "Cars Forever", highestScore: 6705203, playedCount:
850021
id: 8, name: "Jake & Peter Pan", highestScore: 4023134, playedCount:
350230
id: 9, name: "Kong Strikes Back", highestScore: 1050230, playedCount:
450050
id: 10, name: "Mario Kart 2016", highestScore: 10572340, playedCount:
3760879
```

Object-Oriented Programming and Functional Programming

The following screenshot shows the result of executing the previous lines in the Playground:

```swift
public class GameRepository: Repository<Game> {
    public override func getAll() -> [Game] {
        var gamesList = [Game]()
        gamesList.append(Game(id: 1, name: "Invaders 2016",
            highestScore: 1050, playedCount: 3_050))
        gamesList.append(Game(id: 2, name: "Minecraft", highestScore:
            3741050, playedCount: 780_009_992))
        gamesList.append(Game(id: 3, name: "Minecraft Story Mode",
            highestScore: 67881050, playedCount: 304_506_506))
        gamesList.append(Game(id: 4, name: "Soccer Warriors",
            highestScore: 10_025, playedCount: 320_450))
        gamesList.append(Game(id: 5, name: "The Walking Dead Stories",
            highestScore: 1_450_708, playedCount: 75_405_350))
        gamesList.append(Game(id: 6, name: "Once Upon a Time in
            Wonderland", highestScore: 1_050_320, playedCount: 7_052))
        gamesList.append(Game(id: 7, name: "Cars Forever",
            highestScore: 6_705_203, playedCount: 850_021))
        gamesList.append(Game(id: 8, name: "Jake & Peter Pan",
            highestScore: 4_023_134, playedCount: 350_230))
        gamesList.append(Game(id: 9, name: "Kong Strikes Back",
            highestScore: 1_050_230, playedCount: 450_050))
        gamesList.append(Game(id: 10, name: "Mario Kart 2016",
            highestScore: 10_572_340, playedCount: 3_760_879))

        return gamesList
    }
}

var gameRepository = GameRepository()
gameRepository.getAll().forEach({ (game) in print(game) })
```

```
id: 1, name: "Invaders 2016", highestScore: 1050, playedCount: 3050
id: 2, name: "Minecraft", highestScore: 3741050, playedCount: 780009992
id: 3, name: "Minecraft Story Mode", highestScore: 67881050, playedCount: 304506506
id: 4, name: "Soccer Warriors", highestScore: 10025, playedCount: 320450
id: 5, name: "The Walking Dead Stories", highestScore: 1450708, playedCount: 75405350
id: 6, name: "Once Upon a Time in Wonderland", highestScore: 1050320, playedCount: 7052
id: 7, name: "Cars Forever", highestScore: 6705203, playedCount: 850021
id: 8, name: "Jake & Peter Pan", highestScore: 4023134, playedCount: 350230
id: 9, name: "Kong Strikes Back", highestScore: 1050230, playedCount: 450050
id: 10, name: "Mario Kart 2016", highestScore: 10572340, playedCount: 3760879
```

The following line uses the argument shorthand notation, which is equivalent to the last line, and produces the same result:

```
gameRepository.getAll().forEach({ print($0) })
```

Filtering arrays with complex conditions

We can use our new repository to restrict the results retrieved from more complex data. In this case, the `getAll` method returns an array of `Game` instances that we can use with the `filter` method to retrieve only the games that match certain conditions. The following lines declare a new `getGamesWithHighestScoreGreaterThan` method for our previously coded `GameRepository` class:

```
public func getGamesWithHighestScoreGreaterThan(score: Int) -> [Game]
{
    return getAll().filter({ (game) in game.highestScore > score })
}
```

The `getGamesWithHighestScoreGreaterThan` method receives a `score: Int` argument and returns `Array<Game>`. The code calls the `getAll` and `filter` methods for the result with a closure that specifies the required condition for the games in the array to be returned in the new array. In this case, only the games whose `highestScore` value is greater than the `score` value received as an argument will appear in the resulting `Array<Game>`.

The following lines use the `GameRepository` instance called `gameRepository` to call the previously added method and then chain a call to `forEach` to print all the games whose `highestScore` value is greater than 5,000,000:

```
gameRepository.getGamesWithHighestScoreGreaterThan(5_000_000).forEach(
{ print($0) })
```

The following lines show the output generated using the preceding code:

```
id: 3, name: "Minecraft Story Mode", highestScore: 67881050,
playedCount: 304506506
id: 7, name: "Cars Forever", highestScore: 6705203, playedCount:
850021
id: 10, name: "Mario Kart 2016", highestScore: 10572340, playedCount:
3760879
```

The next code shows two versions of the `getGamesWithHighestScoreGreaterThan` method that are equivalent and produce the same results:

```
public func getGamesWithHighestScoreGreaterThan(score: Int) -> [Game]
{
    return getAll().filter({
        (game: Game) -> Bool in
        game.highestScore > score })
}
```

[253]

Object-Oriented Programming and Functional Programming

```
public func getGamesWithHighestScoreGreaterThan(score: Int) -> [Game]
{
    return getAll().filter({ $0.highestScore > score })
}
```

The following lines declare a new `getGamesWithPrefix` method for our previously coded `GameRepository` class:

```
public func getGamesWithPrefix(prefix: String) -> [Game] {
    return getAll().filter({ game in game.name.hasPrefix(prefix) })
}
```

The `getGamesWithPrefix` method receives a `prefix String` argument and returns an `Array<Game>`. The code calls the `getAll` method and calls the `filter` method for the result with a closure that specifies the required condition for the games in the array to be returned in the new array. In this case, only the games whose name includes the string specified in the `prefix` value and is received as an argument or prefix will appear in the resulting `Array<Game>`.

The following line uses the `GameRepository` instance called `gameRepository` to call the previously added method and then chains a call to `forEach` to print all the games whose name starts with `"Mi"`:

```
gameRepository.getGamesWithPrefix("Mi").forEach( { print($0) })
```

The following lines show the output generated by the preceding code:

```
id: 2, name: "Minecraft", highestScore: 3741050, playedCount: 780009992
id: 3, name: "Minecraft Story Mode", highestScore: 67881050, playedCount: 304506506
```

The next code shows two versions of the `getGamesWithPrefix` method that are equivalent and produce the same results:

```
public func getGamesWithPrefix(prefix: String) -> [Game] {
    return getAll().filter({
        (game: Game) -> Bool in
        game.name.hasPrefix(prefix)
    })
}

public func getGamesWithPrefix(prefix: String) -> [Game] {
    return getAll().filter({ $0.name.hasPrefix(prefix) })
}
```

So far, we used the `filter` method to generate a new `Array<Game>`. Sometimes, we just want to retrieve a single element from an `Array` or a similar collection, and we also want to specify a more complex condition. The following lines declare a new `getGameByHighestScoreAndPlayedCount` method for our previously coded `GameRepository` class:

```
public func getGameByHighestScoreAndPlayedCount(highestScore: Int,
playedCount: Int) -> Game? {
    return getAll().filter({ game in game.highestScore == highestScore
&& game.playedCount == playedCount }).first
}
```

The `getGameByHighestScoreAndPlayedCount` method receives two `Int` arguments: `highestScore` and `playedCount`. The method returns an optional `Game`—that is, `Game?`. The code calls the `getAll` and `filter` methods for the result with a closure that specifies the required condition for the games in the array to be returned in the new array. In this case, only the games whose `highestScore` and `playedCount` values are equal to the values received as arguments with the same names will appear in the `Array<Game>` generated by the call to the `filter` method. Then, the call to the first method returns the `first` element in the generated array or `nil` if no elements are found.

The following lines use the `GameRepository` instance called `gameRepository` to call the previously added method to retrieve two games that match the specified `highestScore` and `playedCount` values. The method returns a `Game?`; therefore, the code checks whether the result is a `Game` instance or not in each call using `if` statements:

```
if let game0 = gameRepository.
getGameByHighestScoreAndPlayedCount(4023134, playedCount: 350230) {
    print(game0)
} else {
    print("No game found with the specified criteria")
}
if let game1 = gameRepository.getGameByHighestScoreAndPlayedCount(30,
playedCount: 40) {
    print(game1)
} else {
    print("No game found with the specified criteria")
}
```

The following lines show the output generated with the preceding code. In the first call, there was a game that matched the search criteria. In the second call, there is no `Game` instance included in the array that matches the search criteria:

```
id: 8, name: "Jake & Peter Pan", highestScore: 4023134, playedCount:
350230
No game found with the specified criteria
```

Object-Oriented Programming and Functional Programming

The next code shows two versions of the `getGameByHighestScoreAndPlayedCount` method that are equivalent and produce the same results:

```
public func getGameByHighestScoreAndPlayedCount(highestScore: Int,
playedCount: Int) -> Game? {
    return getAll().filter({
        (game: Game) -> Bool in
        game.highestScore == highestScore && game.playedCount ==
playedCount
    }).first
}

public func getGameByHighestScoreAndPlayedCount(highestScore: Int,
playedCount: Int) -> Game? {
    return getAll().filter({ $0.highestScore == highestScore &&
$0.playedCount == playedCount }).first
}
```

Using map to transform values

The `map` method takes a closure as an argument, calls it for each item in the array, and returns a mapped value for the item. The returned mapped value can be of a different type from the item's type.

The following lines declare a new `getGamesNames` method for our previously coded `GameRepository` class that performs the simplest map operation:

```
public func getGamesNames() -> [String] {
    return getAll().map({ game in game.name.uppercaseString })
}
```

The `getGamesNames` parameterless method returns `Array<String>`. The code calls the `getAll` method and calls the `map` method for the result with a closure that returns the `name` value for each game converted to uppercase. This way, the `map` method transforms each `Game` instance into a `String` with its name converted to uppercase. The result is an `Array<String>` generated by the call to the `map` method.

The following line uses the `GameRepository` instance called `gameRepository` to call the previously added `getGamesNames` method and then chains a call to `forEach` to print all the game names converted to uppercase strings:

```
gameRepository.getGamesNames().forEach( { print($0) })
```

The following lines show the output generated by the preceding code:

```
INVADERS 2016
MINECRAFT
MINECRAFT STORY MODE
SOCCER WARRIORS
THE WALKING DEAD STORIES
ONCE UPON A TIME IN WONDERLAND
CARS FOREVER
JAKE & PETER PAN
KONG STRIKES BACK
MARIO KART 2016
```

The next code shows two versions of the `getGamesNames` method that are equivalent and produce the same results:

```
public func getGamesNames() -> [String] {
    return getAll().map({
        (game: Game) -> String in
        game.name.uppercaseString
    })
}

public func getGamesNames() -> [String] {
    return getAll().map( { $0.name.uppercaseString })
}
```

Swift supports tuples that group multiple values into a single compound value. The following lines declare a new `getUpperAndLowerCaseGamesNames` method for our previously coded `GameRepository` class that performs a map operation that returns a tuple—specifically, a tuple that groups two string values into a single compound value:

```
public func getUpperAndLowerCaseGamesNames() -> [(upper: String,
lower: String)] {
    return getAll().map({
        game -> (String, String) in
        (game.name.uppercaseString, game.name.lowercaseString)
    })
}
```

Object-Oriented Programming and Functional Programming

The `getUpperAndLowerCaseGamesNames` parameterless method returns a tuple with two named `String` values: `[(upper: String, lower: String)`. The first string element in the tuple is named `upper`, and the second one is named `lower`. The code calls the `getAll` and `map` method for the result with a closure that returns a tuple with the first element equal to the `name` value for each game converted to uppercase and the second element with the value converted to lower case. This way, the `map` method transforms each `Game` instance into a `(String, String)` tuple with its name converted to uppercase and lowercase and stored in a compound value. The result is `(String, String)` generated by the call to the `map` method. The method declaration specifies names for each element in the returned tuple, so we will be able to access its members through these specified names.

The following line uses the `GameRepository` instance called `gameRepository` to call the previously added `getUpperAndLowerCaseGamesNames` method and then chains a call to `forEach` to print the `upper` and `lower` elements of the tuple separated by a hyphen:

```
gameRepository.getUpperAndLowerCaseGamesNames().forEach( { print($0.upper, " - ", $0.lower) })
```

The following lines show the output generated by the preceding code:

```
INVADERS 2016      -   invaders 2016
MINECRAFT    -   minecraft
MINECRAFT STORY MODE    -   minecraft story mode
SOCCER WARRIORS    -   soccer warriors
THE WALKING DEAD STORIES    -   the walking dead stories
ONCE UPON A TIME IN WONDERLAND    -   once upon a time in wonderland
CARS FOREVER    -   cars forever
JAKE & PETER PAN    -   jake & peter pan
KONG STRIKES BACK    -   kong strikes back
MARIO KART 2016    -   mario kart 2016
```

The following lines would produce the same results by accessing the tuple elements with `.0` and `.1` for the first and second elements instead of using the `upper` and `lower` names:

```
gameRepository.getUpperAndLowerCaseGamesNames().forEach( { print($0.0, " - ", $0.1) })
```

> Swift allows us to access tuple elements with a dot followed by the element number. The element number starts in 0. However, it is usually convenient to provide names to the elements in order to make the code easier to understand and maintain.

Chapter 7

We can also easily iterate through the upper and lower pairs using a `for` loop:

```
for (upper, lower) in gameRepository.getUpperAndLowerCaseGamesNames()
{
    print("UPPER: \(upper), lower: \(lower)")
}
```

The next lines show the results of executing the previous `for` loop:

```
UPPER: INVADERS 2016, lower: invaders 2016
UPPER: MINECRAFT, lower: minecraft
UPPER: MINECRAFT STORY MODE, lower: minecraft story mode
UPPER: SOCCER WARRIORS, lower: soccer warriors
UPPER: THE WALKING DEAD STORIES, lower: the walking dead stories
UPPER: ONCE UPON A TIME IN WONDERLAND, lower: once upon a time in wonderland
UPPER: CARS FOREVER, lower: cars forever
UPPER: JAKE & PETER PAN, lower: jake & peter pan
UPPER: KONG STRIKES BACK, lower: kong strikes back
UPPER: MARIO KART 2016, lower: mario kart 2016
```

Combining map with reduce

The following lines show an imperative code version of a `for in` loop that calculates the sum of all the `highestScore` values for the games:

```
var sum = 0
for game in gameRepository.getAll() {
    sum += game.highestScore
}
print(sum)
```

The code is very easy to understand. The `sum` variable has a starting value of `0`, and each iteration of the `for in` loop retrieves a `Game` instance from the `Array<Game>` returned by the `gameRepository.getAll` method and increases the value of the `sum` variable with the value of the `highestScore` property.

We can combine the map and reduce operations to create a functional version of the previous imperative code to calculate the sum of all the `highestScore` values for the games. The next lines chain a call to `map` to a call to `reduce` to achieve this goal. Take a look at the following code:

```
let highestScoreSum = gameRepository.getAll().map({ $0.highestScore
}).reduce(0, combine: {
    sum, highestScore in
```

Object-Oriented Programming and Functional Programming

```
    return sum + highestScore
})
print(highestScoreSum)
```

First, the code uses the call to map to transform an Array<Game> into an Array<Int> with the values specified in the highestScore stored property. Then, the code calls the reduce method that receives two arguments: the initial value for an accumulated value and a combine closure that will be repeatedly called with the accumulated value. The method returns the results of the repeated calls to the combine closure.

The closure specified in the combine argument receives sum and highestScore and returns the sum of both values. Thus, the closure returns the sum of the total accumulated so far plus the highestScore value that is processed. We can add a print statement to display the values for both sum and highestScore within the closure specified in the combine argument. The following lines show a new version of the previous code that adds the line with the print statement:

```
let highestScoreSum2 = gameRepository.getAll().map({ $0.highestScore
}).reduce(0, combine: {
    sum, highestScore in
    print("sum value: \(sum), highestScore value: \(highestScore)")
    return sum + highestScore
})
print(highestScoreSum2)
```

The following lines show the results for the previous line, where we can see how the sum value starts with the initial value specified in the initial argument for the reduce method and accumulates the sum completed so far. Finally, the highestScoreSum2 variable holds the sum of all the highestScore values—that is, the last value of sum, 85,912,770 plus the last highestScore value, 10,572,340. The result is 96,485,110:

```
sum value: 0, highestScore value: 1050
sum value: 1050, highestScore value: 3741050
sum value: 3742100, highestScore value: 67881050
sum value: 71623150, highestScore value: 10025
sum value: 71633175, highestScore value: 1450708
sum value: 73083883, highestScore value: 1050320
sum value: 74134203, highestScore value: 6705203
sum value: 80039406, highestScore value: 4023134
sum value: 84862540, highestScore value: 1050230
sum value: 85912770, highestScore value: 10572340
96485110
```

The following screenshot shows the results of executing the previous lines in the Playground:

```
var sum = 0                                                                  0
for game in gameRepository.getAll() {
    sum += game.highestScore                                                 (10 times)
}
print(sum)                                                                   "96485110\n"

let highestScoreSum =                                                        (11 times)
    gameRepository.getAll().map({ $0.highestScore }).reduce(0, combine: {
    sum, highestScore in
        return sum + highestScore                                            (10 times)
})
print(highestScoreSum)                                                       "96485110\n"

let highestScoreSum2 = gameRepository.getAll().map({ $0.highestScore }).     (11 times)
    reduce(0, combine: {
    sum, highestScore in
        print("sum value: \(sum), highestScore value: \(highestScore)")      (10 times)
        return sum + highestScore                                            (10 times)




})
print(highestScoreSum2)                                                      "96485110\n"
```

```
sum value: 0, highestScore value: 1050
sum value: 1050, highestScore value: 3741050
sum value: 3742100, highestScore value: 67881050
sum value: 71623150, highestScore value: 10025
sum value: 71633175, highestScore value: 1450708
sum value: 73083883, highestScore value: 1050320
sum value: 74134203, highestScore value: 6705203
sum value: 80839406, highestScore value: 4023134
sum value: 84862540, highestScore value: 1050230
sum value: 85912770, highestScore value: 10572340
96485110
```

In the previous code, we had to pass a closure expression to the `reduce` method as the method's final argument, and the closure expression is long. We can write it as a trailing closure—that is, a closure expression written after the closing parenthesis of the method call and outside of it. The following lines show a new version of the previous code that uses a trailing closure. Note that the call to `reduce` seems to include just one argument: 0. However, the code included within curly braces after the method call is the combine argument for `reduce`. Take a look at the following lines:

```
let highestScoreSum3 = gameRepository.getAll().map({ $0.highestScore
}).reduce(0) {
```

Object-Oriented Programming and Functional Programming

```
    sum, highestScore in
    print("sum value: \(sum), highestScore value: \(highestScore)")
    return sum + highestScore
}
```

Chaining filter, map, and reduce

We can chain `filter`, `map`, and `reduce`. The following lines declare a new `calculateGamesHighestScoresSum` method for our previously coded `GameRepository` class that chains `filter`, `map`, and `reduce` calls:

```
public func calculateGamesHighestScoresSum(minPlayedCount: Int) -> Int
{
    return getAll().filter({ $0.playedCount >= minPlayedCount }).map({
$0.highestScore }).reduce(0) {
        sum, highestScore in
        return sum + highestScore
    }
}
```

The `calculateGamesHighestScoresSum` method receives a `minPlayedCount` argument of the `Int` type and returns an `Int` value. The code calls the `getAll` and `filter` methods to generate a new `Array<Game>` with only the `Game` instances, whose `playedCount` value is greater than or equal to the value specified in the `minPlayedCount` argument. The code calls the `map` method to transform an `Array<Game>` into an `Array<Int>` with the values specified in the `highestScore` stored property. Then, the code calls the `reduce` method with the initial value for the accumulated value set to `0` and a trailing closure that performs the sum task for `highestScore` that we analyzed in the previous example.

The following line uses the `GameRepository` instance called `gameRepository` to call the previously added `calculateGamesHighestScoresSum` method to calculate the sum of the `highestScores` for the games that were played at least 500,000 times:

```
let highestScoreSumFor500000 = gameRepository.
calculateGamesHighestScoresSum(500_000)
```

Solving algorithms with reduce

We can chain solve algorithms with `reduce` by following a functional approach. The following lines declare a new `getSeparatedGamesNames` method for our previously coded `GameRepository` class that solves an algorithm by calling the `reduce` method:

```
public func getSeparatedGamesNames(separator: String) -> String {
    let gamesNames = getGamesNames()
```

```
        return gamesNames.reduce("") {
            concatenatedGameNames, gameName in
            print(concatenatedGameNames)
            let separatorOrEmpty = (gameName == gamesNames.last) ? "" : separator
            return "\(concatenatedGameNames)\(gameName)\(separatorOrEmpty)"
        }
    }
```

The `getSeparatedGamesNames` method receives a `separator` argument of the `String` type and returns a `String` value. The code calls the `getGamesNames` method and saves the result in the `gamesNames` reference constant. Then, the code calls the `reduce` method with an empty string as the `initial` value for an accumulated value. The code uses a trailing closure to specify the closure expression for `combine`.

The trailing closure receives `concatenatedGameNames` and `gameName`. First, the closure prints the value of `concatenatedGameNames`. This way, we will be able to understand how the algorithm completes the concatenated game names in each execution. Then, an expression determines whether the string specified in `separator` or an empty string has to be used as a separator. In case the `gameName` is equal to the last game in the `Array<String>`, the code uses an empty string because the last game shouldn't have the separator after it. Finally, the code returns a string composed of the names concatenated so far, `concatenatedGameNames`; the game name that is being concatenated, `gameName`; and the separator or an empty string, `separatorOrEmpty`.

The following line uses the `GameRepository` instance called `gameRepository` to call the previously added `getSeparatedGamesNames` method to generate a string with all the uppercase game names separated by a semicolon followed by a space:

```
    print(gameRepository.getSeparatedGamesNames("; "))
```

The following lines show the results for the previous line where we can see how the concatenated game names start with the initial value specified in the `initial` argument for the `reduce` method and accumulates the strings generated so far. Finally, the value returned by the `getSeparatedGamesNames` method includes all the game names in uppercase separated by a semicolon and followed by a space:

```
    INVADERS 2016;
    INVADERS 2016; MINECRAFT;
    INVADERS 2016; MINECRAFT; MINECRAFT STORY MODE;
    INVADERS 2016; MINECRAFT; MINECRAFT STORY MODE; SOCCER WARRIORS;
    INVADERS 2016; MINECRAFT; MINECRAFT STORY MODE; SOCCER WARRIORS; THE WALKING DEAD STORIES;
```

```
INVADERS 2016; MINECRAFT; MINECRAFT STORY MODE; SOCCER WARRIORS; THE
WALKING DEAD STORIES; ONCE UPON A TIME IN WONDERLAND;
INVADERS 2016; MINECRAFT; MINECRAFT STORY MODE; SOCCER WARRIORS; THE
WALKING DEAD STORIES; ONCE UPON A TIME IN WONDERLAND; CARS FOREVER;
INVADERS 2016; MINECRAFT; MINECRAFT STORY MODE; SOCCER WARRIORS; THE
WALKING DEAD STORIES; ONCE UPON A TIME IN WONDERLAND; CARS FOREVER;
JAKE & PETER PAN;
INVADERS 2016; MINECRAFT; MINECRAFT STORY MODE; SOCCER WARRIORS; THE
WALKING DEAD STORIES; ONCE UPON A TIME IN WONDERLAND; CARS FOREVER;
JAKE & PETER PAN; KONG STRIKES BACK;
INVADERS 2016; MINECRAFT; MINECRAFT STORY MODE; SOCCER WARRIORS; THE
WALKING DEAD STORIES; ONCE UPON A TIME IN WONDERLAND; CARS FOREVER;
JAKE & PETER PAN; KONG STRIKES BACK; MARIO KART 2016
```

The following screenshot shows the results of executing the previous lines in the Playground:

Exercises

Add new methods to the `GameRepository` class we created in this chapter. Make sure you create a new method to solve each algorithm and that you use a functional programming approach:

- Retrieve all the games whose average score is lower than a maximum average score received as an argument.
- Generate a string with the first letter of each game name followed by the highest score value. Use a hyphen as a separator for each game name and highest score value pair. That last value pair shouldn't include a hyphen after it.
- Calculate the minimum `playedCount` value.
- Calculate the maximum `playedCount` value.

Test your knowledge

1. The `{ (game: Game) -> Bool in game.highestScore == highestScore && game.playedCount == playedCount }` closure is equivalent to:
    1. `{ $0.highestScore == highestScore && $1.playedCount == playedCount }`
    2. **`{ $0.highestScore == highestScore && $0.playedCount == playedCount }`**
    3. `{ 0 -> 0.highestScore == highestScore && 0.playedCount == playedCount }`

2. The closure `{ return condition($0) }` is equivalent to:
    1. `{ (number: Int) -> Bool in return condition(number) }`
    2. `{ (number -> Bool) -> Int in condition <- (number) }`
    3. `{ 0 -> condition(number) }`

3. A function type specifies:
    1. **The parameter and return types for the function.**
    2. Only the parameter names required for the function.
    3. The required function name and the return value without any details about the parameters.

4. Which of the following lines declare a variable with a function type:
    1. `var condition: { 0 -> Int -> Bool }`
    2. `var condition: Int $0 returns Bool`
    3. **`var condition: (Int -> Bool)`**

5. After we assign a tuple to a variable with this line `var tuple: (key: String, value: String) = ("Name", "Garfield")`, which of the following lines access the first string element in the tuple—that is, the value named key?
    1. `tuple.$0`
    2. `tuple.1`
    3. **`tuple.0`**

Summary

In this chapter, you learned how to refactor existing code to take full advantage of object-oriented code. We prepared the code for future requirements, reduced maintenance cost, and maximized code reuse.

We worked with many functional programming features included in Swift and combined them with everything we discussed so far about object-oriented programming. We analyzed the differences between imperative and functional programming approaches for many algorithms.

Now that you have learned about refactoring code to take advantage of object-oriented programming and include functional programming pieces in our object-oriented code, we are ready to extend and build object-oriented code, which is the topic of the next chapter.

8
Extending and Building Object-Oriented Code

In this chapter, we will put together many pieces of the object-oriented puzzle. We will take advantage of extensions to add features to classes, protocols, and types that we can't modify through source code editing. We will interact with a simple object-oriented data repository through Picker View and consider how object-oriented code is everywhere in an iOS app.

Putting together all the pieces of the object-oriented puzzle

In *Chapter 1*, *Objects from the Real World to Playground,* you learned how to recognize objects from real-life situations. We understood that working with objects makes it easier to write code that is easier to understand and reuse. You learned how to recognize real-world elements and translate them into the different components of the object-oriented paradigm supported in Swift: classes, protocols, properties, methods, and instances.

We discussed that classes represent blueprints or templates to generate the objects, which are also known as instances. We designed a few classes with properties and methods that represent blueprints for real-life objects. Then, we improved the initial design by taking advantage of the power of abstraction and specialized different classes.

In *Chapter 2, Structures, Classes, and Instances*, you learned about an object's life cycle. We worked with many examples to understand how object initializers and deinitializers work. We declared our first class to generate a blueprint for objects. We customized object initializers and deinitializers and tested their personalized behavior in action with live examples in Swift's Playground. We considered how they work in combination with automatic reference counting.

In *Chapter 3, Encapsulation of Data with Properties*, you learned the different members of a class and how they are reflected in members of the instances generated from a class. We worked with instance properties, type properties, instance methods, and type methods. We worked with stored properties, getters, setters, and property observers, and we took advantage of access modifiers to hide data. We also worked with mutable and immutable versions of a 3D vector. We discussed the difference between mutable and immutable classes. Immutable classes are extremely useful when we work with concurrent code.

In *Chapter 4, Inheritance, Abstraction, and Specialization*, you learned how to take advantage of simple inheritance to specialize a base class. We designed many classes from top to bottom using chained initializers, type properties, computed properties, stored properties, and methods. Then, we coded most of these classes in the interactive Playground, taking advantage of different mechanisms provided by Swift. We took advantage of operator functions to overload operators that we could use with the instances of our classes. We overrode and overloaded initializers, type properties, and methods. We also took advantage of one of the most exciting object-oriented features: polymorphism.

In *Chapter 5, Contract Programming with Protocols*, you learned that Swift works with protocols in combination with classes. The only way to have multiple inheritance in Swift is through the usage of protocols. You learned about the declaration and combination of multiple blueprints to generate a single instance. We declared protocols with different types of requirements. Then, we created many classes that conform to these protocols. We worked with type casting to take a look at how protocols work as types. Finally, we combined protocols with classes to take advantage of multiple inheritance in Swift. We combined inheritance for protocols and inheritance for classes.

In *Chapter 6, Maximization of Code Reuse with Generic Code*, you learned how to maximize code reuse by writing code capable of working with objects of different types—that is, instances of classes that conform to specific protocols or whose class hierarchy includes specific superclasses. We worked with protocols and generics. We also created classes capable of working with one or two constrained generic types. We combined inheritance, protocols, and extensions to maximize the reusability of code. We also made classes work with many different types. Generics are very important to maximizing code reuse in Swift.

In *Chapter 7, Object-Oriented Programming and Functional Programming,* you learned how to refactor existing code to take full advantage of object-oriented code. We prepared the code for future requirements, reduced maintenance cost, and maximized code reuse. We worked with many functional programming features included in Swift, and we combined them with everything we discussed so far about object-oriented programming. We analyzed the differences between imperative and functional programming approaches for many algorithms.

Now, you will learn how to extend the existing classes to achieve our goals.

Adding methods with extensions

Sometimes, we would like to add methods to an existing class. We already know how to do this; we just need to go to its Swift source file and add a new method within the class body. However, sometimes, we cannot access the source code for the class, or it isn't convenient to make changes to it. A typical example of this situation is a class, struct, or any other type that is part of the standard language elements. For example, we might want to add a method that we can call in any Int value to initialize either a 2D or 3D point with all its elements set to the Int value.

The following lines declare a simple Point2D class that represents a mutable 2D point with the x and y elements. The class conforms to the CustomStringConvertible protocol; therefore, it declares a description computed property that returns a string representation for the 2D point:

```
public class Point2D: CustomStringConvertible {
    public var x: Int
    public var y: Int

    public var valuesAsDescription: String {
        return "x: \(x), y: \(y)"
    }

    public var description: String {
        get {
            return "(\(valuesAsDescription))"
        }
    }

    init(x: Int, y: Int) {
        self.x = x
        self.y = y
    }
}
```

Extending and Building Object-Oriented Code

The `Point2D` class declares two stored properties: x and y. The `valueAsDescription` computed property returns a string with the values for x and y without a parenthesis. The description computed property encloses the value returned by `valueAsDescription` in parentheses.

The following lines declare a `Point3D` class that inherits from the previously created `Point2D` class and add a z element to the inherited x and y elements:

```
public class Point3D: Point2D {
    public var z: Int

    public override var valuesAsDescription: String {
        return "\(super.valuesAsDescription), z:\(z)"
    }

    init(x: Int, y: Int, z: Int) {
        self.z = z
        super.init(x: x, y: y)
    }
}
```

The `Point3D` class declares the z stored property and overrides the `valueAsDescription` computed property to concatenate the value of the z stored property to the string value of this property in the superclass. This way, the description computed property declared in the `Point2D` superclass will generate the values for x, y, and z enclosed within parentheses.

Now that we have a `Point2D` class and a `Point3D` class, we want to extend the `Int` type to provide methods that generate instances of these classes with all their elements initialized with the `Int` value. Specifically, we want to be able to write the following line to generate a `Point2D` instance with the x and y values initialized to 3:

```
Var point2D1 = 3.toPoint2D()
```

In addition, we want to be able to write the following line to generate a **Point3D** instance with the x, y, and z values initialized to 5:

```
var point3D1 = 5.toPoint3D()
```

The following lines use the `extension` keyword to add two methods to the `Int` standard type—`toPoint2D` and `toPoint3D`:

```
extension Int {
    public func toPoint2D() -> Point2D {
        return Point2D(x: self, y: self)
    }
```

```
    public func toPoint3D() -> Point3D {
        return Point3D(x: self, y: self, z: self)
    }
}
```

The `toPoint2D` method returns a new instance of `Point2D` with the x and y arguments of the initializer set to `self`. In this case, `self` represents the actual value for `Int`. The `toPoint3D` method returns a new instance of `Point3D` with the x, y, and z arguments of the initializer set to `self`.

The following lines use the previously added methods to create instances of both `Point2D` and `Point3D`:

```
print(3.toPoint2D())
print(5.toPoint2D())
print(3.toPoint3D())
print(5.toPoint3D())
```

The following lines show the output generated by the preceding code:

```
(x: 3, y: 3)
(x: 5, y: 5)
(x: 3, y: 3, z:3)
(x: 5, y: 5, z:5)
```

The following screenshot shows the results of executing the previous lines in the Playground:

```
public class Point3D: Point2D {
    public var z: Int

    public override var valuesAsDescription: String {
        return "\(super.valuesAsDescription), z:\(z)"      (4 times)
    }

    init(x: Int, y: Int, z: Int) {
        self.z = z
        super.init(x: x, y: y)
    }
}

extension Int {
    public func toPoint2D() -> Point2D {
        return Point2D(x: self, y: self)                   (2 times)
    }

    public func toPoint3D() -> Point3D {
        return Point3D(x: self, y: self, z: self)          (2 times)
    }
}

print(3.toPoint2D())                                       "(x: 3, y: 3)\n"
print(5.toPoint2D())                                       "(x: 5, y: 5)\n"
print(3.toPoint3D())                                       "(x: 3, y: 3, z:3)\n"
print(5.toPoint3D())                                       "(x: 5, y: 5, z:5)\n"

(x: 3, y: 3)
(x: 5, y: 5)
(x: 3, y: 3, z:3)
(x: 5, y: 5, z:5)
```

Extending and Building Object-Oriented Code

> If you have some experience with Objective-C, you will notice that extensions in Swift are very similar to categories in Objective-C. However, one of the main differences is that extensions in Swift do not have names.

Now, let's imagine that both the `Point2D` and `Point3D` classes are included in an external framework or library and that we aren't able to access the source code. Our code needs to convert instances of `Point3D` to a `(Int, Int, Int)` tuple. It is a nice feature to generate a tuple with named elements. As we consider that we cannot access the source code, we can use the **extension** keyword to add a `toTuple` method to the `Point3D` class. This way, we can easily convert a `Point3D` instance to a tuple. The following lines do the job:

```
extension Point3D {
    public func toTuple() -> (x: Int, y: Int, z: Int) {
        return (x: x, y: y, z: z)
    }
}
```

The following lines create an instance of the `Point3D` class and then call the recently added `toTuple` method to generate a tuple composed of three `Int` values (`Int, Int, Int`). Then, the code prints the string representation of the generated tuple. The next line uses a **let** statement to retrieve the three elements from the tuple generated by another call to the `toTuple` method. Then, the code prints the values for the three retrieved elements. The last two lines use the element names (x, y, and z) and numbers (0, 1, and 2) to access the generated tuple values:

```
var point3D1 = Point3D(x: 10, y: 20, z: 15)
var point3D1Tuple = point3D1.toTuple()
print(point3D1Tuple)
let (point3D1x, point3D1y, point3D1z) = point3D1.toTuple()
print(point3D1x, point3D1y, point3D1z)
print(point3D1Tuple.x, point3D1Tuple.y, point3D1Tuple.z)
print(point3D1Tuple.0, point3D1Tuple.1, point3D1Tuple.2)
```

The following lines show the output generated by the preceding code.

```
(10, 20, 15)
10 20 15
10 20 15
10 20 15
```

The following screenshot shows the result of executing the previous lines in the Playground:

```swift
extension Point3D {
    public func toTuple() -> (x: Int, y: Int, z: Int) {
        return (x: x, y: y, z: z)                              (2 times)
    }
}

var point3D1 = Point3D(x: 10, y: 20, z: 15)                    (x: 10, y: 20, z:15)
var point3D1Tuple = point3D1.toTuple()                         (.0 10, .1 20, .2 15)
print(point3D1Tuple)                                           "(10, 20, 15)\n"
let (point3D1x, point3D1y, point3D1z) = point3D1.toTuple()
print(point3D1x, point3D1y, point3D1z)                         "10 20 15\n"
print(point3D1Tuple.x, point3D1Tuple.y, point3D1Tuple.z)       "10 20 15\n"
print(point3D1Tuple.0, point3D1Tuple.1, point3D1Tuple.2)       "10 20 15\n"
```

```
(10, 20, 15)
10 20 15
10 20 15
10 20 15
```

Adding computed properties to a base type with extensions

Swift allows us to add both computed instance properties and computed type properties to an existing type. These are the only types of properties that we can add to an existing type, so we cannot add simpler stored properties using extensions.

When you need to perform calculations with values that have an associated unit of measurement, it is very common to make mistakes by mixing different units of measurement. It is also common to perform incorrect conversions between the different units that generate wrong results. Swift doesn't allow us to associate a specific numerical value with a unit of measurement. However, we can add computed properties to provide some information about the units of measurement for a specific domain.

> We worked with units when we analyzed the object-oriented approach of the HealthKit framework in *Chapter 1, Objects from the Real World to Playground*. However, in this case, we just want to simplify a sum operation with a specific resistance unit.

Extending and Building Object-Oriented Code

The need to associate quantities with units of measurement in any programming language is easy to understand even in the most basic math and physics problems. One of the simplest calculations is to sum two values that have an associated base unit. For example, say that you have two electrical resistance values. One of the values is measured in ohms and the other in kilo-ohms. To sum the values, you must choose the desired unit and convert one of the values to the chosen unit. If you want the result to be expressed in ohms, you must convert the value in kilo-ohms to ohms, sum the two values expressed in ohms, and provide the result in ohms.

The following code uses variables with a suffix that defines the specific unit being used in each case. You have probably used or seen similar conventions. The suffixes make the code less error-prone because you easily understand that `r1InOhms` holds a value in ohms, and `r2InKohms` holds a value in kilo-ohms. Thus, there is a line that assigns the result of converting the `r2InKohms` value to ohms to the new `r2InOhms` variable. The last line calculates the sum and holds the result in ohms because both variables hold values in the same unit of measurement:

```
var r1InOhms = 500.0
var r2InKohms = 5.2
var r2InOhms = r2InKohms * 1e3
var r1PlusR2InOhms = r1InOhms + r2InOhms
```

Obviously, the code is still error-prone because there won't be any exception thrown or syntax error if a developer adds the following line to sum ohms and kilo-ohms without performing the necessary conversions:

```
// The following line produces a wrong result
var r3InOhms = r1InOhms + r2InKohms
```

There is no rule that assures that all the variables included in the sum operation must use the same suffix—that is, the same unit. There aren't invalid operations between variables that hold values with incompatible units. For example, you might sum a voltage value to a resistance value, and the code won't produce any error or warning.

The following lines use the `extension` keyword to add three get-only computed properties to the `Double` standard type: `ohm`, `kohm`, and `mohm`:

```
extension Double {
    public var ohm: Double { return self }
    public var kohm: Double { return self * 1e3 }
    public var mohm: Double { return self * 1e6 }
}
```

The ohm get-only computed property returns self — that is, the actual value for Double. The kohm get-only computed property returns self multiplied by 1,000. In this case, the code uses the exponential notation, where 1e3 means 10 to the third power — that is, $10 * 10 * 10$. Finally, the mohm get-only computed property returns self multiplied by 1,000,000. In this case, the code uses the exponential notation where 1e6 means 10 to the sixth power — that is, $10 * 10 * 10 * 10 * 10 * 10$.

After we add the previous extensions, we want to perform the following calculation: *500 ohms + 5.2 KOhms + 3.1 MOhms*. If we convert all the values to ohms and express the result in ohms, we must calculate *500 ohms + 5,200 ohms + 3,100,000 ohms*. We can declare three variables with the number followed by a dot and the extension we created to convert the number to the value in a baseline ohm unit. The extension methods will return a Double number that will be always converted to ohms. Then, we can easily calculate the total resistance value in ohms by computing the sum of the three variables.

The following lines declare three variables, and each one uses the get-only computed property to specify the specific unit in which the original value is expressed: ohm, kohm, or mhom. Then, the code prints the real values stored in the three variables: resistance1, resistance2, and resistance3. The three values are stored in ohms because the get-only computed property returns the result of the conversion of each unit to ohms. Then, the code computes the sum of the three variables and stores the result expressed in ohms in the totalResistance variable:

```
var resistance1 = 500.0.ohm
var resistance2 = 5.2.kohm
var resistance3 = 3.1.mohm
print("resistance1 in ohms: \(resistance1)")
print("resistance2 in ohms: \(resistance2)")
print("resistance3 in ohms: \(resistance3)")

var totalResistance = resistance1 + resistance2 + resistance3

print("Total resistance in ohms: \(totalResistance)")
```

The following lines show the output generated after executing the preceding code:

```
resistance1 in ohms: 500.0
resistance2 in ohms: 5200.0
resistance3 in ohms: 3100000.0
Total resistance in ohms: 3105700.0
```

Extending and Building Object-Oriented Code

The following screenshot shows the results of executing the previous lines in the Playground:

```
var r1InOhms = 500.0                                        500
var r2InKohms = 5.2                                         5.2
var r2InOhms = r2InKohms * 1e3                              5200
var r1PlusR2InOhms = r1InOhms + r2InOhms                    5700

extension Double {
    public var ohm: Double { return self }                  500
    public var kohm: Double { return self * 1e3 }           5200
    public var mohm: Double { return self * 1e6 }           3100000
}

var resistance1 = 500.0.ohm                                 500
var resistance2 = 5.2.kohm                                  5200
var resistance3 = 3.1.mohm                                  3100000
print("resistance1 in ohms: \(resistance1)")                "resistance1 in ohms: 500.0\n"
print("resistance2 in ohms: \(resistance2)")                "resistance2 in ohms: 5200.0\n"
print("resistance3 in ohms: \(resistance3)")                "resistance3 in ohms: 3100000.0\n"

var totalResistance = resistance1 + resistance2 + resistance3    3105700

print("Total resistance in ohms: \(totalResistance)")       "Total resistance in ohms: 3105700.0\n"
```

```
resistance1 in ohms: 500.0
resistance2 in ohms: 5200.0
resistance3 in ohms: 3100000.0
Total resistance in ohms: 3105700.0
```

We can take advantage of Swift's flexibility with property names and use the Greek omega letter (Ω) instead of the ohm word in each of the get-only computed properties. You can easily insert the Greek omega letter in OS X by pressing *Alt + Z*. The following lines use the `extension` keyword again to add three get-only computed properties to the `Double` standard type—Ω, KΩ, and MΩ:

```
extension Double {
    public var Ω: Double { return self }
    public var KΩ: Double { return self * 1e3 }
    public var MΩ: Double { return self * 1e6 }
}
```

The following lines declare three variables, and each one uses the get-only computed property to specify the specific unit in which the original value is expressed: Ω, KΩ, or MΩ. Then, the code prints the real values stored in the three variables—`resistance4`, `resistance5`, and `resistance6`—then it computes the sum, and prints the result. The code looks really nice because it is easy to understand the unit in which each resistance value is expressed:

```
var resistance4 = 500.0.Ω
var resistance5 = 5.2.KΩ
```

```
var resistance6 = 3.1.MΩ
print("resistance4 in Ω: \(resistance4)")
print("resistance5 in Ω: \(resistance5)")
print("resistance6 in Ω: \(resistance6)")

var totalResistance456 = resistance4 + resistance5 + resistance6

print("Total resistance in Ω: \(totalResistance456)")
```

The following lines show the output generated after executing the preceding code:

```
resistance4 in Ω: 500.0
resistance5 in Ω: 5200.0
resistance6 in Ω: 3100000.0
Total resistance in Ω: 3105700.0
```

The following screenshot shows the results of executing the previous lines in the Playground:

```
extension Double {                                          500
    public var Ω: Double { return self }                    5200
    public var KΩ: Double { return self * 1e3 }             3100000
    public var MΩ: Double { return self * 1e6 }
}

var resistance4 = 500.0.Ω                                   500
var resistance5 = 5.2.KΩ                                    5200
var resistance6 = 3.1.MΩ                                    3100000
print("resistance4 in Ω: \(resistance4)")                   "resistance4 in Ω: 500.0\n"
print("resistance5 in Ω: \(resistance5)")                   "resistance5 in Ω: 5200.0\n"
print("resistance6 in Ω: \(resistance6)")                   "resistance6 in Ω: 3100000.0\n"

var totalResistance456 = resistance4 + resistance5 +        3105700
    resistance6

print("Total resistance in Ω: \(totalResistance456)")       "Total resistance in Ω: 3105700.0\n"
```

```
resistance4 in Ω: 500.0
resistance5 in Ω: 5200.0
resistance6 in Ω: 3100000.0
Total resistance in Ω: 3105700.0
```

Declaring new convenience initializers with extensions

So far, we always worked with one specific type of initializer for all the classes: *designated initializers*. These are the primary initializers for a class in Swift, and they make sure that all the properties are initialized. In fact, every class must have at least one designated initializer. However, it is important to note that a class can satisfy this requirement by inheriting a designated initializer from its superclass.

There is another type of initializer known as *convenience initializer* that acts as a secondary initializer and always ends up calling a designated initializer. Convenience initializers are optional, so any class can declare one or more convenience initializers to provide initializers that cover specific use cases or more convenient shortcuts to create instances of a class.

Now, imagine that we cannot access the code for the previously declared `Point3D` class. We are working on an app, and we discover too many use cases in which we have to create an instance of a `Point3D` class based on the values found on any of the following:

- A tuple with three `Int` values (Int, Int, Int)
- A single `Int` value that should be used to initialize x, y, and z
- The x and y properties in a `Point2D` instance and an **Int** value that adds the z component

> Swift allows us to add convenience initializers when we extend classes. It isn't possible to add designated initializers using the `extend` keyword.

The following lines use the `extension` keyword to add three convenience initializers to the existing `Point3D` class:

```
extension Point3D {
    convenience init(tuple: (Int, Int, Int)) {
        self.init(x: tuple.0, y: tuple.1, z: tuple.2)
    }

    convenience init(singleValue: Int) {
        self.init(x: singleValue, y: singleValue, z: singleValue)
    }

    convenience init(point2D: Point2D, z: Int) {
```

```
            self.init(x: point2D.x, y: point2D.y, z: z)
    }
}
```

The `convenience` keyword before `init` indicates to Swift that we are declaring a convenience initializer instead of the default designated initializer. The first convenience initializer receives a `tuple` argument of type `(Int, Int, Int)` and calls the designated initializer for the class using `self.init` and providing the values for the three required arguments: x, y, and z. The second convenience initializer receives a `singleValue` argument of the `Int` type and calls the designated initializer for the class with `singleValue` for the three required arguments. The third convenience initializer receives two arguments: `point2D` and z. The first argument is of the `Point2D` type, and the second is of type `Int`. The convenience initializer calls the designated initializer for the class with `point2D.x` for x, `point2D.y` for y, and z for z.

The following lines use the recently added convenience initializers to create instances of the `Point3D` class and print their description:

```
var tuple1 = (10, 20, 30)
var tuple2 = (5, 10, 15)

var point3D3 = Point3D(tuple: tuple1)
var point3D4 = Point3D(tuple: tuple2)
print(point3D3)
print(point3D4)

var point3D5 = Point3D(singleValue: 5)
print(point3D5)

var point2D6 = Point2D(x: 10, y: 11)
var point3D6 = Point3D(point2D: point2D6, z: 12)
print(point3D6)
```

The following lines show the output generated after executing the preceding code:

```
(x: 10, y: 20, z:30)
(x: 5, y: 10, z:15)
(x: 5, y: 5, z:5)
(x: 10, y: 11, z:12)
```

The following screenshot shows the results of executing the previous lines in the Playground:

```swift
extension Point3D {
    convenience init(tuple: (Int, Int, Int)) {
        self.init(x: tuple.0, y: tuple.1, z: tuple.2)
    }
    
    convenience init(singleValue: Int) {
        self.init(x: singleValue, y: singleValue, z: singleValue)
    }
    
    convenience init(point2D: Point2D, z: Int) {
        self.init(x: point2D.x, y: point2D.y, z: z)
    }
}

var tuple1 = (10, 20, 30)
var tuple2 = (5, 10, 15)

var point3D3 = Point3D(tuple: tuple1)
var point3D4 = Point3D(tuple: tuple2)
print(point3D3)
print(point3D4)

var point3D5 = Point3D(singleValue: 5)
print(point3D5)

var point2D6 = Point2D(x: 10, y: 11)
var point3D6 = Point3D(point2D: point2D6, z: 12)
print(point3D6)
```

```
(x: 10, y: 20, z:30)
(x: 5, y: 10, z:15)
(x: 5, y: 5, z:5)
(x: 10, y: 11, z:12)
```

Defining subscripts with extensions

Let's consider that we still cannot access the code for the previously declared `Point3D` class. We are working on an app, and we discover that it would be nice to access the x, y, and z values of a `Point3D` instance with `[0]`, `[1]`, and `[2]`. We can easily add a subscript by extending the `Point3D` class.

The following lines use the `extension` keyword to a subscript to the existing `Point3D` class:

```swift
extension Point3D {
    public subscript(index: Int) -> Int? {
        switch index {
```

```
            case 0: return x
            case 1: return y
            case 2: return z
            default: return nil
            }
        }
    }
```

The following lines use the recently added subscript to access the elements of a `Point3D` instance:

```
var point3D7 = Point3D(x: 10, y: 15, z: 4)
if let point3D7X = point3D7[0] {
    print("X or [0]: \(point3D7X)")
}
if let point3D7Y = point3D7[1] {
    print("Y or [1]: \(point3D7Y)")
}
if let point3D7Z = point3D7[2] {
    print("Z or [2]: \(point3D7Z)")
}
```

The following lines show the output generated after executing the preceding code:

```
X or [0]: 10
Y or [1]: 15
Z or [2]: 4
```

Working with object-oriented code in apps

So far, we created and extended classes in the Playground. In fact, we could execute the same sample code in the Swift REPL. The Swift REPL is a read-eval-print loop, also known as an interactive language shell, where we can enter expressions or pieces of code, make Swift evaluate them, and prints the results.

Now, we will create a simple iOS app based on the Single View Application template with Xcode. We will recognize the usage of object-oriented code included in the template—that is, before we add components and code to the app. Then, we will take advantage of the `GameRepository` class we created in the previous chapter and use it to populate a UI element.

Extending and Building Object-Oriented Code

Navigate to **File** | **New** | **Project...** in Xcode. Then, navigate to **iOS** | **Application** on the left-hand side of the **Choose a template for your new project** dialog box. Select **Single View Application** on the right-hand side and click on **Next**, as shown in the following screenshot:

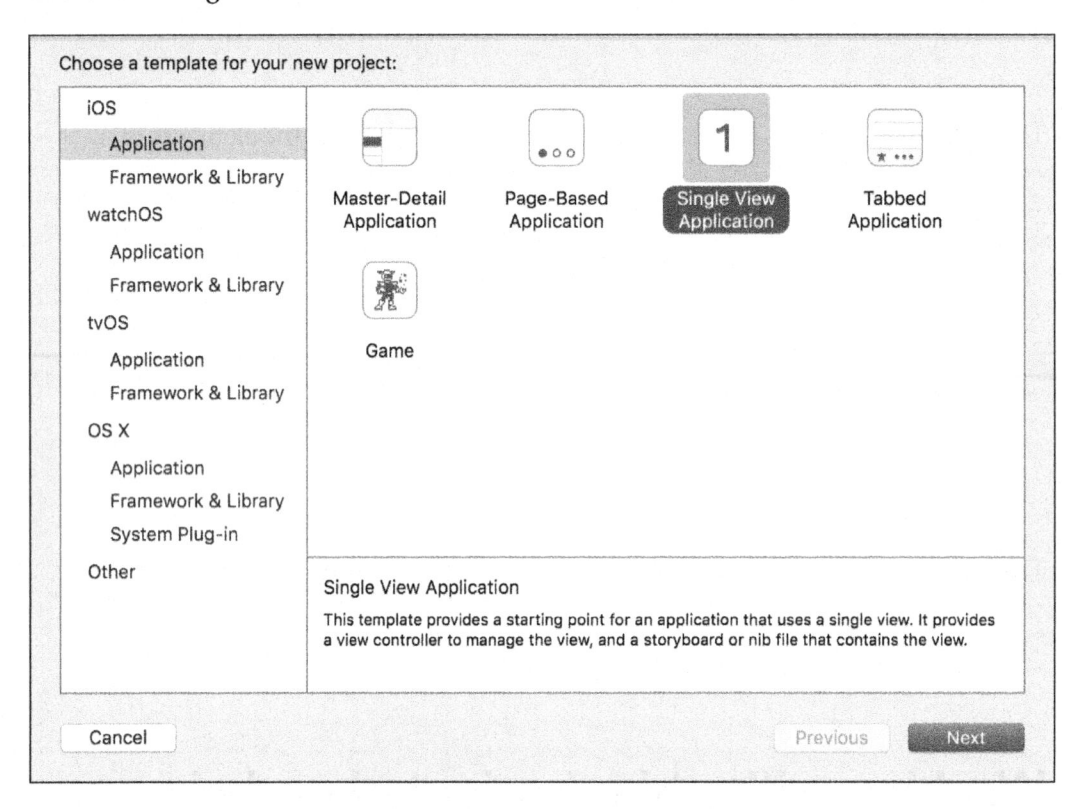

Enter Chapter 8 in **Product Name** and select **Swift** in language and **Universal** in **Devices**, as shown in the next screenshot. This way, we will create an app that can run on both iPad and iPhone devices. Then, click on **Next**:

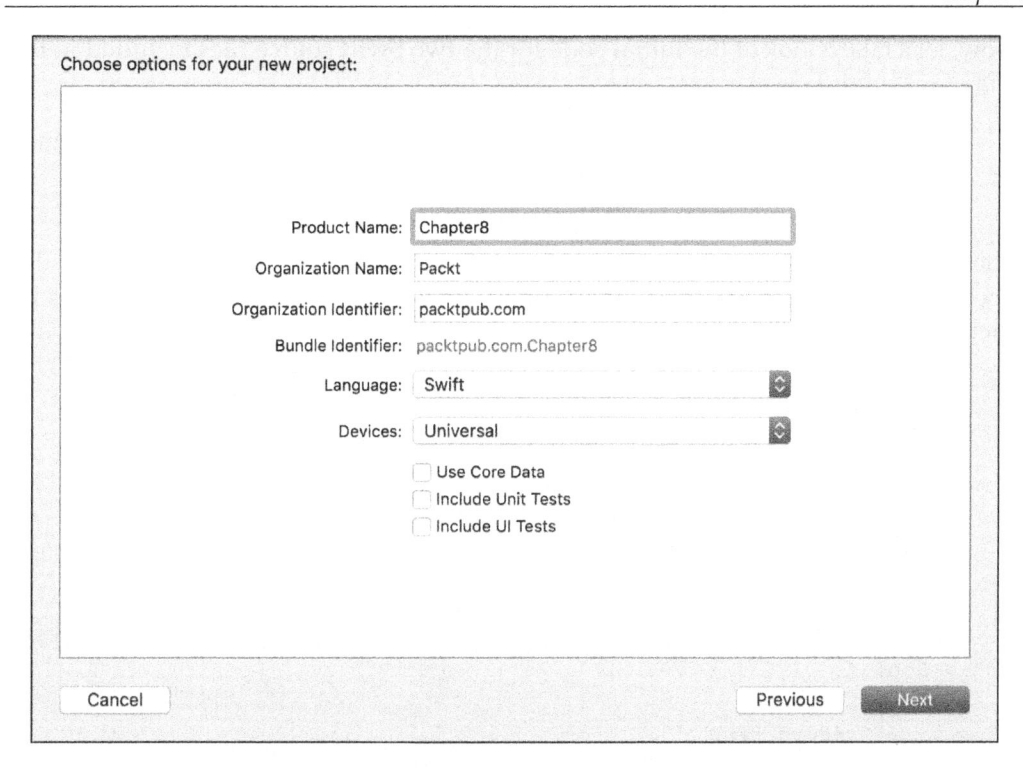

Select the desired folder in which you want to create the new project folder, make sure **Don't add to any project or workspace** is selected in the **Add to** drop-down list in case this option is shown in the dialog box, and click on **Create**. Xcode will create the new project and all the related files. The following screenshot shows the project navigator located on the left-hand side of the Xcode window:

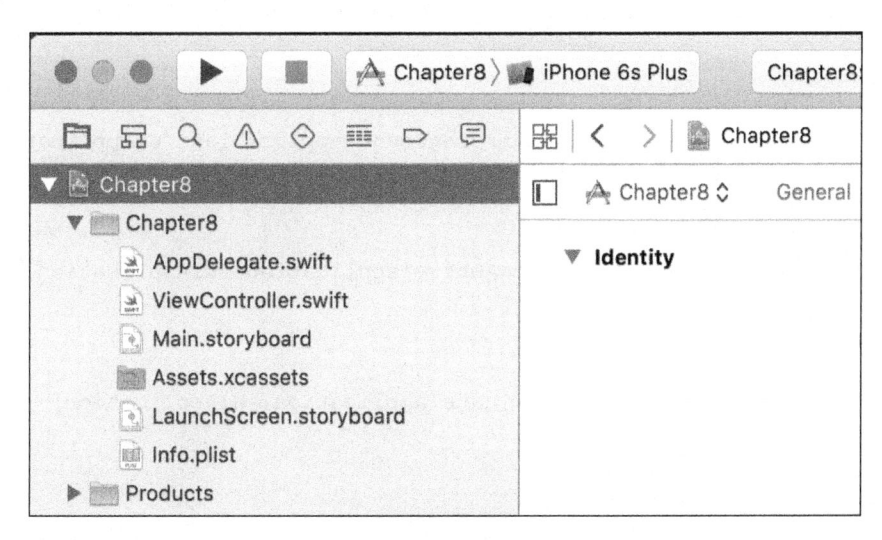

Extending and Building Object-Oriented Code

Now, let's take a look at the initial code for the two Swift source files included in the `Chapter8` module:

- `AppDelegate.swift`: This declares the `AppDelegate` class, and it is the entry point to our application
- `ViewController.swift`: This declares the `ViewController` class

The following lines show the initial code for the `AppDelegate.swift` source file that declares the `AppDelegate` class without the comments that the template includes in each method:

```swift
import UIKit

@UIApplicationMain
class AppDelegate: UIResponder, UIApplicationDelegate {

    var window: UIWindow?

    func application(application: UIApplication,
didFinishLaunchingWithOptions launchOptions: [NSObject: AnyObject]?)
-> Bool {

        return true
    }

    func applicationWillResignActive(application: UIApplication) {

    }

    func applicationDidEnterBackground(application: UIApplication) {

    }

    func applicationWillEnterForeground(application: UIApplication) {

    }

    func applicationDidBecomeActive(application: UIApplication) {

    }

    func applicationWillTerminate(application: UIApplication) {

    }
}
```

The `@UIApplicationMain` attribute included at the top of the declaration of the `AppDelegate` class indicates that the class is designated as the delegate of the shared `UIApplication` object in any iOS app. The `AppDelegate` class is a subclass of the `UIResponder` class and conforms to the `UIApplicationDelegate` protocol. The class declares a `window` stored property of the `UIWindow` type optional (`UIWindow?`) and six instance methods. All the methods receive an `application` argument of the `UIApplication` type, which is another subclass of `UIResponder`. The `application` argument will always be the same instance of `UIApplication` that represents the current iOS app—that is, our app. The `application` method receives a second argument named `launchOptions` that provides a dictionary with keys indicating the reason that your app was launched for. This method is the only one that has code and just returns `true`.

The following lines show the initial code for the **ViewController.swift** source file that declares the `ViewController` class without the comments that the template includes in each method:

```
import UIKit

class ViewController: UIViewController {

    override func viewDidLoad() {
        super.viewDidLoad()
    }

    override func didReceiveMemoryWarning() {
        super.didReceiveMemoryWarning()
    }
}
```

The `ViewController` class is a subclass of the `UIViewController` class and overrides two parameterless instance methods: `viewDidLoad` and `didReceiveMemoryWarning`. Both methods include a line of code that calls the method with the same name in its superclass.

It is important to take into account that the `UIViewController` class—that is, the superclass for `ViewController`—is a subclass of the `UIResponder` class and conforms to the following protocols: `NSCoding`, `UIAppearanceContainer`, `UITraitEnvironment`, `UIContentContainer`, and `UIFocusEnvironment`.

Extending and Building Object-Oriented Code

We just created a new project based on a template, and we are already working with classes that have superclasses, conform to protocols, declare stored properties, define instance methods, and override inherited instance methods. Everything you learned in the previous chapters is extremely useful to adding object-oriented code to the initial templates for any kind of app or application, and it is also useful to understand how to interact with the different object-oriented frameworks based on our targets.

Click on **Main.storyboard** in the Project Navigator on the left-hand side of the Xcode window. The editor will switch to a design view that displays how the view will look. Click on **View Controller** under **View Controller Scene**. Make sure that you see the **Utilities** pane on the right-hand side and check the values for **Identity Inspector**. The value for **Class** will be **ViewController** under **Custom Class**, as shown in the following screenshot:

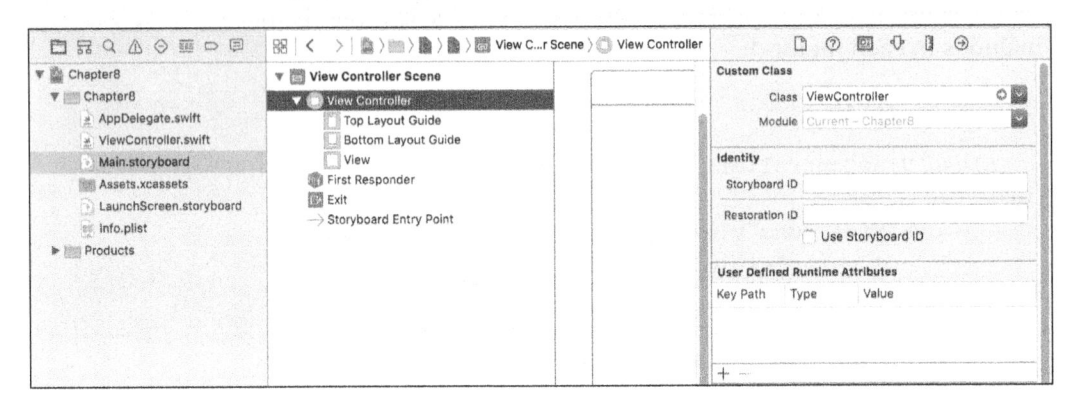

The previously introduced `ViewController` class is the custom class associated with the **View Controller** tab in the main storyboard for the iOS app. We will add code to this class later.

Now, we want to add and connect a simple UI element that will allow us to make a selection from multiple choices—specifically a `UIPickerView` instance. A picker view uses a spinning-wheel or slot-machine metaphor to show one or more sets of values. We can select the desired values by rotating the wheels and making the desired row of values align with a selection indicator.

Make sure that the **Object Library** tab is visible in **Library View**, which Xcode displays in the bottom half of the **Utilities** pane on the right-hand side. You just need to click on the **Show the Object Library** button at the top of the bottom half. Click on the **Filter** textbox located at the bottom and type `Picker`. **Object Library** will display all the objects that contain `Picker`, and one of them is **Picker View**, as shown in the following screenshot:

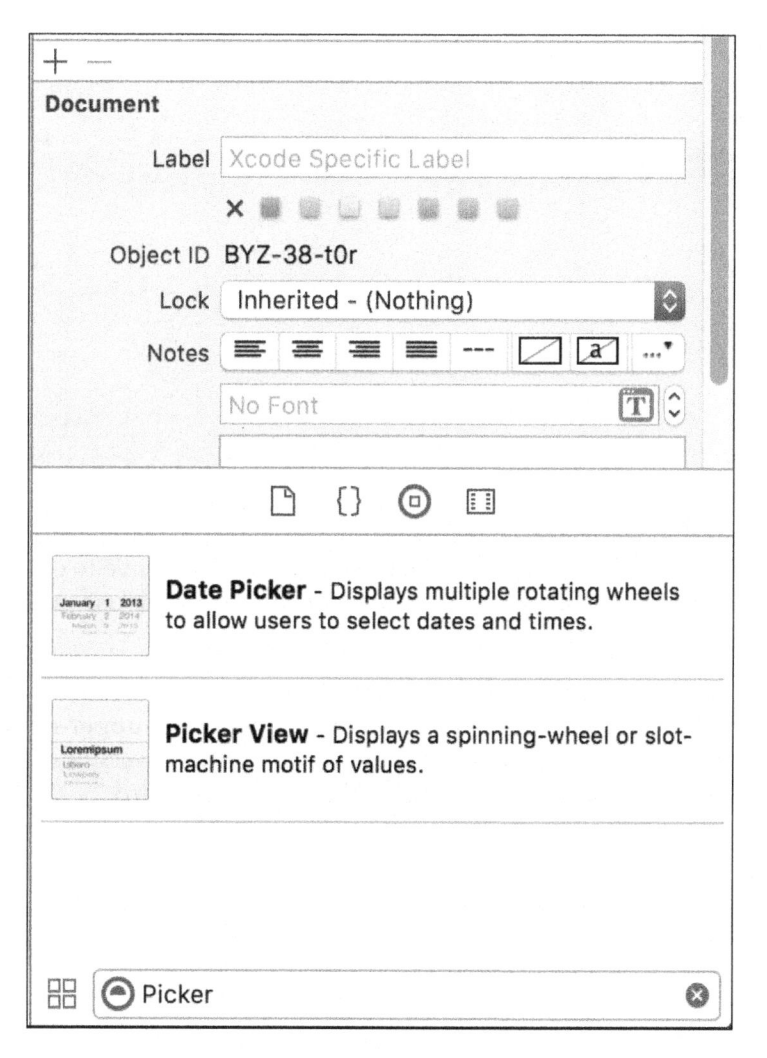

Extending and Building Object-Oriented Code

Drag **Picker View** from the previously shown list to the rectangle that defines the view in the preview. This way, we will have a **Picker View** component on the view in the main storyboard, as shown in the following screenshot. Note that the class is `UIPickerView`:

We added a **Picker View** component on the view. Now, we have to expose the component to make it accessible through code in the previously analyzed `ViewController` class.

Navigate to **View** | **Assistant Editor** | **Show Assistant Editor** in the Xcode menu or simply click on the button with two intersecting circles in the upper-right corner (the second button). Xcode will display the source code for the `ViewController` class on the right-hand side of the view preview for the main storyboard.

Press the *Ctrl* key and hold it while you drag the recently added **Picker View** component from the view to the blank line after the `ViewController` class declaration. Xcode will display a line and a tooltip with the following legend at the position to which you are dragging the mouse: **Insert Outlet or Outlet Collection**. Release the *Ctrl* key, and Xcode will display a pop-up dialog box asking us for a name for the new property and `IBOutlet` that it will create. Enter `picker` in the **Name** textbox and then click on **Connect**:

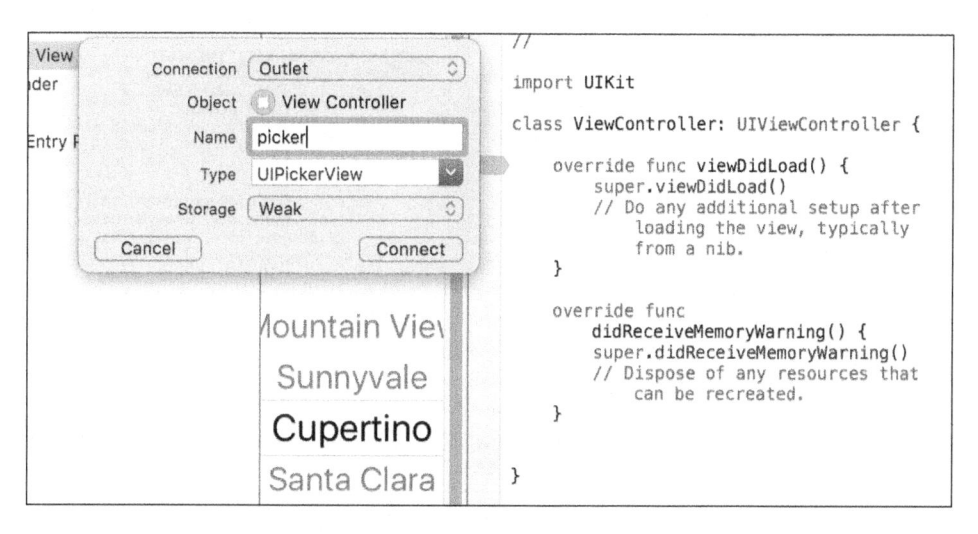

After we click on the **Connect** button, the following highlighted line will appear within the `ViewController` class body:

```
class ViewController: UIViewController {

    @IBOutlet weak var picker: UIPickerView!
```

The new line uses the `@IBOutlet` decorator to indicate the outlet connection. The line declares a `picker` stored property as a weak reference to an implicitly unwrapped optional `UIPickerView`. The `weak` keyword indicates Swift to use a weak reference that allows the possibility of the object that the property points to become `nil`.

The exclamation mark (`!`) after the `UIPickerView` class name indicates that Xcode wants Swift to treat `picker` as an implicitly unwrapped optional `UIPickerView` class. This way, the optional will be automatically unwrapped whenever the property is used. However, if it points to `nil`, it will trigger a runtime error.

Extending and Building Object-Oriented Code

You will notice there are two small circles on the left-hand side of the new line of code. If you let the cursor hover over this small icon, Xcode will highlight the **Picker View** component in the view connected to this property. If you click on the icon, Xcode will display a tooltip with the story board name, **Main.storyboard**, and the related component, **Picker**, as shown in the following screenshot:

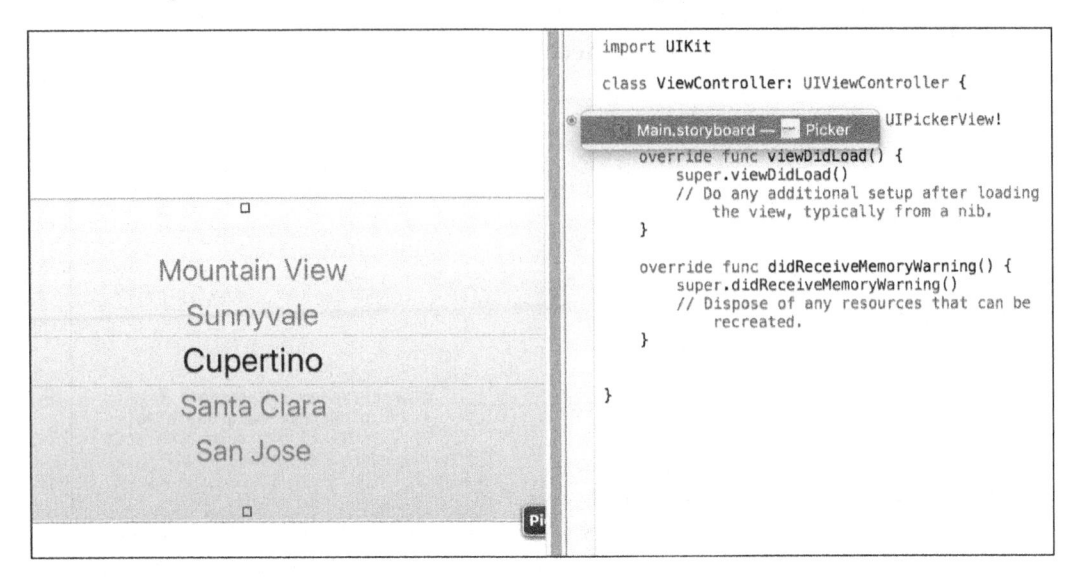

We can easily interact with the **Picker View** component through the recently added `picker` property in our `ViewController` class.

Adding an object-oriented data repository to a project

Now, we will add one protocol and many classes we created in the previous chapter to generate the `GameRepository` class. We want to display a list of game names in the **Picker View**. We will add the following Swift source files in the project within the `Chapter8` group:

- `EntityProtocol.swift`
- `Entity.swift`
- `Repository.swift`
- `Game.swift`
- `GameRepository.swift`

Click on the **Chapter8** group in **Project Navigator** (the icon represents a folder). Do not confuse it with the **Chapter8** project that is the parent for the **Chapter8** group. Navigate to **File** | **New** | **File...** and select **Swift File** as the template for your new file. Then, click on **Next** and enter **EntityProtocol** in the **Save As** textbox. Make sure that **Chapter8** with the folder icon is selected in the **Group** drop-down menu, as shown in the next screenshot, and then click on **Create**. Swift will add the new `EntityProtocol.swift` source file to the **Chapter8** group within the **Chapter8** project:

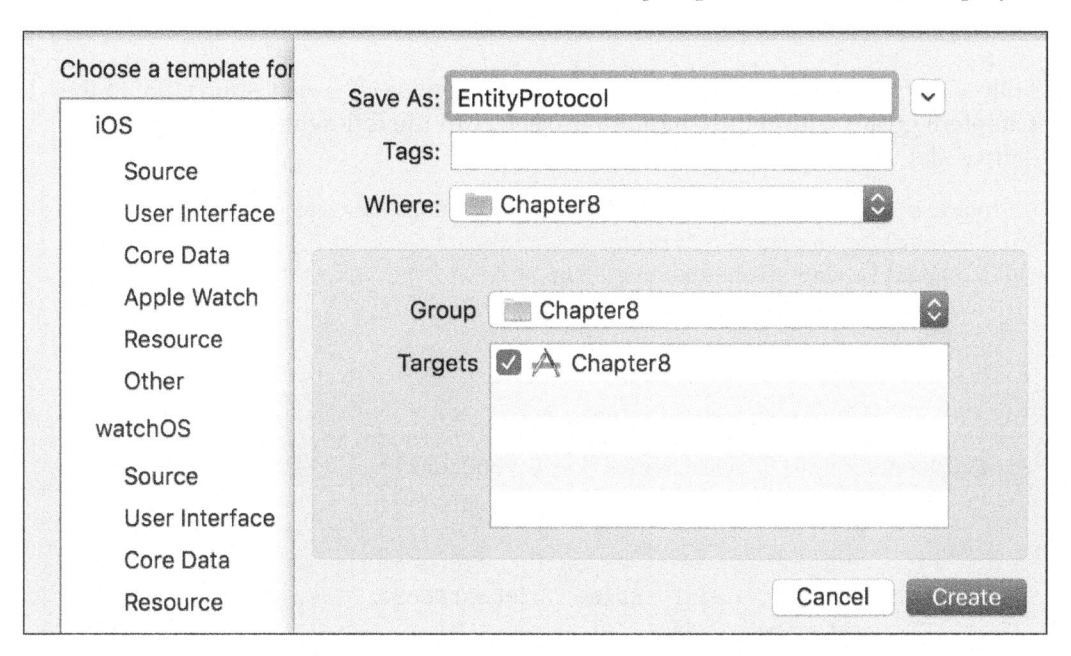

Add the following code for the recently created `EntityProtocol.swift` source file:

```
public protocol EntityProtocol {
    var id: Int { get }
}
```

Follow the previously explained steps to add a new `Entity.swift` source file to the **Chapter8** group within the **Chapter8** project. Add the following code to the new source file:

```
public class Entity: EntityProtocol {
    public let id: Int

    init(id: Int) {
        self.id = id
    }
}
```

Extending and Building Object-Oriented Code

Follow the previously explained steps to add a new `Repository.swift` source file to the **Chapter8** group within the **Chapter8** project. Add the following code to the new source file:

```
public class Repository<T: EntityProtocol> {
    public func getAll() -> [T] {
        return [T]()
    }
}
```

Follow the previously explained steps to add a new `Game.swift` source file to the **Chapter8** group within the **Chapter8** project. Add the following code to the new source file:

```
public class Game: Entity, CustomStringConvertible {
    public var name: String
    public var highestScore: Int
    public var playedCount: Int
    
    public var description: String {
        get {
            return "id: \(id), name: \"\(name)\", highestScore: \(highestScore), playedCount: \(playedCount)"
        }
    }
    
    init(id: Int, name: String, highestScore: Int, playedCount: Int) {
        self.name = name
        self.highestScore = highestScore
        self.playedCount = playedCount
        super.init(id: id)
    }
}
```

Follow the previously explained steps to add a new `GameRepository.swift` source file to the **Chapter8** group within the **Chapter8** project. Add the following code to the new source file:

```
public class GameRepository: Repository<Game> {
    public override func getAll() -> [Game] {
        var gamesList = [Game]()

        gamesList.append(Game(id: 1, name: "Invaders 2016", highestScore: 1050, playedCount: 3_050))

        gamesList.append(Game(id: 2, name: "Minecraft", highestScore: 3741050, playedCount: 780_009_992))

        gamesList.append(Game(id: 3, name: "Minecraft Story Mode", highestScore: 67881050, playedCount: 304_506_506))

        gamesList.append(Game(id: 4, name: "Soccer Warriors", highestScore: 10_025, playedCount: 320_450))

        gamesList.append(Game(id: 5, name: "The Walking Dead Stories", highestScore: 1_450_708, playedCount: 75_405_350))

        gamesList.append(Game(id: 6, name: "Once Upon a Time in Wonderland", highestScore: 1_050_320, playedCount: 7_052))

        gamesList.append(Game(id: 7, name: "Cars Forever", highestScore: 6_705_203, playedCount: 850_021))

        gamesList.append(Game(id: 8, name: "Jake & Peter Pan", highestScore: 4_023_134, playedCount: 350_230))

        gamesList.append(Game(id: 9, name: "Kong Strikes Back", highestScore: 1_050_230, playedCount: 450_050))

        gamesList.append(Game(id: 10, name: "Mario Kart 2016", highestScore: 10_572_340, playedCount: 3_760_879))

        return gamesList
    }
}
```

Extending and Building Object-Oriented Code

We have added all the necessary source files to include the protocol and the classes that allow us to work with the `GameRepository` class in our app. The following screenshot shows the **Project Navigator** with all the new files added to the **Chapter8** group. In this case, we will add all the files to the same group. However, in more complex apps, it would be convenient to split the files in different groups to have a better organization of the code:

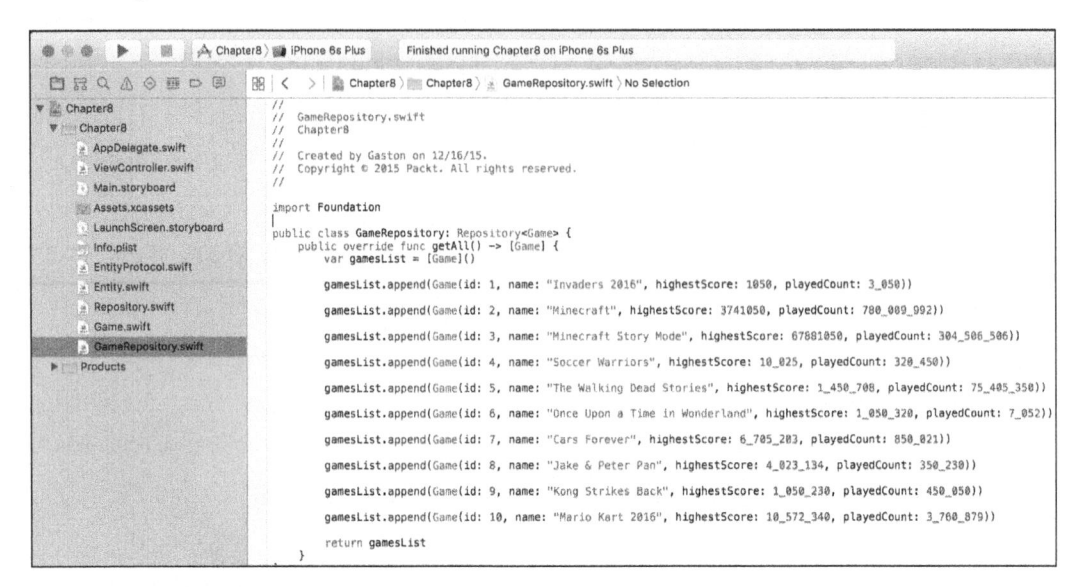

Interacting with an object-oriented data repository through Picker View

Now, we have to add code to the `ViewController` class in the `ViewController.swift` source file to make the class conform to two additional protocols: `UIPickerViewDataSource` and `UIPickerViewDelegate`. The conformance to the `UIPickerViewDataSource` protocol allows us to use the class as a data source for the `UIPickerView` class that represents the Picker View component. The conformance to the `UIPickerViewDelegate` protocol allows us to handle the events raised by the `UIPickerView` class.

The following lines show the new code for the `ViewController` class:

```
class ViewController: UIViewController, UIPickerViewDelegate,
UIPickerViewDataSource {

    @IBOutlet weak var picker: UIPickerView!
```

```swift
    private var gamesList: [Game] = [Game]()

    override func viewDidLoad() {
        super.viewDidLoad()
        // Do any additional setup after loading the view, typically from a nib.
        picker.delegate = self
        picker.dataSource = self

        let gameRepository = GameRepository()
        gamesList = gameRepository.getAll()
    }

    override func didReceiveMemoryWarning() {
        super.didReceiveMemoryWarning()
        // Dispose of any resources that can be recreated.
    }

    func numberOfComponentsInPickerView(pickerView: UIPickerView) -> Int {
        // Return the number of columns of data
        return 1
    }

    func pickerView(pickerView: UIPickerView, numberOfRowsInComponent component: Int) -> Int {
        // Return the number of rows of data
        return gamesList.count
    }

    func pickerView(pickerView: UIPickerView, titleForRow row: Int, forComponent component: Int) -> String? {
        // Return the data for the row. In this case, we don't have columns
        return gamesList[row].name
    }

    func pickerView(pickerView: UIPickerView, didSelectRow row: Int, inComponent component: Int) {
        // Retrieve the game for the selected row
        let selectedGame = gamesList[row]
        print("Selected game name: \(selectedGame.name). Highest score: \(selectedGame.highestScore)")
    }
}
```

Extending and Building Object-Oriented Code

We made changes to the class declaration to make it conform to the two additional protocols. We declared a private `gamesList` stored property of the `Array<Game>` type. We used the `[Game]` shortcut for this type. We then added the following lines to the overridden `viewDidLoad` method:

```
picker.delegate = self
picker.dataSource = self

let gameRepository = GameRepository()
gamesList = gameRepository.getAll()
```

The code assigns the current instance of the `ViewController` class identified by `self` to the `picker.delegate` property. We can do this because the `ViewController` class conforms to the `UIPickerViewDelegate` protocol. Then, the code assigns the current instance of the `ViewController` class to the `picker.dataSource` property. We can do this because the `ViewController` class conforms to the `UIPickerViewDataSource` protocol. This way, we can specify the data source and delegate for **Picker View**.

Then, we will create an instance of the `GameRepository` class and save `Array<Game>` with the list of games returned by the `getAll` method in the `gamesList` property. This way, we will be able to use `gamesList` later.

Then, we implemented two methods declared in the `UIPickerViewDataSource` protocol:

- `func numberOfComponentsInPickerView(pickerView: UIPickerView) -> Int`: This returns the number of columns to display in **Picker View**. In this case, we just want to display the name for each game, so we added code to this method to return 1.
- `func pickerView(pickerView: UIPickerView, numberOfRowsInComponent component: Int) -> Int`: This returns the number of rows to be displayed in each component or column. In this case, we just have one column, and we will display the number of games included in `gamesList Array<Game>`. Thus, we added code to this method to return `gamesList.count`.

Finally, we implemented two methods declared in the `UIPickerViewDelegate` protocol:

- `func pickerView(pickerView: UIPickerView, titleForRow row: Int, forComponent component: Int) -> String?`: This returns the data for the row to be displayed in **Picker View**. In this case, we just want to display the name for each game, so we added code to this method to return the `name` property for the `gamesList` element at the received `row` value.

- `func pickerView(pickerView: UIPickerView, didSelectRow row: Int, inComponent component: Int)`: Whenever the user makes a change to the Picker View selection, this method is executed, and the `row` argument includes the value for the selected row. We use the `row` value to retrieve the `Game` instance corresponding to the same index value for the `gamesList` array and then call `print` to display the selected game `name` and `highestScore` property values on the target output.

Now, we can debug the iOS app on an installed iOS simulator, such as an iPhone 6s Plus. Click on the **Play** button in the upper-left corner of the Xcode window. Once the simulator launches and the app begins its execution, you will see the **Picker View** component displaying all the game names. When we select a game in the **Picker View**, the target output will display the selected game name and its highest score, as shown in the following screenshot:

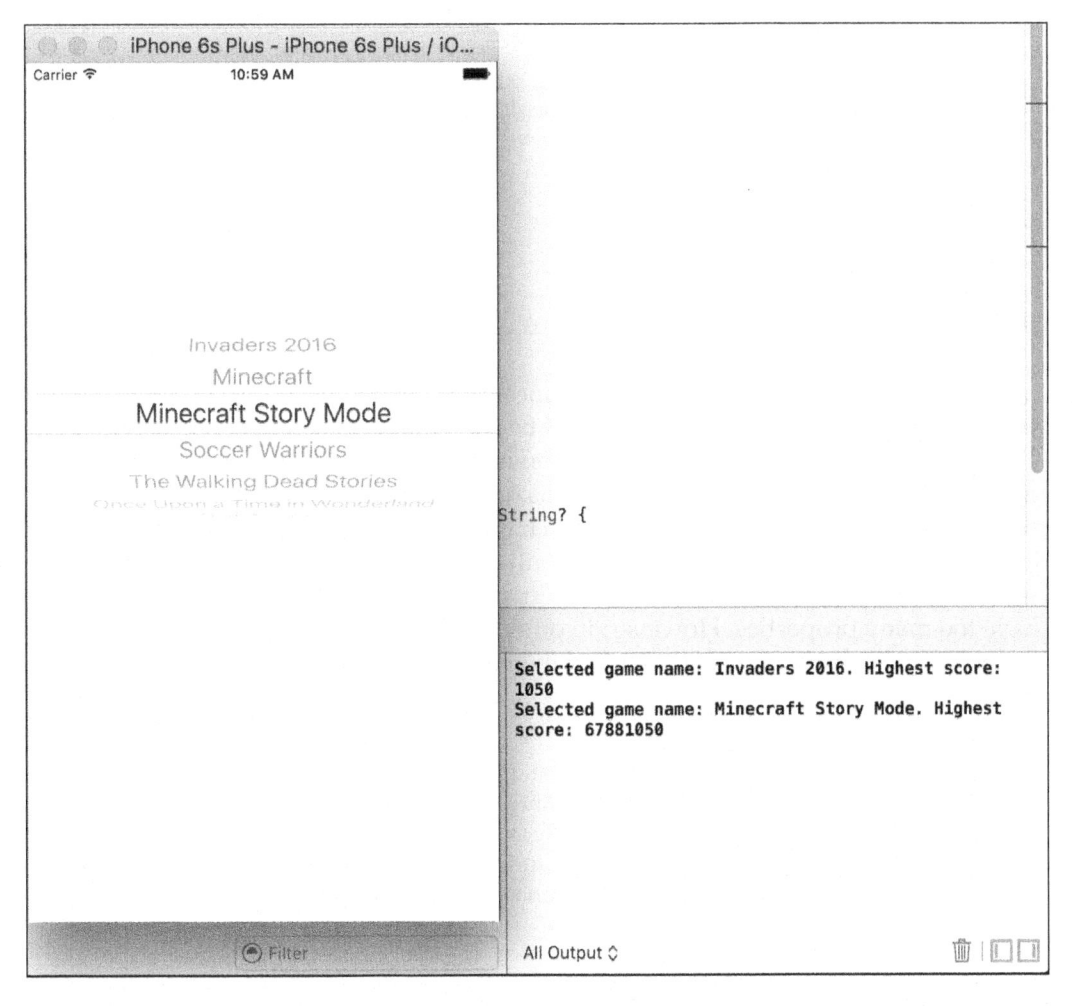

Extending and Building Object-Oriented Code

Go to the Xcode editor for the `ViewController.swift` source file and move the cursor to the following line in the `ViewController` class:

```
print("Selected game name: \(selectedGame.name). Highest score: \
(selectedGame.highestScore)")
```

Navigate to **Debug | Breakpoint | Add Breakpoint at Current Line**. Go back to the simulator and select a different game name from **Picker View**. Xcode will hit the break point, and we will be able to inspect the value for the `selectedGame` constant that references an instance of `Game`. The debugger will display the ID property as part of `Chapter8.Entity` because this property is inherited from the `Entity` class. The values for the other properties defined in the `Game` class are listed after the `id` property, as shown in the following screenshot:

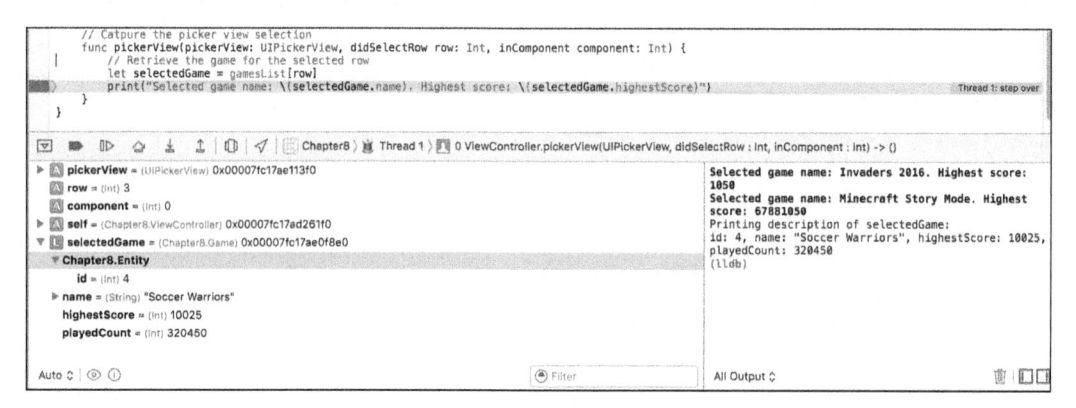

In this case, we have just a few `Game` instances in the game list. However, we must take into account that sometimes, it won't be convenient to have all the instances alive in case they have a big impact on memory consumption. We can transform the data from the instances to instances that have less memory footprint and retrieve the entire instances by a related ID when we change the selection in **Picker View**. For example, we can generate instances that only have a few stored properties instead of working with instances with all the properties. In this case, the `Game` instance doesn't have too many properties. However, in other cases, we might have instances that have dozens of properties, and many of them might be other instances with dozens of properties.

> Object-oriented code is great. However, we don't have to forget memory footprint as the number of required instances to keep alive increases in certain use cases. In our previous example, it doesn't make sense to transform the `Game` instances into simpler values because the code won't cause any memory issues.

Exercises

Use the recently created iOS app as the baseline and extend it to provide the following features:

- Add a text box to allow the user to enter the text that the game names must match in order to be displayed as an option in **View Picker**
- After the user selects a game in **View Picker**, display a new view that shows the highest score and the played count for the chosen game

Test your knowledge

1. We can add the following type of initializers to a class with extensions:
    1. Convenience initializers.
    2. Designated initializers.
    3. Primary initializers.

2. We can add the following type of properties to a class with extensions:
    1. Read/write stored type properties.
    2. Primary properties.
    3. Computed instance properties and computed type properties.

3. Convenience initializers are:
    1. Optional.
    2. Required.
    3. Required only in superclasses.

4. A convenience initializer acts as:
    1. A required initializer that doesn't need to call any other initializer.
    2. A secondary initializer that doesn't need to call any other initializer.
    3. A secondary initializer that always ends up calling a designated initializer.

5. If we declare the type for a property as `UIPickerView!`, Swift will treat the property as:
    1. An implicitly wrapped optional.
    2. An implicitly unwrapped optional.
    3. An exact equivalent of `UIPickerView?`.

Summary

In this chapter, you learned how to add methods, computed properties, convenience initializers, and scripts using extensions and without editing the original source code for the original classes or types. Then, we analyzed the initial object-oriented code in the Single View Application template for an iOS app.

We added a simple UI element to the template and then we added classes that we tested in the Swift Playground in the previous chapter. We interacted with a simple object-oriented data repository through Picker View and discussed how object-oriented code is everywhere in an iOS app.

Now that you have learned to write object-oriented code in Swift, you are ready to use everything you learned in real-life applications that will not only rock, but also maximize code reuse and simplify maintenance.

Exercise Answers

Chapter 1, Objects from the Real World to Playground

Q1	3
Q2	2
Q3	1
Q4	2
Q5	3

Chapter 2, Structures, Classes, and Instances

Q1	2
Q2	1
Q3	1
Q4	3
Q5	1

Exercise Answers

Chapter 3, Encapsulation of Data with Properties

Q1	1
Q2	3
Q3	1
Q4	2
Q5	2

Chapter 4, Inheritance, Abstraction, and Specialization

Q1	1
Q2	2
Q3	1
Q4	2
Q5	3

Chapter 5, Contract Programming with Protocols

Q1	2
Q2	3
Q3	1
Q4	1
Q5	3

Chapter 6, Maximization of Code Reuse with Generic Code

Q1	1
Q2	3
Q3	2
Q4	1
Q5	2

Chapter 7, Object-Oriented Programming and Functional Programming

Q1	2
Q2	1
Q3	1
Q4	3
Q5	3

Chapter 8, Extending and Building Object-Oriented Code

Q1	1
Q2	3
Q3	1
Q4	3
Q5	2

Index

A

actions
  recognizing, to create methods 17, 18
API objects
  working with, in Xcode Playground 26-30
array filtering
  functional version, creating 245-247
arrays
  filtering, with complex conditions 253-256
associated types
  adding, in protocols 213
  declaring, in protocols 202-204
  inheriting, in protocols 213
attributes 14
**automatic reference counting
        (ARC) 33, 36, 37**

B

base types
  extending, to conform custom
        protocols 223, 224

C

classes
  about 33, 34
  declaring 37
  declaring, that inherit from another
        class 90-96
  declaring, that works with two constrained
        generic types 206-208
  downcasting with 155-159
  existing classes, generalizing with
        generics 214-222
  generating, to create objects 11-14
  instances, creating 45
  organizing, UML diagrams used 20-25
class hierarchies
  creating 83-86
class inheritance
  combining, with protocol
        inheritance 166-177
code
  refactoring 229-241
computed properties
  adding to base type, with
        extensions 273-277
  generating, with getters 54-60
  generating, with setters 54-62
constants
  recognizing, to create properties 14-16
constrained generic type
  class, declaring 190-194

D

data repository
  creating, with generics 248-252
  creating, with protocols 248-252
deinitialization
  about 36
  customizing 41-44
deinitializer 49

E

equivalent closures
  writing, with simplified code 247, 248

[305]

extensions
  computed properties, adding to base type 273-277
  convenience initializers, declaring 278, 279
  used, for adding methods 269-272
  used, for defining subscripts 280, 281

F

fields 14
filter
  chaining 262
functions
  about 241, 242
  function types, within classes 243, 244

G

generic class
  using, for multiple types 195-201
  using, with two generic type parameters 209-212
generic code 181, 182
getters
  about 50
  combining 62-65
  used, for generating computed properties 54-62
  used, for transforming values 69

I

immutable classes
  building 78-81
inheritance
  about 88-90
  and protocols, combining 144-151
initialization
  about 34, 35
  customizing 38-40
initializers
  about 49
  convenience initializers, declaring with extensions 278, 279
instance methods 50
instance properties 50
instances 33, 34

Integrated Development Environment (IDE) 1

M

map
  chaining 262
  combining, with reduce 259-261
  used, for transforming values 256-259
methods 17
  adding, with extensions 269-272
  downcasting with 155-159
  overloading 96-100
  overriding 96-100
  protocols, receiving as arguments 152-155
  requirements, specifying 164-166
mutable classes
  creating 74-77

N

nested types 50

O

object-oriented code
  in apps, working with 281-290
object-oriented data repository
  adding, to project 290-294
  interacting with, Picker View used 294-298
objects
  capturing, from real world 4-11
operator functions
  declaring, for specific subclasses 126, 127
operator overloading 121-126

P

parametric polymorphism 181, 182
Picker View
  used, for interacting with object-oriented data repository 294-298
polymorphism 108-121
properties
  about 14
  overriding 101, 102
  requirements, specifying 162-164
property observers 65-68

protocols
  and inheritance, combining 144-151
  associated types, adding 213
  associated types, inheriting 213
  class, declaring that conforms to multiple protocols 184-188
  classes, declaring 137-142, 186-188
  custom protocols, conforming 223, 224
  declaring 133-136
  declaring, to be used as constraint 183
  initializer requirements, combining with generic types 201, 202
  instances, treating as different subclass 159-161
  multiple inheritance 142, 144
  subclasses, declaring 188-190
  working, in combination with classes 131-133

R

reduce
  chaining 262
  map, combining 259-261
  used, for solving algorithms 262, 263

S

setters
  about 50
  combining 62-65
  used, for generating computed properties 54-62
  used, for transforming values 69, 70
stored properties
  declaring 51-53
structures 33, 34

subclass
  about 88
  declaring, that inherit conformance to protocols 188-190
  members overriding, controlling 103-108
subscripts
  about 49
  defining, extensions used 280, 281
  used, for creating shortcuts 204, 205

T

typecasting
  working with 108-121
type methods 49, 50
type properties
  about 49
  used, for creating values 70-74

U

Unified Modeling Language (UML)
  about 16
  UML diagrams, used for organizing classes 20-25
User eXperiences (UXs) 4
User Interfaces (UIs) 4

V

values
  transforming, with getters 69, 70
  transforming, with setters 69, 70
variables
  recognizing, to create properties 14-16

X

Xcode Playground 2

Thank you for buying
Object–Oriented Programming with Swift 2

About Packt Publishing

Packt, pronounced 'packed', published its first book, *Mastering phpMyAdmin for Effective MySQL Management*, in April 2004, and subsequently continued to specialize in publishing highly focused books on specific technologies and solutions.

Our books and publications share the experiences of your fellow IT professionals in adapting and customizing today's systems, applications, and frameworks. Our solution-based books give you the knowledge and power to customize the software and technologies you're using to get the job done. Packt books are more specific and less general than the IT books you have seen in the past. Our unique business model allows us to bring you more focused information, giving you more of what you need to know, and less of what you don't.

Packt is a modern yet unique publishing company that focuses on producing quality, cutting-edge books for communities of developers, administrators, and newbies alike. For more information, please visit our website at www.packtpub.com.

About Packt Open Source

In 2010, Packt launched two new brands, Packt Open Source and Packt Enterprise, in order to continue its focus on specialization. This book is part of the Packt Open Source brand, home to books published on software built around open source licenses, and offering information to anybody from advanced developers to budding web designers. The Open Source brand also runs Packt's Open Source Royalty Scheme, by which Packt gives a royalty to each open source project about whose software a book is sold.

Writing for Packt

We welcome all inquiries from people who are interested in authoring. Book proposals should be sent to author@packtpub.com. If your book idea is still at an early stage and you would like to discuss it first before writing a formal book proposal, then please contact us; one of our commissioning editors will get in touch with you.

We're not just looking for published authors; if you have strong technical skills but no writing experience, our experienced editors can help you develop a writing career, or simply get some additional reward for your expertise.

Mastering Swift 2

ISBN: 978-1-78588-603-4   Paperback: 408 pages

Dive into the latest release of the Swift programming language with this advanced Apple development book for creating exceptional iOS and OS X applications

1. Harness the latest and most advanced features of Swift 2 to develop quality iOS and OSX applications.

2. Comprehensive coverage of all the advanced features of Swift and guidance on advanced design techniques.

3. Dive deep into protocol extensions, learn new error handling model, and use featured Swift design patterns to write more efficient code.

Swift 2 Design Patterns

ISBN: 978-1-78588-761-1   Paperback: 224 pages

Build robust and scalable iOS and Mac OS X game applications

1. Learn to use and implement the 23 Gang of Four design patterns using Swift 2.

2. Design and architect your code for Swift application development.

3. Understand the role, generic UML design, and participants in the class diagram of the pattern by implementing them in a step-by-step approach.

Please check www.PacktPub.com for information on our titles

[PACKT] open source
community experience distilled

Swift High Performance

ISBN: 978-1-78528-220-1   Paperback: 212 pages

Leverage Swift and enhance your code to take your applications to the next level

1. Build solid, high performance applications in Swift.
2. Increase your efficiency by getting to grips with concurrency and parallel programming.
3. Use Swift to design performance-oriented solutions.

Learning Object-Oriented Programming

ISBN: 978-1-78528-963-7   Paperback: 280 pages

Explore and crack the OOP code in Python, JavaScript, and C#

1. Write reusable code that defines and makes objects interact with one another.
2. Discover the differences in inheritance and polymorphism in Python, JavaScript, and C#.
3. Capture objects from real-world elements and create object-oriented code that represents them.

Please check **www.PacktPub.com** for information on our titles

Lightning Source UK Ltd.
Milton Keynes UK
UKOW07f1918081116

287087UK00014B/343/P